A Social Hi…
of Educat…
the Muslim …ed

From the Prophetic Era to Ottoman Times

Dr. Amjad M. Hussain

Ta-Ha Publishers Ltd.

First Published in January 2013

Ta-Ha Publishers Ltd.
Unit 4, The Windsor Centre
Windsor Grove, West Norwood
London, SE27 9NT, UK
www.tahapublishers.com

Written by: Dr. Amjad M. Hussain
Edited by: Abdassamad Clarke
General Editor: Dr. Abia Afsar-Siddiqui

A catalogue record of this book is available from the British Library

ISBN-13: 978-1-84200-130-1

Cover design and Typeset by: N.A. Qaddoura
Printed and bound by: IMAK Ofset, Turkey

Anas related that the Prophet Muḥammad ﷺ said:

﴾A person who goes out in search of knowledge
is in the way of Allah and remains so
until he returns.﴿[1]

[1] Imam Abu Zakariya Yahya bin Sharaf an-Nawawi, S. M. Madni Abbasi (tr.), *Riyadh as-Ṣaliheen, Kitāb al-'Ilm,* No. 1385, Vol. II, (New Delhi: Kitab Bhavan), 1986, p. 655.

J 3
W21

Contents

Acknowledgements

It is when searching for light in the shadows of the past that the lanterns of the future are lit.

All praise and gratitude belong to Allah ﷻ Who made it possible for me to complete this book.

I dedicate this work to my late mother Abidah and my late sister Shabnum, may Allah have mercy upon them and grant them a place in Paradise.

I would like to thank my wife Shaheen Kausar for her love and support and my brother Khalid Hussain for his faith in me. I would also like to thank family and friends who have supported me in my many endeavours over the years and Ta-Ha Publishers for their assistance in the preparation of my first book.

Finally, I would like again to express my gratitude to my wife Shaheen Kausar for her immense editorial work on this book, without which it would never have reached this stage.

Notes on Transliteration

The following rules of transliteration are used:

Arabic	Roman	Arabic	Roman	Arabic	Roman
ا	a	ز	z	ق	q
ب	b	س	s	ك	k
ت	t	ش	sh	ل	l
ث	th	ص	ṣ	م	m
ج	j	ض	ḍ	ن	n
ح	ḥ	ط	ṭ	و	w
خ	kh	ظ	ẓ	ه	h
د	d	ع	‘	ي	y
ذ	dh	غ	gh	ة	h
ر	r	ف	f	ء	’

ـَ	(*fatḥah*)	a	ا	(alif)	ā
ـِ	(*kasrah*)	i	ي	(yā’)	ī
ـُ	(*ḍammah*)	u	و	(wāw)	ū

Transliteration will involve only Arabic words in *italics*. Other words of foreign origin will be written in *italics only* without transliteration, with the exception of original Arabic words that are plural through the use of English grammar such as madrasahs, *khanqahs* etc.

Introduction

The aim of this book is to map and evaluate the evolution of Islamic education as a social phenomenon from the time of the Prophet Muḥammad ﷺ to the end of the Ottoman Caliphate. In it I will attempt to investigate what particular social role education played in the history of Islam, insha'Allāh. It is well known that knowledge, both revealed and acquired, and the quest for this knowledge have played a vital part in forming Islamic civilisation. Therefore, it is important to ask a number of questions regarding this crucial quest for knowledge. For example, what is the basis of this pursuit called 'Islamic education'? How has Islamic education evolved throughout history and what social impact has it had on various societies? Have these various historical social changes throughout the ages had an effect on how Islamic education was perceived and presented? How does this affect contemporary Islamic education and its role in society?

There are currently many fine works which introduce the reader to the political history of Islam. In contrast, very few books have been written dealing with the history of Islamic education; some of these have spoken about a minor component of Islamic education, whereas others have not looked at it chronologically or socially, but rather they have compacted centuries together without any social analysis.[1] Therefore, this book will attempt a chronological survey of Islamic education focusing on social analysis of the different epochs. Since this is a very wide area of study, the book has been restricted to cover only the major Sunni Caliphal Islamic educational centres of Islamic history from Madīnah to Damascus, Baghdad, Cairo, and finally Istanbul. This edition of the book will therefore not be able to cover fully the social history of Islamic education in Moghul India, Safavid Iran and Muslim Spain even though these places will be touched upon. The study will demonstrate that it is not possible for the educational system of a civilisation with a life-span of over a thousand years to remain stagnant and totally devoid of any change, either positive or negative. I aim to identify and demonstrate evolutionary changes in Islamic education throughout the history of Islam.

Western historians and educators have long maintained that the instruction and preparation of young people for society is a major concern of mankind.[2] According to some sociologists, the word 'education' is synonymous with the word 'socialisation', meaning 'the learning of practices by which an individual becomes a member of an existing society'.[3] Education has an influence on every aspect of society. As a result it may be argued that if education changes in a society, that society as a whole will change. R. E. Sullivan explains this phenomenon by stating, "If anything happened in any historical period to change the character of education, it follows that the period has significance in the total stream of human history."[4]

1 See: Ahmad Shalaby, *The History of Muslim Education*, (Karachi: Indus Publication), 1979 and Mehdi Nakosteen, *History of Islamic Origins of Western Education*, (Colorado: University Of Colorado Press), 1964.

2 Williams Boyd (ed.), *The History of Western Education*, (Edinburgh: Black), 1966, p. 1.

3 W. Outhwaite and T. Bottomore, *The Blackwell Dictionary of Twentieth Century Social Thought*, (USA: Blackwell), 1993, p. 188.

4 Pierre Riche, *Education and Culture in the Barbarian West: From the Sixth through the Eight century*, (Colombia: University of South Carolina Press), 1978, p. xvi.

Therefore taking the above principle into account it is surprising that the mass of historical work by Westerners relating to the history of education seems to be totally unaware of the history of Islamic education. In most works on the history of education there seems to be a major gap of one thousand years involving educational theories and advances from the Muslim lands. In works such as *A History of Education* by Franklin Verzelius Newton Painter, it is possible to see an astonishing jump from the fall of the Eastern provinces of the Byzantine Empire in the seventh century to the Italian Renaissance in the twelfth century.[5] The total exclusion of the contribution made in the field of education by Islamic civilisation from the time of the Umayyads to the Ottoman Caliphate is simply staggering.[6]

In the light of there being little or no mention of Muslim education in Western history books, there is a need to comprehend the similarities and the differences between Muslim and non-Muslim perceptions of the nature of education. The definitions of education by Islamic scholars are as numerous and diverse as the various concepts that Western scholars have of education. The major difference between the two groups of educators seems to lie in what they perceive as the appropriate way to educate the individual and what that entails. Western civilisation historically commenced in Greece, where Plato presented the first theory of education in the West. This theory of education, not being derived from divine revelation, was based purely on rationalism, whilst in Islamic civilisation the various theories of education were based upon the newly revealed *dīn* of Islam in seventh century Arabia.[7] Consequently, that meant that theories regarding Islamic education were derived not only from the human intellect but also from divine revelation. It is from this revelation that Muslim scholars coined and expressed the purposes of Islamic education.

5 Franklin Verzelius Newton Painter, *A History of Education,* (BiblioBazaar), 2009.

6 See: John Adamson, *A Short History of Education,* (Cambridge: University of Cambridge Press), 1991.

7 Hamza Y. Hanson, *Lambs to the Slaughter,* (California: Ihya Production), 2000, p. 14.

The majority of scholars agree that three Arabic terms express the meaning of education in the Islamic sense. Two of these terms are taken from the Qur'an and the third is derived from the *ḥadīth* literature.[8] The first term '*tarbiyah*', which means 'fostering growth', derives from the Qur'an and its root is '*rabā*', which means to 'increase and grow'.[9] In the Qur'an Allah ﷻ says:

وَٱخْفِضْ لَهُمَا جَنَاحَ ٱلذُّلِّ مِنَ ٱلرَّحْمَةِ وَقُل رَّبِّ ٱرْحَمْهُمَا كَمَا رَبَّيَانِى صَغِيرًا ۝

"Take them under your wing, out of mercy, with due humility and say: 'Lord, show mercy to them as they did in looking after me when I was small'."[10]

The first term therefore indicates that Islamic education is there to nurture a person. The second term for education used in the Qur'an is '*ta'līm*' and it comes from the root word '*ilm*, which means 'knowledge'.[11] It has been used in the Qur'an in:

ٱلَّذِى عَلَّمَ بِٱلْقَلَمِ ۝ عَلَّمَ ٱلْإِنسَـٰنَ مَا لَمْ يَعْلَمْ ۝

"He who taught by the pen, taught man what he did not know."[12]

This term specifically means the imparting of knowledge. The last term, '*ta'dīb*', derives from the *ḥadīth* reporting that Prophet Muḥammad ﷺ said:

---

8 Seyyed Hossein Nasr, *Traditional Islam in the Modern World*, (London: KPI), 1987, p. 123.

9 Zaid bin Ngah, *The Practice of the Prophet Muhammad in Tarbiyah: Its significance for the formation of the first Muslim community*, (M.Phil: University of Birmingham), 1996, p. 34.

10 Abdalhaqq and Aisha Bewley, *The Noble Qur'an : a New Rendering of Its Meaning in English*, (London: Ta-Ha Publishers), 2011, Sūrat al-Isrā' 17:24.

11 Ngah, op. cit., p. 35.

12 Ibid., Sūrat al-'Alaq 96:4-5.

أَدَّبَنِي رَبِّي فَأَحْسَنَ تَأْدِيبِي

My Lord educated[13] me and then made my education[14] most excellent."[15]

The root of *'ta'dīb'* is *adab* , which in a wider sense implies good manners and ethics.[16,17] The *ḥadīth* narrated by Jābir ibn 'Abdullāh ﵁ illustrates beautifully the meaning of manners and ethics as education. Jābir narrated that the Prophet ﷺ said, "Enjoining all that is good is a *ṣadaqah.*"[18]

The traditions of the Prophet Muḥammad ﷺ contain numerous sayings concerning knowledge and education. He ﷺ himself called upon individuals to educate themselves when he said, as is narrated by Anas ﵁, "The quest for knowledge is incumbent upon every Muslim"[19,20] and Abū ad-Dardā' ﵁ narrated that the Prophet ﷺ said, "The learned

13 *Addabanī* ['educated me'] is from the same root as *ta'dib.*

14 Ibid.

15 'Abd ar-Rahman al-Qasim (comp. and ed.), *Ibn Taymiyya Fatawa*, Vol. 18, (Beirut: Dar al-Kutub al-Ilmiyyah), 1398 AH, p. 375 and also see Muhammad al-Zarkashi, *Ibn Taymiyya Fatawa*, (Beirut: Dar al-Kutub al-Ilmiyyah), 1406 AH, p. 160. Also see: Syed M. Naquib al-Attas, *The Concept of Education in Islam: A Framework for an Islamic Philosophy of Education*, (Jeddah: Hodder and Stoughton), 1979, p. 144.

16 *Adab*, in addition to 'good manners and ethics', means 'literature' or the 'literary and philological sciences' as we will see later in the book. The high importance of literary studies in Islam is because without them the student will have a poor grasp of the Arabic language and thus make gauche mistakes in his understanding of the Qur'an and the *ḥadīth* - Ed.

17 Ngah, op. cit., p. 38.

18 Muhammad ibn Ismail ibn al-Mughira al-Bukhari, Muhammad Muhsin Khan (tr.), *Sahih al-Bukhari – The translation of the meaning of Sahih al-Bukhari, Kitāb al-Adab*, No. 50, Vol. 8, (New Delhi: Kitab Bhavan), 1984.

19 Abu Muhammad ibn Yazid ibn Majah al-Rabi al-Qazwini, *Sunan Ibn Majah, Kitāb al-'Ilm*, No. 224, (Beirut: Dar al-Maarifah), 1996. Also see: Muhammad ibn 'Abdullah Khatib at-Tabrizi, Abdul Hameed Siddiqui (tr.), *Mishkat al-Masabih, Kitāb al-'Ilm*, Vol. 1, No. 218, (Lahore: Islamic Publication Ltd.), 1979, p. 136.

20 Both men and women are intended by the *ḥadīth.*

are the heirs of the prophets, and the prophets leave neither dinar nor dirham; they only leave knowledge, and he who takes it takes an abundant portion."[21] Other *ḥadīth* mention specifically education as it relates to ethics and manners, for example, 'Abdullāh ibn 'Amr narrated that the Messenger of Allah ﷺ neither spoke in an insulting manner nor did he ever deliberately utter evil. He used to say, "The most beloved to me amongst you is the one who has the best character and manners."[22] The majority of these reports were recorded under the title *Kitāb al-'ilm* ['The Book of Knowledge'] in a variety of *ḥadīth* collections, thus reflecting the intimate and important connection between character, good behaviour, courtesy and knowledge.

Islamic education has been described as a tool of the society whose purpose is to help a person become an ethical, moral and spiritual being; a person that is multi-dimensional and has a direction that is positive and healthy.[23]

The three Arabic terms for education and their relative importance have not always been equally balanced throughout history. The idea of disciplining the soul, the mind and the body has from time to time in history been overruled by the idea either of simply disciplining the mind and imparting knowledge or conversely just fostering spiritual growth.

Perhaps the best way to define the word 'education' is to demonstrate the relationship between the three indispensable foundations that make up the basic education of any civilisation, i.e. the teacher, the student and the aim or philosophy of the education provided. The term 'Islamic education' is sometimes misinterpreted when looked at from a Western point of view, for it is often misunderstood to be

---

21 Abu Dawoud, Ahmad Hasan (tr.), *Sunan Abu Dawoud, Kitāb al-'Ilm,* Chapter 1369, No. 3634, Vol. III, (New Delhi: Al-Madinah Publications), 1985, p. 1034.

22 Muhammad bin Ismail bin al-Mughira al-Bukhari, Muhammad Muhsin Khan (tr.), *Sahih al-Bukhari -The translation of the meaning of Sahih al-Bukhari,* Book of the Companions of the Prophet, No. 104, Vol. 5, (New Delhi: Kitab Bhavan), 1984.

23 Hanson, op. cit., p. 14.

a complete interconnected system run by a religious establishment. In addition, the misunderstanding of the term 'Islamic education' is further exacerbated by the false impression that this kind of education only provides for instruction in 'religious' sciences and does not cater for the sciences that are not revealed. Arguably, this is not the case with education in Islamic civilisation.

In all examples of education during the early Islamic period, as in other civilisations, there was self-evidently a relationship between the student, the teacher and the philosophy of education. However, learning ethics and morals, education, and the acquisition of knowledge (whether religious or not) were private and un-systematic activities. Hence, no single educational authority granted qualifications, if any existed. Moreover, education was not under state control. It is astonishing that, in comparison with our contemporary period, classical Islamic Caliphal government allowed unprecedented and consequently unequalled freedom to the populace, as illustrated by the following passage:

> Other than collecting taxes, the government did not interfere in the daily affairs of society. People were born, educated, married; they made their living and bequeathed their wealth; they engaged in trade and other kinds of business – all without interference from the central government. Virtually all of daily life was under the purview of Islamic law, articulated and administered by legal scholars who operated for the most part independent of the central government.[24]

In different periods of Islamic history it is possible to find a high number of elementary schools that taught pupils how to read, write and calculate. However, these were all separate from each other and

---

24 Tamara Sonn, *Islam, A Brief History*, 2nd edition, (Oxford: Wiley-Blackwell), 2010, p. 50.

were mostly independent of state authorities. At higher levels of education, students had to travel long distances to various teachers in order to learn from them. There were higher education institutions in the later ‘Abbasid period which became famous for various sciences and scholars. Nevertheless, it is important to remember that education in Islamic civilisation was not based on one system, but on many independent methods of education imparting knowledge from various sources. In the majority of earlier cases, educational authorities did not give out qualifications, but instead the teacher or the scholar decided when the student had learnt what he required. It is also important to keep in mind that to acquire knowledge during the era of early Islam, one could only learn from teachers/scholars; there were few books, since paper was in short supply and indeed almost non-existent until approximately 751 CE, when Muslim armies encountered the Chinese who taught them the art of paper-making.[25]

One of the aims of this book is to show how various educational institutions changed over time and evolved into other institutions with different curricula and administrations. Therefore, it is very important to understand from the outset that when talking about the history of ‘Islamic education’, I mean the ‘history of education in the Muslim world’. In other words, it is a social history of how peoples of the Islamic civilisation were educated.

It is also important to point out that early Islamic civilisation was not alone in possessing an education system that was not state controlled, an idea so alien to the contemporary world. Historical research shows that certain aspects of the Byzantine education system were very similar to that of the later Islamic world. Since the Islamic world inherited much of the Eastern Byzantine social system, it is highly plausible that some characteristics of Byzantine education may have influenced the Islamic educational system.

---

25 S. M. Imamuddin, *Arabic Writing and Arab Libraries,* (London: Ta-Ha Publishers), 1983, p. 7.

Looking at the education of Byzantium we find it comprised of three stages: primary, intermediate and higher education.[26] However, much like the education of the Muslims, the organisation of education in Byzantium was far removed from the education of today. In the Byzantine period, pupils would be sent to a teacher throughout all three stages and not to a building that was designated as a school. Teachers normally either rented a place or used their own house as a place of teaching. Primary level pupils were sent to a teacher known as a *grammatistes* (elementary teacher). At secondary-level, the pupils were yet again not sent to a designated building but to the *grammatikos*,[27] and finally those who wanted to continue their higher education went to a *sophist* who was also referred to as the *rhetor*. These people did not grant degrees. If the student wanted to learn, he had to travel to different places to find a suitable *sophist*; all types of higher education in Byzantium were only found in the big metropolises and so learning at this time was synonymous with travel. If a Byzantine student wanted to study law he would go to Beirut, whereas the study of medicine would lead him to Alexandria ; philosophy was studied in Athens and Alexandria and if a student wanted to learn art, letters and literature, he would go to the city of Gaza.[28] This way of acquiring knowledge and education increased considerably during Muslim times.

So these are the essential elements that came to comprise Islamic education. Thus, the term 'Islamic education' in this book indicates a distinct system of education in which all the religious and non-revealed sciences were taught and refers to all the institutions utilised for educational purposes from the time of the Prophet ﷺ to the Ottoman period.

---

26 Cyril Mango, *Byzantium, the Empire of New Rome,* (London: Weidenfield and Nicholson), 1950, p. 125.

27 N. H. Baynes and L. B. Moss (eds.), *Byzantium: An Introduction to East Roman Civilisation,* (Oxford: Clarendon Press), 1949, p. 204.

28 Mango, op. cit., p. 126.

Chapter One

Islamic Education in the First Community

The origins of 'Islamic education', as with all Islamic traditions, can be traced back to the time of the Prophet Muḥammad ﷺ. To comprehend Islamic education it is vital to explore and explain its origins and thus the immense transformation of pre-Islamic life in Arabia that occurred due to the arrival of the revelation.

Pre-Islamic Instruction

Prior to the revelation to Muḥammad ﷺ, in general the Arabs did not have a literary education. According to the polymath scholar Ibn Khaldūn (d. 1406), the Arabs had no art or science in pre-Islamic Arabia.[1] However, it is important not to write off the Arabs of the pre-Islamic period as ignorant and foolish, even though, with regards to their religious and moral attitudes, their period has been dubbed 'the period of ignorance'. According to various historical sources they did in fact have a form of education or rather, it can be argued, instruction. Just as with the Spartans of Ancient Greece, the Arab concept of

1 Ibn Khaldun, Franz Rosenthal (tr.), *The Muqaddimah,* (London: Routledge and Kegan Paul), Vol. 2, 1967, pp. 401-403.

instruction was based upon training youth of a certain background to become traders and/or warriors, not as ideal citizens of a polis but, as ideal members of their tribes.[2] In the Arabian Peninsula the ideal tribal member would train to become an Arab warrior or a trader with an eloquent Arabic tongue. In the early stage of a child's life he would be given to foster parents in the desert, so that it would be possible for him to be strengthened by that environment and so that he would acquire the eloquence of the pure Arabic language. The example can be given of the Prophet ﷺ himself, who during his childhood was sent to foster parents in the desert.[3] His ﷺ uncles also gave him martial training and he became a skilled archer, swordsman and wrestler.[4] It can be assumed that most Arabs were trained in such a way to differing degrees since their lifestyle required both the rigorous way of life of the warrior and the ability to trade.

Other qualities that brought honour and prestige to people in this society were the ability to speak eloquently and an aptitude for poetry. Before the advent of Islam, the only craft the Arabs had was poetry and they had no other sciences. Thus, Arabic poetry became the means of distinguishing the individual as a noble and 'educated' man of the desert. As Ibn Khaldūn states:

> The Arabs appreciated poetry very highly. It was distinguished in their speech through certain nobility, because it alone possessed harmony. They made poetry the archive of their history, their wisdom, their nobility and the touchstone of their natural gift for expressing themselves correctly, choosing the best methods of expression.[5]

---

[2] Williams Boyd, *The History of Western Education,* Edmund J. King (ed.), (Edinburgh: Black), 1966, p. 3.

[3] Martin Lings, *Muḥammad ﷺ,* (Hemel Hempstead: George Allen and Unwin), 1983, pp. 23-26.

[4] Karen Armstrong, *Muhammad: A Western Attempt to Understand Islam,* (London: Victor Gollancz), 1991, p. 79.

[5] Ibn Khaldun, op. cit., pp. 401-403.

The Arabs also included the science of genealogy (*'ilm al-ansāb*) and the tales of Arab battles (*ayyam al-'Arab*) in their poetry.[6]

The Education of Christians and Jews

Three pre-Islamic Arab communities distinguished themselves from the rest. These were the Lakhmids of Hirah (present-day Iraq), whose rulers were often the vassals of the Persian throne; the Ghassanids of Huran (in present-day Syria), whose kingdom was a protectorate of Byzantium; and the land of the Yemen, which was a prize always fought over by both Abyssinia and Persia.[7] Although these nations were less fortunate politically than their Hijaz neighbours in respect of independence, this contact with other civilisations enabled them to boast of a literary education. Thus, Christian Arabs in these three communities were often educated, due to their contact with the outside world.

Archaeologists have found preserved Syriac writings of Christian Arabs who resided along the northern borders of Arabia in the sixth and seventh centuries.[8] There is historical evidence that the Jews of pre-Islamic Arabia lived in a number of Arab cities (including Yathrib which later became *THE* city par excellence, the Madīnah of the Prophet ﷺ) and were educated in reading the Torah in Hebrew. Even

6 Munir-ud-din Ahmed, *Muslim Education and the Scholar's Social Status up to the 5th century Muslim Era,* (Zurich: Verlag Der Islam), 1968, p. 31.

7 K. Seeman, 'Education in Islam: From the Jahiliyyah to Ibn Khaldun', *Muslim World,* (Binghamton: State University of New York), Vol. 56, 1966, pp. 188-198.

8 Charles Cutler Torrey, *The Jewish Foundation of Islam,* (New York: Ktav Publishing House), 1933, p. xiv. *Note:* Charles Cutler Torrey in this book seems to be trying to convince the reader that Islam is based upon Judaism, an argument already dealt with by the Qur'an at some length. He further contends that Muḥammad ﷺ somehow got to read and learn from Jewish books given by certain unnamed rabbis; hence the conclusion that Muḥammad ﷺ must himself have written the Qur'an basing it upon Judaism. Even though this book is filled with Orientalist bias, nevertheless, it is useful for the detailed information regarding the pre-Islamic period.

though they had a Jewish religious lifestyle, they had become accustomed to the Arab tribal system[9] and spoke the Arabic language.[10] In his book *Futūḥ al-Buldān*, Aḥmad ibn Yaḥyā al-Balādhurī (d. 892) wrote that according to his sources a number of Jews had taught some of the Arabs of Madīnah to read and write.[11] However, this teaching seems to have been a bare minimum, since, according to the *Ṭabaqāt* of Ibn Sa'd (d. 845), only thirteen people of Madīnah knew the art of Arabic writing before the arrival there of the Prophet Muḥammad ﷺ.[12]

Hence, there is no doubt that the majority of the Arabs confined themselves to their own religious and social customs and had very little contact of a pedagogic nature with either the Jews or the Christians. In addition, both the Jews and the Christians had their own exclusive educational systems, which were either Jewish or Christian in origin and which did not spread outside their circles to include Arab polytheists.

Textual Evidence of Education in the Qur'an and Sunnah

It is important to understand the difference between instruction in the pre-Islamic era and the new approach towards education after Islam. This does not mean that after the spread of Islam the Arabs became masters in all the sciences and arts *en masse.* Yet, Islam signifies the decisive turning point in their philosophy of life in which Islamic education came very much to the fore. The Qur'an without doubt was historically the first Arabic literary work found in Arabia

---

9 It is highly probable that a significant proportion of these Jews were Judaised Yemeni Arabs, as maintained by the Arabs' own histories and recent DNA studies – Ed.

10 Ibid., p. 37.

11 C. E. Bosworth, P. J. Bearman, Th. Bianquis, E. Van Donzel and W. P. Heinrichs (eds.), *Encyclopaedia of Islam,* Vol. 1, (Leiden: E. J. Brill), 1997. See: 'Classical Arabic'.

12 Muhammad Zubayr Siddiqi, *Hadith Literature*, (Cambridge: The Islamic Texts Society), 1993, p. 26.

and the *raison d'être* for the immense social changes in the seventh century across most of the known world.[13] Thus, everything started to change in Arabia when the Prophet Muḥammad ﷺ came down from the mountain in Makkah for the first time with the revelation from Allah ﷻ. In fact one may argue that the first revelation was the first edification in Islam.[14] Allah ﷻ states in the Qur'an:

> *Recite: In the Name of your Lord Who created, created man from clots of blood. Recite: And your Lord is the Most Generous, He Who taught by the pen, taught man what he did not know.*[15]

Consequently, the first step in Islam was the command to read and the second drew attention to the importance of writing. In the next twenty-three years of the Prophet's ﷺ life, Allah revealed many *ayats* in the Qur'an concerning knowledge and its importance for mankind.[16] Some examples of these are: "*And say: 'My Lord, increase me in knowledge*'"[17] and "*You have only been given a little knowledge.*"[18] These verses may seem contradictory at first, but by looking closely at them one can see that they are complementary. In combination they sum up the Muslim's duty to seek knowledge through study, reading and writing, and through supplicating Allah for increase in knowledge while nevertheless believing that knowledge lies with Allah ﷻ alone.

The Qur'an and *ḥadīth* do not simply contain descriptions of education as a conveyance of information. As mentioned earlier, scholars

---

[13] Muhammad Hamidullah, 'Signs of Punctuation in the Copies of the Holy Qur'an: A Suggestion', *Al-'Ilm Journal of the Centre for Research in Islamic Studies*, (South Africa: University of Durban-Westville), Vol. 4, 1994, p. 1.

[14] Fazlur Rahman, *Muḥammad: The Educator of Humankind,* (London: The Muslim Schools Trust), 1980, pp. 117-126.

[15] Sūrat al-'Alaq 96:1-5.

[16] Hamidullah, *Khutabat-e-Bahaawalpoor* (*Essays of Bahaawalpoor*), (Islamabad: Idarah Tahqiqat Islami), 1997, p. 295.

[17] Sūrah Ṭā Hā 20:114.

[18] Sūrat al-Isrā' 85:17.

with insight have shown that both the Qur'an and *ḥadīth* use three main concepts to describe Islamic education:

- '*tarbiyah* - nurturing and fostering the growth of the student';
- '*ta'līm* - imparting knowledge'; and
- '*ta'dīb* - disciplining him or her and helping them to acquire *adab* or courtesy'.[19]

Numerous examples of the importance given to the spiritual, mental and physical aspects of life can be found in the lifestyle of the Prophet Muḥammad ﷺ. The importance of acquiring etiquette and manners is demonstrated in numerous books written by Muslim scholars dealing with topics such as the correct courtesy due to Allah, the Messengers, oneself, parents, children, siblings, community and the correct manner of eating, attending a gathering, travelling and even sleeping. The Prophet ﷺ taught his Companions to eat together when he said, as narrated by Waḥshī ibn Ḥarb ؓ, "If you gather together at your food and mention Allah's name, you will be blessed in it,"[20] and he said to one youth when eating, as narrated by 'Umar ibn Abī Salamah ؓ, "Come near, my son, mention Allah's name, eat with your right hand and eat from what is near you."[21] The Prophet ﷺ specifically mentioned that all the learning and teaching of the rites of Islam have spiritual as well as moral and physical benefits. In narratives of the Prophet's life there are found descriptions of him racing with his wife 'Ā'ishah ؓ, playing with children and encouraging sport for the sake of amusement and for fitness.[22] It seems that for adults, sports such as archery and riding

---

[19] Al-Attas, op. cit., pp. 1-15.

[20] Abu Dawoud, Ahmad Hasan (tr.), *Sunan Abu Dawoud, Kitāb al-Aṭ'imah,* Chapter 1418, No. 3755, Vol. III, (New Delhi: Al-Madina Publications), 1985, p. 1063.

[21] Abu Dawoud, Ahmad Hasan (tr.), *Sunan Abu Dawoud, Kitāb al-Aṭ'imah,* Chapter 1423, No. 3768, Vol. III, (New Delhi: Al-Madina Publications), 1985, p. 1063.

[22] Fahmeeda Hameed, *A Critical Study and Analysis of the Scholarly Achievements of 'A'ishah,* (PhD: Lampeter), 2000, p. 5.

were encouraged not only in preparation for the defence of Islam and its polity, but also as a form of exercise during times of peace.

Schools in Makkah

Did any school or private education exist during the Prophet Muḥammad's ﷺ life in Makkah and were people taught to read and write and learn various sciences? According to most sources, the Muslims remained in Makkah for thirteen years from the first revelation until the emigration to Madīnah.[23] Did the Prophet ﷺ encourage education in Makkah during those thirteen years? The answer to this question is two-fold: first, the activity of the Muslims in memorising and understanding the Qur'an and living in accordance with the revelation was in itself profoundly edifying and educational. The Prophet ﷺ was transforming the Arabs of his time, both town-dwellers and nomads, into becoming reflective people who believed in the Oneness of Allah. In the Makkan period the basic beliefs of Islam, such as in the Unity of Allah, in the Prophets and Messengers, the Revealed Books, the Last Day, the Garden and the Fire, and the Divine Decree, were fully developed. It was, however, in Madīnah that the Ummah with its social structures and its laws was built up through revelation.[24] The political situation in Makkah at this time would not have allowed the Messenger of Allah ﷺ to establish education nor would it have encouraged or even permitted open study circles. When the Prophet ﷺ first brought the message to the people of Makkah they did not take him seriously as a critic of their way of life. However, this attitude changed drastically when people started accepting Islam in growing numbers. Muslims began to be persecuted, which lasted until the Muslims emigrated to Madīnah. Looking at the sources

---

[23] Al-Tabari, Ismail K. Poonawala (tr.), *The History of Al-Tabari,* (Los Angles: State University of New York Press), Vol. VI, 1990, p. 156.

[24] W. M. Watt, *Muhammad at Mecca,* (Karachi: Oxford University Press), 1953, pp. 152-153.

concerning both the lives of the Prophet ﷺ and of the Muslims in Makkah it is therefore evident why such an institution could not have been established at this stage.

However, there are many sources that point to the house of Arqam in Makkah, near the foothills of Mount Safa, as the first seat of Islamic learning. Arqam ibn Abū Arqam[25] ؓ was one of the Prophet's ﷺ Companions in Makkah and his house was used by the Messenger of Allah ﷺ to teach Muslims about their *dīn*.[26] This learning was carried out in secret and the instructions were basic in comparison to what was to be taught later on in Madīnah. These teachings were mostly related to the matters of belief and stories of the ancient peoples and their prophets. Numerous *ḥadīths* describe the Prophet ﷺ teaching his Companions manners, the etiquette for various situations, the importance of a good diet, physical training, and many more issues related to everyday life. Thus, the starting point of Islamic edification by Muḥammad ﷺ was in his capacity as the Prophet of Allah. He taught his Companions the principles of Islam and, when the *ṣalāh* was revealed, the correct way to perform it, and he taught them the divine revelation.[27] During the early years of the revelation, Dār al-Arqam became the main place where the majority of this education took place. 'Umar ibn al-Khattab ؓ, during the sixth year of the revelation, may have been one of the last people to have embraced Islam within the doors of Dār al-Arqam. Most historical evidence points towards Dār al-Arqam being used for three years before the infamous boycott of Banū Hāshim, when it was finally abandoned.

It was in Madīnah that the first Muslim *dawlah* was created and therefore it was here that the parameters of the social structures of

---

[25] His son, 'Abdullāh ibn al-Arqam, was to become the scribe who would write out the famous letters which were sent by the Prophet ﷺ to such persons as the Emperor of Byzantine and the Shahanshah of Persia.

[26] Al-Attas, op. cit., p. 99.

[27] Ahmed, op. cit., p. 30.

Islam were revealed. In Madīnah, the Qur'an and the embodiment of its message in practice by the Messenger of Allah ﷺ served as the main inspirations of Muslim life, and the Qur'anic revelation started to be revealed about matters of importance to the community and repeatedly exhorted the Muslims to support community efforts.[28] The description of Madīnah as a Qur'anic city state is most apt, because it was in Madīnah that the first Muslim milieu was created.

Schools in Madīnah

According to the Orientalist William Muir, the first six months of the Prophet's ﷺ residence in Madīnah were occupied in construction of the mosque and houses for the emigrants. He mentions the mosque as a building with a prayer hall and doors leading to the apartments of his wives. In addition:

> ....to the north of the building the ground was open. On that side a place was appropriated for the poorer followers of Muhammad, who had no home of their own. They slept in the mosque and had a sheltered bench or pavement outside.[29]

According to Victor Danner, these people were the *Ahl aṣ-Ṣuffah* ['The People of the Veranda'], who led a contemplative and saintly life in the Prophet's mosque in Madīnah.[30] However, Hamidullah argues that the *Ṣuffah* was neither used just as a place for poorer Muslims to sleep at night nor simply for those who wanted to lead a saintly life. He maintains that in addition to these uses it was a place of study. It may be argued that the *Ṣuffah* was in fact a blueprint for the students' dormitory in the history of Islamic education. The *bayt al-māl*, the

---

28 Marshall G. S. Hodgson, *The Venture of Islam*, (Chicago: The University of Chicago Press), 1974, p. 183.

29 William Muir, *Life of Mahomet*, (Osnabruck: Biblio Verlag), Vol. VIII, 1988, p. 21.

30 Seyyed Hossein Nasr (ed.), *Islamic Spirituality*, (London: SCM Press), 1985, p. 245.

Prophet's ﷺ household and those in Madīnah who were wealthy, provided the people of the *Ṣuffah* with food and other necessities. The people of *Ṣuffah* were also known to work in order to be able to provide for themselves while studying.[31] At this *Ṣuffah* there were said to have also been lessons in poetry. A specific day was chosen by the Prophet ﷺ himself to teach the women of Madīnah separately.

It is also clear from the *ḥadīth* collections that the Prophet ﷺ taught his followers spiritual, physical and religious knowledge. Furthermore, within a short time, Islamic education started to be taught in the other mosques of Madīnah. According to Hamidullah, during the lifetime of the Prophet ﷺ there were at least nine mosques in Madīnah which had study circles that served in providing education for the inhabitants.[32] The Prophet ﷺ himself ordered the various mosques of Madīnah to open their own study circles so that the central mosque would not be overcrowded. In addition, he believed that all the children around Madīnah should have a mosque close to their vicinity so it could be easy for them to go and receive an education.[33]

The First Method of Education – *Ḥalaqah* (Study Circle)

Education at the time of the Prophet Muḥammad ﷺ was divided into two different categories which entailed two methods. The first method was based upon education in study circles at the mosques, especially in the Prophet's Mosque. Here the students learned Islam, i.e. the Qur'an, Sunnah and *sharīʿah*; poetry and the art of reading and writing.[34] The students would form a circle, referred to as a '*ḥalaqah*', around the teacher. It was named thus because the teacher sat against a wall or a pillar and the students would make a semi-circle around

---

31 Hamidullah, op. cit., 1997, pp. 202-205.

32 Ibid.

33 Hamidullah, op. cit., 1997, p. 206.

34 Ghulam Ahmad Harery, *Islami Dastor-i-Hajaat* (*Islamic Way of Life*), (Lahore: Takhliq Markaz), 1991, p. 147.

him/her. The semi-circle was formed according to rank, thus the most advanced students sat closer to the teacher.[35] This unique educational experience would be a constant phenomenon in the history of Islamic education, be it in the mosque, *kuttāb, maktab,* or madrasah.[36]

One of the most famous teachers of writing and reading in the *Ṣuffah* was the Companion 'Ubādah ibn aṣ-Ṣāmit ﵁ who, in the Caliph 'Umar's ﵁ time, was sent to teach Islam to the inhabitants of Palestine.[37] He also taught the Qur'an to his students by the instruction of the Prophet ﷺ.[38] Another teacher of reading and writing in the *Ṣuffah* was the Companion 'Abdullāh ibn Sa'd ibn al-'Āṣ ﵁ of Makkah, who was personally instructed by the Prophet ﷺ to teach the people of Madīnah.[39] According to some sources, the Prophet ﷺ also assigned Ash-Shifā bint 'Abdullāh al-Qurashiyyah al-'Adawiyyah ﵂ to teach reading and writing to his wife Ḥafṣah ﵂. According to the Companion Anas ﵁, seventy of the people of *aṣ-Ṣuffah* (*Aṣḥāb aṣ-Ṣuffah*) would sometimes go to a teacher at night and engage in study until daylight.[40] Thus, there is evidence that there was a group of teachers in the *Ṣuffah* who taught students the Qur'an, the Sunnah and literacy.

Some historians including Ghuinaima have described the *Ṣuffah* or the mosque of Madīnah as a university.[41] The *Ṣuffah,* from the evidence cited above, was a place of learning for all who had a desire to learn and were able to attend, a place of teaching and learning and not only of scholarship, which would figure to a greater degree later in the history of Islamic education. Hence, the *Ṣuffah* cannot be viewed as a

---

35 Nakosteen, op. cit., p. 45.

36 Ahmed, op. cit., p. 53.

37 Harery, op. cit., p. 147.

38 Abu Amina Yasir Qadri, *An Introduction to the Sciences of the Qur'an,* (Birmingham: Al-Hidayah), 1999, p. 128.

39 Siddiqi, op. cit., p. 26.

40 Harery, op. cit., p. 148.

41 George Makdisi, *The Rise of Colleges,* (Edinburgh: Edinburgh University Press), 1981, p. 293.

madrasah or university since its level of organisation was more closely related to that of a school. Nevertheless, the mosque of Madīnah can be seen as the origin and cornerstone of all Islamic education. H. A. Jawad summarises the status of the *Ṣuffah* in Islamic history eloquently as, "In the course of time, the simple pattern of the Prophet's school developed into a comprehensive and coherent educational system, fully integrated into the social and economic way of life."[42]

The sources reveal that the Prophet ﷺ personally devoted much time to teaching, and he taught his Companions and followers regularly. He gathered them in the *Ṣuffah* to teach them the *dīn* and cognate subjects[43] such as manners, ethics, law, spirituality and *tajwīd.* The Prophet ﷺ, in his lessons, introduced the initiative of teaching by repetition. According to Anas ؓ, "Whenever the Prophet ﷺ said a thing, he would repeat it thrice so that people could understand it properly from him and whenever he asked permission to enter, (he knocked the door) thrice with greeting."[44] In this way he ﷺ conveyed the importance of teachers being patient with their students at all times and speaking clearly and repeatedly to help them understand. The Prophet ﷺ argued that it was imperative to teach people at suitable times and not to have long sessions, in case students fall prey to boredom and lose all enthusiasm for further learning. As narrated by Ibn Mas'ud ؓ, "The Prophet ﷺ used to take care in his teachings by selecting a suitable time, so that we might not become bored."[45] Another concept introduced amongst the Companions was that a

---

42 H. A. Jawad, *Muḥammad the Educator: An Authentic Approach,* The Islamic Quarterly, (London: The Islamic Cultural Centre), Vol. xxxiv, No. 2, 1990, p. 118.

43 Seeman, op. cit., p. 192.

44 Muhammad bin Ismail bin al-Mughira al-Bukhari, Muhammad Muhsin Khan (tr.), *Sahih al-Bukhari -The translation of the meaning of Sahih al-Bukhari, Kitāb al-'Ilm,* Chapter 30, No. 95, Vol. I, (New Delhi: Kitab Bhavan), 1984.

45 Muhammad bin Ismail bin al-Mughira al-Bukhari, Muhammad Muhsin Khan (tr.), *Sahih al-Bukhari -The translation of the meaning of Sahih al-Bukhari, Kitāb al-'Ilm,* Chapter 12, No. 68, Vol. I, (New Delhi: Kitab Bhavan), 1984.

good teacher is the one who begins by teaching simple subjects of knowledge before touching difficult ones.[46] There is also evidence in the sources that the Prophet ﷺ allowed the teaching of poetry (the first non-religious subject besides literacy) at the *Ṣuffah*.[47] He also allocated certain times specifically for women to learn from him. According to a narration by Abū Sa'īd al-Khudrī ﷺ, "Some women requested the Prophet ﷺ to fix a day for them as the men were taking all his time. On that he promised them one day for religious lessons and commandments."[48] However, this does not mean that women were not allowed to attend other lessons with the men; it just means that they wanted a specific day for themselves as they thought the Prophet's ﷺ time was very limited.

Some academics such as Seeman have argued that the Prophet's ﷺ main teaching techniques were influenced largely by pre-Islamic society. That may be contended, but when looking at some of his main initiatives in education, there is no doubt that the Prophet ﷺ was introducing revolutionary ideas far in advance of his time. Many of his methods could not in any case be from the pre-Islamic society; for example, his action in giving women the right to learn as equals. Moreover, some of his means were explicitly frowned upon by the pre-Islamic traditionalists.

After the Prophet ﷺ passed on, his Companions continued to apply his methods, while at the same time, following his example, developing further techniques of teaching. The Companions understood the most important basis of his education system, i.e. that they needed

---

46 Muhammad bin Ismail bin al-Mughira al-Bukhari, Muhammad Muhsin Khan (tr.), *Sahih al-Bukhari - The translation of the meaning of Sahih al-Bukhari, Kitāb al-'Ilm*, Chapter 11, Vol. I, (New Delhi: Kitab Bhavan), 1984, p. 59.

47 Poetry has a high importance as a subject since it is the highest expression of human use of language and thus a vital tool in acquiring the Arabic language.

48 Muhammad bin Ismail bin al-Mughira al-Bukhari, Muhammad Muhsin Khan (tr.), *Sahih al-Bukhari - The translation of the meaning of Sahih al-Bukhari, Kitāb al-'Ilm*, Chapter 36, No. 101, Vol. I, (New Delhi: Kitab Bhavan), 1984.

to continue the work of the Prophet ﷺ by following his example but without making the education system stagnant by merely adhering to blind imitation of his example. In subsequent years, Islamic literature became filled with educational theories. For example, Caliph 'Umar ibn al-Khaṭṭāb ؓ was known to say that children should also be taught subjects such as poetry, history and the social sciences, which guarantee the success of society, and he followed the Messenger of Allah ﷺ in emphasising the importance of physical education for children such as horsemanship, archery and swimming.[49] Another Companion to continue the Prophet's ﷺ work in education was 'Abdullāh ibn 'Abbās ؓ; he copied the Prophet's idea of a suitable amount of time for study about which he said, "Teach only for as long as the students look at you with their eyes fully open, but once students start to turn their eyes away from you their attention has strayed."[50] Ibn 'Abbās ؓ also developed in his advanced teaching classes, the notion of free time given to students to do whatever they wanted between each lecture.[51] The fourth caliph, 'Alī ؓ, emphasised the importance of discussion and review of the student's lessons to ensure that the student had not forgotten or made a mistake in his/her understanding. 'Alī ؓ stressed the idea of asking questions; he used to say, "Knowledge is a treasure, and its keys are the questions asked, so ask questions. As the question is rewarded by its answer, so is the person who asked the question, his teacher, the listener and the bystander."[52]

The Second Method of Education – *Riḥlah* (Travel)

The other method of education in Madīnah introduced by the Prophet ﷺ concerned those people who came to Madīnah from the outlying

---

[49] Khalid F. Oadah, *The Madrasah System in Mediaeval Time*, (PhD: Cardiff University), 1998, p. 25.

[50] Ibid., p. 34.

[51] Oadah, op. cit., p. 34.

[52] Ibid., pp. 37-38.

lands of Arabia. According to Ibn 'Abbās ﷺ, an envoy from nearly every tribe of Arabia came to the Prophet ﷺ and enquired about Islam and acquired knowledge of the Islamic sciences from him.[53] These envoys stayed in Madīnah for a short time, learning about the different revealed sciences of Islam, then returned to their respective tribes with this knowledge. One famous example of this was the Companion Mālik ibn al-Ḥuwayrith ﷺ, who after learning about Islam was told by the Prophet ﷺ, "Go back to your family, stay with them, and teach them and exhort them to good."[54]

There is no doubt that travelling in search of knowledge was an essential of education from ancient times. It is possible to find examples of this practice in various societies such as Persia, Rome and China. Here it is argued that *riḥlah* (travelling for knowledge) was an ancient tradition mostly existent outside the Arabian Peninsula, which because of the encouragement of the Prophet ﷺ, started to be used specifically for the acquisition of knowledge of the *dīn*. However, this approach to education was due to a socio-geographical situation and not because of a religious command. Since there was only one Prophet ﷺ and only one Madīnah al-Munawwarah, every Muslim who desired to learn from him had to visit him personally. Another variation of this method (*riḥlah*) was that the Messenger of Allah ﷺ himself sent selected Muslims to the people who had recently accepted Islam to teach them about their new *dīn*.[55] He is known to have taken this action even while he was resident in Makkah: "The Prophet ﷺ, before his migration to Madīnah, had sent a teacher there to arrange for the education of the Muslims."[56]

---

[53] Harery, op. cit., p. 148.

[54] Muslim bin al-Hajjaj, Abdul Hamid Siddiqi (tr.), *Sahih Muslim, Kitab al-Salat,* No. 1423, (New Delhi: Kitab Bhavan), 1984.

[55] Seeman, op. cit., p. 192.

[56] Hamiuddin Khan, *History of Muslim Education: Vol. I (712-1750),* (Karachi: Academy of Educational Research), 1967, p. 21.

After the Prophet ﷺ, some of the Companions spread throughout the newly conquered lands. This led to a great deal of travelling for those Muslims who were new to the *dīn* and wished to learn more about it. They would undertake journeys to visit the Companions and, later on, their successors. Thus, by the first century of Islam, a number of learned men and women were held in esteem by the Muslims in different parts of the Islamic world. Those desiring *riḥlah* were provided with the opportunity to visit many new centres of knowledge in addition to Madīnah such as Kufa, Basra, Damascus and Jerusalem. Eminent scholars amongst the Companions of the Prophet ﷺ, such as Abū ad-Dardā' ؓ in Damascus, Anas ibn Mālik ؓ in Basra, Abū Idris ؓ in Emesa, and Ḥudhayfah ؓ in Kufa, settled in these cities to teach. Many others stayed in Madīnah, including 'Ā'ishah ؓ. Almost all of these Companions were seen teaching in the mosques in study circles (*ḥalaqāt*).[57]

Pre-Islamic Literacy in Arabia

At this juncture it must be pointed out that, even if education as a concept is very wide, the modern world very often limits the meaning of the word 'education' to literacy and numeracy. Education in literacy then signifies the modern world's social progress, which is seen as being indicated by the percentage of literate citizens. According to H. W. F. Saggs, literacy is the most highly valued skill in the modern world. He states, "The word 'education' is normally used in the limited sense of education in literacy; and the percentage of literate citizens has become a yardstick of the social progress for developing countries."[58]

In this sense of education, pre-Islamic Arabia had very few people who knew the art of reading and writing.[59] According to the *Encyclo-*

---

57 Siddiqi, op. cit., p. 28.

58 H. W. F. Saggs, *Civilization before Greece and Rome*, (London: B.T. Batsford), 1989, p. 98.

59 Mohammed Monir Morsi, *The Islamic Education: Its Foundation and Development in the Arab World*, (Cairo : Alam Alkutub), 1974, p. 4.

paedia of Islam, various sources point out that seventeen individuals of the Quraysh were literate at the time of the Opening of Makkah (*Fatḥ Makkah*) to Islam. One of these seventeen individuals was the future Caliph Mu'āwiyah ibn Abī Sufyān ﷺ, who served the Prophet Muḥammad ﷺ as a scribe of the revelation after the Opening (*Fatḥ*) of Makkah to Islam.[60]

According to the *Encyclopaedia of Islam*, the first record of written Arabic was found in the Christian Temple of Rammin Sinai, dating from approximately 300 CE. Muslim tradition names the poet 'Adi ibn Zayd ibn Ḥammād, a Christian of Hirah, as one of the first people to write in Arabic. He lived in approximately 500 CE. The Arabic written language during this period was still in an early evolutionary stage.[61] According to Ibn Khaldūn, it was the Himyarite script from the Southern Kingdom (Yemen) that was transmitted to Hirah by the family of Al-Mundhir. He further states, "From Hirah, the inhabitants of Taif and the Quraysh learned writing."[62] The historians, al-Balādhurī (d. 892) in his book *Futūḥ al-Buldān* and Qudāmah ibn Ja'far (d. 948) in his book *Al-Kharāj*, elaborate on the story of how Ḥarb ibn Umayyah was taught to write Arabic by Aslam ibn Sidrah in Hirah. The story narrates that Aslam desired to marry Ḥarb's daughter. For her dowry, he taught her father the art of writing in order that he would be able to keep records in trade.[63] Al-Balādhurī and Qudāmah ibn Ja'far further tell us that after Ḥarb was taught the art of reading and writing, he passed on this knowledge to his son Abū Sufyān who then taught his son Mu'āwiyah ﷺ. In other words, all these sources emphasise that literacy in Arabic only commenced in Makkah during the time of Ḥarb ibn Umayyah one generation before the birth of the Prophet Muḥammad ﷺ.[64]

---

[60] Bosworth, op. cit., Vol. IX, p. 265.

[61] C. E. Bosworth, P. J. Bearman, Th. Bianquis, E. Van Donzel and W. P. Heinrichs (eds.), *Encyclopaedia of Islam*, Vol. 1, (Leiden: E. J. Brill), 1997. See: 'Classical Arabic'.

[62] Ibn Khaldun, op. cit., p. 379.

[63] Hamidullah, op. cit., 1997, p. 298.

Hamidullah maintains that according to Ibn Ḥajar (d. 1448), there were also a number of women who were familiar with the art of reading and writing. He specifically mentions Ash-Shifā bint 'Abdullāh al-Qurashiyyah al-'Adawiyyah ﵂ who was related to 'Umar ibn al-Khaṭṭāb ﵁ and who was literate before the hijrah to Madīnah. After she moved to Madīnah, the Prophet ﷺ placed her in a venue in the bazaar so that she could use her literacy and numeracy in this context. Later on during the Caliph 'Umar's period he appointed her to be in charge of a part of the administration of the marketplace.

There are very few examples of pre-Islamic literary activity in Makkah, but the hanging of written parchments on the wall of the Ka'bah containing the best Arabic poetry of the time, the 'seven hanging [poems]', is one such example. Another example is the use of writing on a *ṣaḥīfah* – a page or a scroll – when the Makkans boycotted the clan of the Prophet Muḥammad ﷺ, even though many of them were not Muslims. They wrote the conditions concerning this boycott, which were: "No one is to give their daughter in marriage to them, nor marry them their daughters, nor buy anything from them or sell them anything nor even talk to them."[65] This *ṣaḥīfah* then hung inside the Ka'bah so that it could be seen to be both a legal and a sacred boycott, according to their rights as pagan Arabs.[66] When looking at the various sources it is clear that literacy in pre-Islamic Arabia was almost confined to the élite of Makkah, but that in addition, as mentioned earlier, there were thirteen people in Madīnah who are recorded as having been literate before the arrival of the Messenger of Allah ﷺ.[67] According to the *Ṭabaqāt* of Ibn Sa'd these thirteen were Abū 'Abs, Aws ibn Khawlī, Al-Mundhir ibn 'Amr, Ubayy ibn Ka'b, 'Abdullāh ibn Rawāḥah, Al-Ḥuḍayr al-Katā'ib, Usayd ibn Ḥuḍayr,

---

64 Ibid., p. 298.

65 Hamidullah, op. cit., 1997, p. 301.

66 Ibid.

67 Siddiqi, op. cit., p. 26.

Bashir ibn Sa'd, 'Abdullāh ibn Zayd, Ma'n ibn 'Adī, Sa'd ibn ar-Rabī', Sa'd Ibn 'Ubādah and Rāfi' ibn Mālik.[68] It is important to note that the Himyarite script was written with separated letters, and so literacy in Arabic, which was a very new thing at the time of the Prophet ﷺ, was at best rudimentary in its form.[69] Ibn Khaldūn describes it thus:

> Arabic writing at the beginning of Islam was therefore, not of the best quality or of the greatest accuracy and excellence. It was not even of medium quality, because the Arabs possessed the savage desert attitude and were not familiar with crafts.[70]

However, there were also individuals who lived in the Hijaz at the time of the Prophet Muḥammad ﷺ who had been educated outside the Arabian Peninsula. These included Companions such as Salmān al-Farsī ﵁. All of these Companions had been educated in their own societies before embracing Islam.

In conclusion, the Arabs belonged to a predominantly illiterate society and only a certain number of people, as mentioned above, were familiar with the art of literacy. At this time, Arabic writing was deficient and not fully advanced, in contrast with spoken Arabic, which was at its peak. Even though written Arabic had started to gain currency before the time of the Prophet Muḥammad ﷺ, it was the *waḥyī* – revelation – that would make literary Arabic a global phenomenon.

The Growth of Literacy after the Revelation

From the many accounts of the Messenger of Allah ﷺ encouraging the Arabs to learn to read and write, we can conclude that he ﷺ wanted the Muslims to be literate so that his followers could record and transmit

---

68 Ibid.

69 Hamidullah, op. cit., 1997, pp. 298-299.

70 Ibn Khaldun, op. cit., p. 382.

the knowledge of Islam to subsequent generations. Thus, younger Companions such as 'Alī, Ibn 'Abbās and 'Abdullāh ibn 'Amr ﷺ were inspired to learn to read and write at an early age.[71] The following examples emphasise this point: after the Battle of Badr, the Prophet ﷺ proposed to the captives that those who were literate could buy their freedom by each teaching ten Muslim children to read and write.[72] One of the results of this initiative was Zayd ibn Thābit ﷺ, who was taught literacy by one of the captives of Badr and who in his later years became the Prophet's ﷺ foremost scribe and a great scholar of the Qur'an.[73]

At this point the statement of the Orientalist William Muir about this incident has to be examined critically: he contends that most of the captives knew how to read and write, especially those amongst them who were poor. He states, "Some of the poorest Makkan captives taken at Badr were offered their release on condition that they could teach a certain number of the ignorant citizens of Madīnah to write."[74] From the earlier accounts of life before Islam in Arabia, it is evident that most Makkans could not read and write, especially those who were poor. It is also apparent from the nature of the social system before Islam that poor people could not have been given any educational advantage over the nobility. There is no doubt that certain members of the upper class were taught how to read and write, and that they also included a number of women.[75] However, there is no historical evidence found that the bulk of the poor of Makkah knew how to

71 Siddiqi, op. cit., p. 26.
72 Hamidullah, op. cit, 1997, p. 207.
73 Siddiqi, op. cit., p. 26.
74 Muir, op. cit., Vol. I, p. ix.
75 Khabbāb ibn al-Aratt and 'Umar ibn al-Khaṭṭāb ﷺ both knew the art of reading and writing as is evident from the famous incident concerning 'Umar's conversion to Islam. The account describes 'Umar going to Dār al-Arqam intent on killing the Prophet ﷺ. On his way he meets Nu'aym ibn 'Abdullāh an-Nahhām ﷺ who diverts him from his intention by stating that 'Umar's own sister Fāṭimah bint al-Khaṭṭāb has become a Muslim. He immediately changes direction and goes to

read or write. Additionally, Muir has used the word 'poor' about the captives of Badr, whereas the Prophet's offer was made explicitly to 'any person' who knew how to read and write to teach ten children. Evidently, if all of them knew how to read and write then he would have simply asked each of them to teach ten children. The result of Muir's contention is merely to reduce the Prophet's achievement as an educator, ignoring the fact that he not only allowed children from all backgrounds to learn how to read and write but encouraged them.

Another example of the Messenger of Allah's initiative with regards to literacy can be seen as early as his entrance to Madīnah: he ordered the writing of the contract, made in Madīnah in the early period of his arrival there, between the Emigrants, the Helpers and the Jews ;[76] he also sent letters to foreign rulers and made written treaties.[77] Moreover, in the later period of revelation, Allah in the Qur'an commands Muslims to write down trade agreements, "*You who believe, when you take on a debt for a specified period, write it down.*"[78] The *ayah* also speaks of not finding scribes to write the *'aqd* (contract) for the people, when Allah says, "*If you are on a journey and cannot find a*

---

his sister's house, forcing himself into the house where he hears the recitation of the Qur'an. Fāṭimah, in fear of him, hides the manuscript copy of Surah Ṭā Hā that Khabbāb was reading with her husband Sa'īd ibn Zayd ibn 'Amr ibn Nufayl and herself. 'Umar hits out at his sister in rage and instantly feels consumed with shame. Then his sister challenges him to read the Qur'an and hear its arguments. After reading the Qur'an from the manuscript, 'Umar then goes to Dār al-Arqam to declare the *shahādah* in front of the Prophet. For more information see: Ibn Isḥāq, A. Guillaume (tr.), *The Life of Muhammad,* (Karachi: Oxford University Press), 1996, pp. 156-157 and At-Tabari, Ismail K. Poonawala (tr.), *The History of at-Tabari,* (Los Angles: State University of New York Press), 1990.

76 Ibn Ishaq, *The Life of Muhammad,* A. Guillaume (tr.), (Karachi: Oxford University Press), 1996, p. 231.

77 The Treaty of Ḥudaybiyyah was a written treaty of peace between the Makkans and Madinans for ten years and letters to the Roman, Abyssinian and Persian rulers were written by the orders of the Prophet to invite them to Islam. For more information see: Shibli Nu'mani, *Sirat-un-nabi,* (Delhi: Idarah-i Adabyat-i), 1979, pp. 132-154.

78 Sūrat al-Baqarah 2:282.

writer..." which shows that not everyone had acquired literacy during the Prophet's ﷺ lifetime, although by this time, writing was seen as a commendable art to learn and master for all who desired to do so. By the end of his life the Messenger of Allah ﷺ had twenty-four scribes for the Qur'an, including Abū Bakr, 'Umar, 'Uthmān, 'Alī and Zayd ibn Thābit ﷺ.[79]

Hence, in the history of the city of the Prophet ﷺ, the emphasis on reading and writing is apparent as early as the commencement of Islam in the city itself, alongside the *Ṣuffah,* and the compact made between the inhabitants of Madīnah and the various treaties. The art of writing gained so much importance that it began to be utilised in people's trade and personal life. A number of the Companions, after learning the art of literacy, set out to write down the sayings of the Prophet ﷺ. As a result quite a few of the Companions owned written collections (*ṣaḥīfāt*) in the Prophet's ﷺ lifetime. These included the *ṣaḥīfāt* of 'Abdullāh ibn 'Amr, 'Alī ibn Abī Ṭālib, Jābir ibn 'Abdullāh, Abū Rāfi', Ibn 'Abbās, Itbān ibn Mālik al-Anṣārī, Samurah ibn Jundub and Abū Hurayrah ﷺ.[80]

However, here we must mention that according to a *ḥadīth,* the writing down of anything besides the Qur'an had been explicitly forbidden. It was the *ḥadīth* master Ibn Qutaybah (d. 889) in his book *Ta'wīl Mukhtalif al-Ḥadīth* who explained this contradiction by reasoning that either the prohibitive *ḥadīth* belonged to an earlier period of the prophethood and thus is abrogated by later permissions which were also granted and recorded in acceptable *ḥadīth* or, alternatively, the prohibition was specifically meant for only those Companions who were not proficient in literacy.[81] Historical evidence

---

[79] Qadhi, op. cit., p. 29.

[80] Siddiqi, op. cit., p. 25.

[81] Ibid., pp. 25-26. See also Abu Dawoud, Ahmad Hasan (tr.), *Sunan Abu Dawoud, Kitāb al-'Ilm,* Chapter 1371, Nos. 3639 and 3640, Vol. III, (New Delhi: Al-Madina Publications), 1985, p. 1035.

gives support to Ibn Qutaybah's argument concerning the abrogation of the prohibitive *ḥadīth* by dating the *ḥadīth* allowing the writing of traditions to the episode of Abū Shāh ﷺ. According to the *ḥadīth* reported by Abū Hurayrah, Abū Shāh ﷺ asked the Prophet ﷺ at the Opening of Makkah to Islam to have the Prophet's ﷺ address written down; the Prophet ﷺ told his Companions to have the address written down.[82] There is no doubt that the episode of Abū Shāh ﷺ postdates the narrations concerning the prohibition of writing down *ḥadīth.*

Muslim literacy became a vehicle for teaching (*ta'līm*) and through the transmission of knowledge it was possible to receive *tarbiyah* and *ta'dīb,* but literacy in itself was never seen as 'education', and the percentage of literate citizens did not stand as a benchmark of social progress. Rather it was the instruction of the Muslim person that was the centre of education and in order to obtain this the Muslims needed to be familiar with the arts of reading and writing among other things. According to the scholar Hamidullah, the positive attitude towards knowledge in general is evident from the earliest time in Madīnah, when the Messenger of Allah ﷺ started to encourage certain individuals to learn foreign languages. He states that some Jews of Madīnah used to come to the Messenger of Allah ﷺ to argue. The Prophet ﷺ sometimes referred to their Torah, but when asked about the relevant verses the Jews would deliberately not translate them into Arabic. Once when this happened, 'Abdullāh ibn Salām ﷺ, who had converted from Judaism to Islam, pointed this out. At this, the Prophet ﷺ encouraged Zayd ibn Thābit ﷺ to learn Hebrew. Another example is the Companion 'Abdullāh ibn 'Amr ibn al-'Āṣ ﷺ, the son of the famous general, who learnt the Syriac language, with encouragement from the Prophet ﷺ, in order to understand the Bible.[83] Thus, when Islam spread outside Arabia, a certain number of

82 Abu Dawoud, Ahmad Hasan (tr.), *Sunan Abu Dawoud, Kitāb al-'Ilm,* Chapter 1371, Nos. 3641 and 3642, Vol. III, (New Delhi: Al-Madina Publications), 1985, p. 1036.

83 Hamidullah, op. cit., 1997, pp. 208-209.

Muslims, in the same tradition as their predecessors, were quick to educate themselves in foreign languages.

Summary

In summary, it is vital to comprehend that the only sciences the Arabs learnt at this point were the sciences of the *dīn,* with the sole exception of poetry, since this was all the knowledge they possessed at this time. These revealed sciences covered a wide variety of topics such as Qur'an, the Sunnah, *ḥadīth* studies, jurisprudence, worship, the rules of trade and manners, indeed the basis for an entire civilisation and all the sciences needed for individuals and for society. These sciences were not categorised at this time and were therefore taught unsystematically under the wider term '*dīn*'. Due to the encouragement of the Prophet Muḥammad ﷺ, a number of individuals of the older generation and a large number of young people also acquired literacy skills. The youth were in the forefront of learning, reading and writing, which was used in the context of the Qur'an and the Sunnah. Allah ﷻ says in the Noble Qur'an regarding the Prophet ﷺ, "*For this We sent a Messenger to you from among you to recite Our Signs to you and purify you and teach you the Book and Wisdom and teach you things you did not know before.*"[84] This verse demonstrates that the Prophet ﷺ not only taught Muslims knowledge but also how to achieve spiritual wellbeing. Hence, the philosophy of the early community was the use of *ta'līm, ta'dīb* and *tarbiyah,* i.e. learning all the sciences that were available to them, which were about being ethical and moral in all situations, and acting upon the laws laid down by Allah.

These three specific educational terms were not in common use amongst people at that time; they were later coined from the Qur'an and Sunnah by historians and educators who looked back to the sources and the earliest era of Islam for inspiration. Thus, *ta'līm, ta'dīb*

[84] Sūrat al-Baqarah 2:151.

and *tarbiyah* were embodied in action and practice in Madīnah in the Prophet's ﷺ time but were not articulated as a written educational theory. When the Messenger of Allah ﷺ and the Muslims opened Makkah to Islam in the year 630 CE, all of Arabia gave their allegiance to him ﷺ within a short time.[85]

By this time the Prophet ﷺ had introduced two different styles of education in the whole of Arabia; one was the study circles (*ḥalaqāt*) that were based in the mosques, where students of all ages met together at various times to learn different subjects (including poetry) and literacy from a teacher. The second style of learning was based upon students travelling (*riḥlah*) to a known teacher or place where teachers or people of knowledge were known to be, which in this case was the Prophet ﷺ and his city, and here they learned what they required before returning home. Another variation of this second style of learning (*riḥlah*) was that the Prophet ﷺ himself sent teachers to various places where education was needed.

Even if education and learning at this time were centred on the sciences of the *dīn*, the emphasis of learning in Islam was materially conveyed in the central symbol of a Book i.e. the Qur'an. Thus, even at this time, secular learning was seen as inseparable from religious practice, as can be seen by the example of poetry and literacy being taught in the mosques of Madīnah. Moreover, it has always been recognised that Islam, with its fundamental teachings prohibiting usury and other unjust transactions, also has teachings about mundane matters such as the marketplace and economic matters in general. Islam combines knowledge of the secular and the religious, the spiritual and the mundane.

Muhammad ﷺ was their Prophet, thus his actions were copied by his Companions ؓ and recorded by them by committing to memory or in a written form. He was a man chosen by Allah whom they wanted

[85] Hodgson, op. cit., p. 196.

to copy in all aspects of life, i.e. in how to pray, how to eat, how to sleep, and even how to teach and learn. His example in all matters (including education) was seized upon by his Companions:

> It was Muhammad's ﷺ unique position as a prophet of God, which gave the impetus to achieve his success. The Muslims took everything he said or did seriously. The same was the case in the field of education. His method of teaching and what he taught, even the way he used to sit among people were copied throughout the Muslim history.[86]

This whole phenomenon was termed the *Sunnah,* the Way of the Prophet ﷺ. Education by and under the supervision of the Prophet ﷺ in Makkah and Madīnah lasted as long as his Prophethood, which was around twenty-three years, from 610 to 632 CE. The history of education in the Prophet's ﷺ time parallels the build-up (edification) of the first Islamic society. In Makkah the revelation dealt with the central principles of Islam; the Muslims were few in numbers and they were persecuted and for that reason education dealt with matters for the first thirteen years that were more basic and fundamental in comparison to the later years. In contrast in Madīnah, education became more advanced in terms of societal and legal matters because of various factors such as the freedom the Muslims had in their new polity, for example the freedom to build mosques that included study circles. Revelation became more focused on social structures such as law, ethics and community. For the Muslims, their studies of Islam became more sophisticated; moreover, the Prophet ﷺ was able at this point to apportion considerable time to boost literacy and education. Thus, the Prophet ﷺ became a school in himself, teaching the Muslims to take care of both their spiritual and physical wellbeing.

[86] Ahmed, op. cit., p. 30.

In the history of Islamic education the period under the Prophet ﷺ was the primary stage of education; a 'stage of foundation', and his two methods of education were so influential on the first Islamic community that they have been ever present in Islamic education up to the present day. The change of this rudimentary Arab society to a society governed by a written divine law in less than twenty-three years in itself shows the transformation Islam effected in the Arabs. However, at this point this new society did not stand out in the world as a high and significant culture. The Persians and the Byzantines, the world powers of this time, did not see the new Muslim power in Arabia as anything but a petty disturbance. In retrospect, it can be seen that the early community of Islam was a revolutionary society which did not hesitate to trust that it could replace the old systems of the world with its new way of life:

> Some of the early Muslims began to imagine replacing the former societies of all mankind with a new society based on their new ideals. At length we have something approaching a total social experiment -perhaps one of the few really major ones in history. To be sure this did not begin to mature till the very end of the period; with its maturing, we enter the realm of Islamicate civilisation proper. But its seeds were present in the small group of early Muslims.[87]

[87] Hodgson, op. cit., p. 196.

Chapter Two

From the Foundation to the Formative Period

The Prophet Muḥammad ﷺ passed on in the year 632 CE. This chapter is not written with the intention to explain or to analyse the succession of the Prophet ﷺ; neither is it an attempt to study this period with regard to the battles fought and the treaties made between the Muslims and the conquered; this has been adequately treated in the past. In this chapter, the epoch of the *Khulafā ar-Rāshidūn* and subsequent periods are important in view of their impact on the educational system left by the Prophet ﷺ.

The period of the Rightly Guided Caliphs spans approximately thirty years, from 632 to 661 CE. According to most historians the epoch of Abū Bakr aṣ-Ṣiddīq ibn Abī Qaḥāfah (573-634), 'Umar ibn al-Khaṭṭāb (580/81-644), 'Uthmān ibn 'Affān (576-656) and 'Alī ibn Abī Ṭālib (598/600-661) ﷺ, can be divided into two main periods: the first is of expansion and openings whereas the second consists of mutual recrimination and civil war. Both these periods are thus designated in view of the political activities of that time. The first period is deemed to have started in 632 CE with the accession of Abū Bakr ﷺ to the Caliphate and lasted two years. 'Umar ﷺ succeeded him and ruled the

Muslim world (inclusive of Persia and the one-time realms of Eastern Byzantium) as caliph for ten years (r. 634-644). After his death, 'Uthmān ﷺ became the Caliph and remained so for the next twelve years (r. 644-656). Many historians refer to the first six years of 'Uthmān's ﷺ rule as a part of the first period, and the following six years as the beginning of the second period. The last of the Rightly Guided Caliphs was 'Alī ﷺ who ruled for barely four years (r. 656-661). The end of his rule was also the end of the second period, although arguably it ended six months later with the agreement his successor, his son al-Ḥasan, negotiated with Mu'āwiyah to cede him the Caliphate.[1]

Education and *al-Khulafā ar-Rāshidūn*

Those historians who have written about this period have not specifically treated the history of the community's social structure. Thus, the picture drawn in this chapter is derived from very diverse sources that mention education haphazardly while writing largely about political history. Interestingly, many modern historians who have dealt with this kind of social history have argued that this period was not beneficial to Islamic education. They have repeatedly stressed that "the first Muslim conquerors were in no way patrons of learning"[2] and that later on "the Umayyads were suspicious of learning, they were not interested in books and scholarship."[3]

This is a preconception of the historians that does not in any way do justice to the early period of Islamic civilisation after the death of the Prophet ﷺ. It can easily be countered by looking more closely at the state of society in the early Islamic period. During the time of Abū Bakr ﷺ few changes seem to have occurred in the sphere of education. However, this has to be attributed to the short span of time for which

---

1 M. A. Shaban, *Islamic History: A New Interpretation*, (Cambridge: Cambridge University Press), 1971, p. 69.

2 Nakosteen, op. cit., p. 143.

3 Ibid.

he ruled, i.e. two years, in which a great deal of attention was paid to dealing with the wars of apostasy (*riddah*).[4] It is therefore reasonable to assume that at the time of Abū Bakr 🙵, the educational model of the Messenger of Allah 🙵 was not modified.

However, there is one change within the literary sphere which was of major importance and that was the collection, on the insistence of his advisor 'Umar ibn al-Khaṭṭāb 🙵, of the written copy of the Qur'an. It was of major literary historical consequence since this was the first book ever written down in the Arabic language, although this accomplishment did not have a direct impact on education until later. Only one copy was compiled and then left with Ḥafṣah 🙵, the wife of the Prophet 🙵.[5]

According to some historians of education it was at the time of the Caliph 'Umar 🙵 that the existent educational system was developed.[6] According to Hamiuddin Khan, 'Umar ibn al-Khaṭṭāb 🙵 established schools in all the lands newly opened to Islam and paid teachers' salaries.[7] According to these sources, this may be the first time elementary schools (*kuttāb*) are mentioned in Islamic history. In addition, other sources cite the Caliph 'Umar 🙵 as having sent ten teachers to Kufa. There is also evidence of him sending other teachers to the various new areas converted to Islam.[8] However, by looking closely at the historical evidence concerning elementary schools as separate institutions, it is conclusive that the above-mentioned sources do not specifically indicate that he set up the *kuttāb* outside the mosque system. Rather, the evidence seems to support the theory that the Caliph 'Umar 🙵 set up study circles for children and adults in the newly built

---

[4] Shaban, op. cit., p. 69.
[5] Masud ul Hasan, *History of Islam, Vol. 1*, (Lahore: Islamic Publications), 1998, pp. 98-107.
[6] Oadah, op. cit., p. 25.
[7] Khan, op. cit., p. 23.
[8] Oadah, op. cit., p. 25.

mosques in these new Islamic lands. He then advanced the teaching profession by setting salaries for these teachers, which gave value to teachers as governmental employees.

The historical evidence instead demonstrates that it was Imam Mālik (710-795) in Madīnah who separated children's education from the mosque. Special rooms attached to the mosques were utilised to teach them. Later, the *kuttāb* became an institution that was independent of the mosque.[9] Therefore, it is more plausible that the inception of the *kuttāb* occurred at the time of the Umayyads.

However, 'Umar ؓ did improve education and adapt it. In addition to building various mosques for educational purposes and sending teachers to them with established salaries, he also contributed to the educational system by the creation of a governmental department, the *dīwān*[10] "which registered the names of the beneficiary of pensions, dealt with correspondence and finance,"[11] thus indirectly providing a motive for people to educate themselves in literacy and arithmetical sciences. Later, under the Umayyads and especially under the 'Abbasids, it is possible to witness a new class of secretaries working in numerous inns. In many ways they also generated and developed literary sciences that became highly influential in society.[12]

'Umar ؓ was the founder of the 'garrison towns': Basra and Kufa in Iraq, Fusṭāṭ in Egypt and other towns in Khurasan. These garrison towns were destined to become principal cities boasting higher education institutions for centuries.[13] Another governmental position that 'Umar ؓ enhanced was the appointment of the *qāḍī* (judge) for

---

9   Ibid., p. 91.
10   *Dīwāns*, initially registers of all the Muslims, became governmental departments of various functions, and grew immensely in the 'Abbasid period.
11   Imamuddin, op. cit., p. 5.
12   M. J. C. Young and R. B. Serjeant (eds.), *Religion, Learning and Science in the Abbasid Period*, (Cambridge: Cambridge University Press), 1990, p. 155.
13   Albert Hourani, *A History of the Arab People*, (London: Faber and Faber), 1991, p. 24.

various regions of the newly opened lands. He chose Abū ad-Dardā' as *qāḍī* in Madīnah, Shurayḥ in Basra and Abū Mūsā al-Ash'arī in Kufa ﷺ.[14] He followed the Prophet's ﷺ example and confirmed the necessity of the *qāḍī* learning Islamic law. In his letter to Abū Mūsā ﷺ, 'Umar ﷺ wrote about the importance of the primary sources of law, i.e. the Qur'an and Sunnah, and the secondary sources, *qiyās* and *ijtihād*. He continued the letter by giving him advice on how to use all these sources in an environment such as Kufa.[15]

Furthermore, it was at the time of 'Umar ﷺ, in the year 636 CE, that the famous academy of medicine of Jundi-Shapur in Persia was taken over by the Muslims. King Shapur founded the city in the third century CE and in it he developed a medical institute. After the Islamic conquest, the medical institute (*bimaristan*) of Jundi-Shapur continued to flourish and had considerable support from the caliphs. Accordingly, all *bimaristans* (and medical academies) throughout the Muslim world were modelled upon the *bimaristan* of Jundi-Shapur.[16] 'Umar ﷺ let the academy continue without disrupting it and in the 'Abbasid period it was possible to witness a number of new *bimaristans* made on the model of Jundi-Shapur.

The Caliph 'Uthmān ﷺ followed the policies of his predecessors and all the regions were provided with mosques and teachers to educate children and adults. During his Caliphate, disputes about the correct recitation of the Qur'an occurred. The Caliph and his advisors felt that such disputes could lead to disunity and found it imperative to establish an utterly authentic standard text (*muṣḥaf*) that could easily be disseminated across the Caliphate. 'Uthmān appointed Zayd ibn Thābit, who had compiled the first copy under the rule of Abū Bakr,

---

14 Abdur Rahman I. Doi, *Shari'ah: The Islamic Law*, (London: Ta-Ha Publishers), 1997, p. 14.

15 Ibid.

16 Richard N. Frye, *The Golden Age of Persia*, (London: Phoenix Press), 2000, p. 22.

and several other Companions ؓ to use Ḥafṣah's ؓ copy of the Qur'an to prepare a single authoritative text. A number of copies were made and sent to provincial centres of the Caliphate to be further copied and used. The Caliph 'Uthmān ؓ ordered the Muslims to burn any other variant copies circulating in their provinces. Thus, the main contribution of the Caliph 'Uthmān ؓ in the sphere of education, was the standardisation of the written copy (*muṣḥaf*) of the Qur'an. This was carried out within the first six years of his Caliphate. He made six copies and sent them to various provinces, accompanied by a number of Qur'an teachers.[17]

From the rule of Abū Bakr ؓ through to the sixth year of 'Uthmān's rule, eighteen years were spent in fighting the Byzantine and Persian Empires and the consolidation of lands under Muslim rule. Education was still at a foundational stage, but political changes in society began to stir changes in the educational system. Formal instruction in both the Qur'an and the Sunnah increased in these years and there is evidence that the rise of Islam also increased spiritual learning. However, these developments came to an abrupt stop in the last six years of 'Uthmān's era ؓ (650-656) and during the four years of 'Alī's ؓ rule due to civil war.

There is no doubt that formal education was still in its early years and in these approximately thirty years it did not specifically change to a great extent, neither were any new institutions of Islamic education founded. However, in the theory of Islamic education, there was a certain amount of development by various Companions and successors. 'Alī ؓ emphasised the importance of discussion and review of the student's lessons to ensure that the student had not forgotten or made a mistake in his understanding of the teaching. Furthermore, he emphasised the importance of Arabic grammar when he said, "Cleave to the grammar of Arabic and to poetry for they undo the two knots

[17] Qadhi, op. cit., p. 136.

of the tongue: barbarism and ungrammatical language."[18] Indeed, 'Alī
⚜ initiated the first work on Arabic grammar written by Abū'l-Aswad
ad-Du'ali, and he himself gave him the first lines of the composition
and acted as its final editor.[19]

In addition to 'Alī's ⚜ advancement of educational theory, 'Umar
ibn al-Khaṭṭāb ⚜ had seen to it that in addition to the study of Islam,
children should also be taught subjects such as poetry, which teaches
the highest human expression of language and is thus vital for
understanding the supreme example of divine language as well as the
ḥadīth and the great works of Islamic scholarship and history, which
teach the nature of society and civilisation, and physical education
such as horsemanship and swimming.[20] This latter kind of education
seems to have been seen as the responsibility of parents and not of
the teachers nor of the mosques. Thus, most children in a desert
area like the Hijaz would learn the arts of sword-fighting, archery
and horseback riding from experts of their own tribe and clan at the
insistence of their parents.

'Abdullāh ibn 'Abbās⚜ also developed Islamic education by pointing
out the necessity of free time given to students between each class.[21]
The spread in understanding of the Qur'an, the rise of ḥadīth literature
and the emphasis on literacy in these years shows the serious attitude
developed towards education and respect for the learned.

Consequently, this period may still be included in 'the period of the
foundation of Islamic education' since no new institutions of education
were founded and it is normally acknowledged that the time of al-
Khulafā ar-Rāshidūn is part of the beginning of Islamic civilisation.[22]

---

[18] George Makdisi, *The Rise of Humanism in Classical Islam and the Christian West*,
(Edinburgh: Edinburgh University Press), 1990, p. 123.

[19] Jalāl ad-Dīn as-Suyūṭī, *History of the Khalifahs*, (London, Ta-Ha Publishers), 1995,
p. 200.

[20] Oadah, op. cit., p. 25.

[21] Ibid.

[22] Hourani, op. cit., p. 25.

Although many historians have separated the life of the Messenger of Allah ﷺ from the history of the four Rightly Guided Caliphs ؓ, the fact remains that all of this period was the formative time for Islamic civilisation. The influence of the Byzantine and Persian education systems did not fully make their effects felt upon Islamic civilisation until the Umayyad period, the period of 'growth and ripening'.[23]

At this juncture it is important to focus briefly on Nakosteen's charge in his book *History of Islamic Origins of Western Education* that 'Umar ibn al-Khaṭṭāb ؓ burnt down the library in Alexandria.[24] It seems that the story of the library's destruction in Alexandria by 'Amr ibn al-'Āṣ on the order of 'Umar ؓ first appeared in Arabic literature in the latter half of the thirteenth century CE. This account was narrated by Abū al-Faraj and when this story was told he cited no source in evidence. Nevertheless, the tale continued to be retold by Abū al Fidā in the early fourteenth century and then by Makrizi in their respective books.[25] According to historians such as Ali this story is fabricated and this is supported by European historians such as Gibbon and Renaudot who regarded the story as suspect.[26]

It seems that to lay this rumour to rest there is a need for a point-by-point refutation of the story told by Abū al-Faraj. This was successfully done by the historian Alfred J. Butler in the late Seventies. His argument is divided into seven points, which are extensively researched, and are briefly presented here.

The first point is that the tale originally made its appearance, without a source to ensure its authenticity, five hundred years after the event supposedly occurred.

---

[23] Haider Bammate, *Muslim Contribution to Civilization*, (Takoma Park: Crescent Publication), 1962, p. 9.

[24] Nakosteen, op. cit., pp. 143-144.

[25] Alfred J. Butler, *The Arab Conquest of Egypt*, (Oxford: Clarendon Press), 1978, pp. 401-403.

[26] K. Ali, *A Study of Islamic History*, (Lahore: Al-Fazal Market), 1986. Also see: J. B. Bury, Gibbon's Decline and Fall, (London), 1896.

Second, the story has many illogical features. Even if one believes for a moment in the destruction of the library at the Caliph's orders, there is still the task to explain how, according to the tale of Abū al-Faraj, such a number of books could reasonably have been carried from the library to the city. Furthermore, they are supposed to have been burnt in the baths of the city and served as fuel for as long as six months. This is not scientifically possible since it is a well known fact that a large proportion of the books in the library were written on vellum. Vellum is a material that cannot burn as fuel, and as Butler puts it, "all the Caliph's orders could not make books of vellum burn."[27]

The third point exposes the story as an absurdity when it is disclosed that the principal witness to the event who recounts this story, John Philopounus, died long before the Arabs invaded Egypt.

Fourth is the historical fact that either the fire caused by Julius Caesar's attack on Alexandria centuries before destroyed the whole of the library[28] or that the library perished at a date no less than four hundred years before the Muslim conquest. The Serapeum Library in Alexandria inherited a number of the books that survived from the original library. This Serapeum Library was itself destroyed in the year 391 CE which is in scholarly circles a confirmed historical event of antiquity. Hence, there is indisputable historical evidence that the library did not even exist for at least two and a half centuries before the Muslim conquest.

The fifth point is that there is virtually no mention of the Alexandrian Library in any Byzantine literature in the fifth, sixth and seventh centuries.

Butler further argues that even if the library did still exist (which would have been miraculous after the preceding arguments), Cyrus the

[27] Butler, op. cit., pp. 404-405.

[28] Sometimes referred to as the Elder or Mother Library in contrast with the Serapeum Library, which is referred to as the Daughter Library.

Governor of Alexandria, who surrendered Alexandria to the Muslim Arabs, had the right according to the treaty he signed to transfer valuables in Alexandria to Constantinople. The market value of books in the library would have been enormous if it existed. Moreover, eleven months lapsed from the signing of the Treaty until the entry of the Arabs into Alexandria during which time all sea passages to Constantinople were open and unhindered.

The final point against the story of Abū al-Faraj is that if the library had been destroyed by the Arabs, Bishop John of Nikiou, a famous contemporary historian, would not have passed over it in silence since all his work regarding the conquest of Alexandria is detailed.[29]

Education during the Time of the Umayyads

> ....it is the Umayyad caliphs to whom Muslim historians are often rather unfair, who deserve the honor of being the first to promote the development of the Islamic civilisation.[30]

The Umayyads ruled the Muslims from their capital city Damascus for ninety years. The beginning of the Umayyad dynasty started with the Caliph Mu'āwiyah ﵁ whose rule lasted for approximately nineteen years (661-680). He is already well known in the educational history of Islam as being one of the few people of Makkah who were literate before Islam, and after his acceptance of Islam he was well known to have been one of the scribes of the Prophet ﷺ.[31]

According to Hourani, the Umayyads and the later caliphs were seen in a rather different light from the first four Caliphs who are known to the majority of the Muslims as '*ar-Rāshidūn*'[32] or 'The Rightly

---

29 Butler, op. cit., pp. 401-426.

30 Bammate, op. cit., p. 8.

31 Bosworth, op. cit., Vol. IX, p. 265.

32 *Rāshidūn* has a more active sense than 'rightly guided' which might be rendered somewhat cumbersomely as 'who took the right way' - Ed.

Guided'.[33] Primarily, the Umayyads bequeathed a hereditary system and allegedly adopted a lifestyle[34] that was questionable, and this continued with subsequent dynasties, but while the majority of the people did accept the caliphs as leaders, they were never perceived as 'Rightly Guided'.[35] This view also seems to have affected Islamic education, which had been in the hands of rulers such as *ar-Rāshidūn* after the demise of the Messenger of Allah ﷺ.[36] During the Umayyad period, it transferred to a new social class entitled *'ulamā'* (people of knowledge) in the society. They were recognised as the true inheritors of the Prophet ﷺ from the *ḥadīth* reported by Abū ad-Dardā' ﵁, "The *'ulamā'* are the heirs of the prophets, and the prophets did not leave a dinar or a dirham as legacy but they left knowledge as legacy."[37] Even though the government continued to sponsor and develop education, it did so now in parallel with the new social class of scholars.

This is not to say that the caliphs after the 'Rightly Guided' did nothing to encourage Islamic education. In fact the most important change in the educational system from the government came from the Caliph 'Abd al-Mālik ibn Marwān (646-705) who made it compulsory in 690 CE to use the Arabic language in administration throughout all the provinces, which bolstered the use and teaching of the Arabic language across the Caliphate. Another caliph who had a strong impact on education was the Caliph 'Umar ibn 'Abd al-'Azīz (682-720). He boosted the teaching of the Sunnah, *fiqh* and the *ḥadīth* and it may

---

33 Hourani, op. cit., p. 25.

34 It is difficult to assess the period fairly since we receive all information through an 'Abbasid filter, and the 'Abbasids had led a massive propaganda campaign against the Umayyads and then massacred them - Ed.

35 The main exception is the Caliph 'Umar ibn 'Abd al-'Azīz of the Umayyads. Others have been mentioned, most notably Mu'āwiyah ibn Abī Sufyān ﵁ whom some of the *'ulamā'* such as Qadi 'Iyad considered one of *al-Khulafā ar-Rāshidūn* - Ed.

36 Hourani, op. cit., p. 25.

37 Abu Dawoud, Ahmad Hasan (tr.), *Sunan Abu Dawoud, Kitāb al-'Ilm*, Chapter 1369, No. 3635, Vol. III, (New Delhi: Al-Madina Publications), 1985, p. 1034, (re-translated by the editor).

be argued that his interest in the subject was ultimately the origin for the compilation of major collections beginning with early works such as the *Muwaṭṭa'* of Imam Mālik and culminating in the six famous *ḥadīth* collections.[38] Other caliphs also contributed: for example, Mu'āwiyah رضي الله عنه invited the Christian physician Ibn Athal to his palace to translate a medical book into Arabic and later caliphs invited Muslim scholars to have debates with Jewish and Christian scholars concerning religious dogmas and a wide range of other matters.[39]

It was not its work in the arena of education that led to the downfall of the Umayyad dynasty but its political intrigues. The Umayyads' grip on power had always been unstable, since their rise to power originated from civil war and the death of popular figures such as 'Alī and Hussein رضي الله عنهما. Their policies concerning non-Arabs, who were treated as second-class citizens (being clients of Arab tribes and economically dependent),[40] and later rulers' being seen as inconsistent with Islamic law led to widespread discontent and a wish for change, which appeared in the form of the revolution by the 'Abbasids in 750 CE. Therefore, the rise of education in the Umayyad period should not be seen as the success of the Umayyad government alone but rather the success of an entire civilisation, including the general public, but specifically the scholars who were willing to use the educational ways inherited from the Prophet ﷺ and others adapted from the social systems of Persia and Byzantine.

As we have seen, education was not simply in the hands of the Caliphate, and in order for it to adorn itself with the mantle of success, it was rather due to scholars and teachers that an education system started to take shape. They were strongly opposed to government control over education and believed that learning was the inheritance

38 Hourani, op. cit., p. 25.
39 Ibid.
40 Frye, op. cit., p. 104.

of the prophets. Since this period, there has always been a distance, sometimes cordial and sometimes hostile, between scholars, who see themselves as inheritors of the prophets, and the state.

'Schools for Education' and 'Schools of Law'

When writing about education, it is almost impossible not to confuse the two terms 'school of law' and 'school for education'.

> In the history of Islamic institutions the development of the 'schools of law' presents a number of problems, including the very term translated here as 'school', namely *madhhab*.[41]

For the historical study of education, the term 'schools of law', which is given as the translation of *madhhab*, offers a major terminological problem, since it can be misunderstood to mean an educational institution. In his book, *Rise of Colleges,* Makdisi indicates the difference between a school of law and a college of law (madrasah). Accordingly, the latter is an educational institution, which arose in the eleventh century approximately, where specific *madhāhib* were taught. In contrast, the 'schools of law' or the *'madhāhib'* are technically an opinion or a thesis of jurisprudence by one individual master for his disciples. This does not mean that the *madhāhib* are educational institutions; they were in fact legal opinions taught in the early years of Islam at a *ḥalaqah* in the mosque by such figures as Imam Abū Ḥanīfah (699-765), Imam Mālik (711-795), and Imam al-Layth ibn Sa'd (712-791).[42]

Although it is a confusion caused by translating *'madhhab'* as 'school of law' and it does not arise in the Arabic language, the solution concerning the terminology 'school of law' and 'school of education'

---

41 Makdisi, op. cit., 1981, p. 1.

42 Makdisi, op. cit., 1981, p. 4.

lies in the book, *The Rise of Humanism in Classical Islam and the Christian West,* which Makdisi wrote after *The Rise of Colleges.* Here he gives excellent justification for changing the term 'school of law' to 'guild of law', which removes the confusion concerning the word 'school'. He also says that the term 'guild of law' should be used for circles (*ḥalaqah*) held in mosques and 'college of law' for the madrasah, to avoid confusion between the history of Islamic education and the history of Islamic law.

It has to be remembered that the early 'guilds of law' were neither definite organisations nor did they have a uniformity of doctrine. They arose when the Islamic conquests led to territorial expansion, the intermingling of Arabs and non-Arabs, and material development. This gave rise to the frequent use of *ijtihād* and as a result, there was urgent necessity for a methodology.

> At this stage the jurists felt the need for devising a set of some criteria to remove disagreement on the disputed points. They were based on the Arabic grammar, syntax, theology, the textual material of legal relevance in the authoritative sources, and acquaintance with the methods used by the Companions.[43]

Thus, the science of the principles of jurisprudence (*uṣūl al-fiqh*) was developed for the first time in an organised manner. The evolution of the *madhāhib*/guilds of law began during the early Umayyad period.[44] In the beginning these *madhāhib* were based upon their geographical settings, i.e. the Madani, Basran, Kufan and Syrian guilds.[45] From these

43 Ahmad Hasan, *Principles of Islamic Jurisprudence*, (Islamabad: International Islamic University), 1993, p. 17.

44 Abu Ameenah Bilal Philips, *The Evolution of Fiqh*, (International Islamic Publishing House), 1988, pp. 48-49.

45 Makdisi, op. cit., 1990, p. 2.

geographical origins in the later Umayyad and early ʻAbbasid periods there arose the four *madhāhib*[46] of today and many other *madhāhib* that did not survive up to the present day.[47]

Many masters taught their legal doctrines to their students in various mosque *ḥalaqahs.* For example, in the *Jāmiʻah al-Madīnah al-Manṣūr,* the first mosque to be constructed in Baghdad (762-766), *ḥalaqāt* were being taught by different guilds of law, such as the Ḥanbalī, Ḥanafī, Shāfiʻī and Ẓāhirī. It was possible to find most *madhāhib* teaching their legal doctrines in mosques around the Muslim world in this manner.[48] Hence, the *madhāhib*/guilds of law were not educational institutions but legal doctrines, which in the early centuries of Islam were taught in a mosque *ḥalaqah.* According to Makdisi, all the guilds of law were basically opinions/theses that needed to be defended. Many of the *madhāhib* started to die out slowly due to the lack of support by disciples and their inability to defend their doctrines. The survival of the four *madhāhib* and the disappearance of all other guilds of law is considered to have happened around the twelfth to thirteenth century.[49] This implies that in the first four centuries of Islam, an abundance of guilds of law were teaching their legal doctrines and formulating them in the mosques but that by the time the madrasah came along in the eleventh and twelfth century, it was mostly the four present-day *madhāhib* that were left to teach their legal doctrines.

The Establishment of the Elementary Schools

Change, or as Haider calls it 'growth and ripening', occurred in Islamic education in three different ways. Primarily, there was the introduction of new educational institutions; secondly, the rise of different

---

46 These are the Ḥanafī, Shāfiʻī, Ḥanbalī and Mālikī guilds of law.

47 Abdul Aziz bin Muḥammad, *Zakat and Rural Development in Malaysia,* (Malaysia: Berita Publishing), 1993, p. 60.

48 Ahmed, op. cit., p. 116.

49 Makdisi, op. cit., 1981, pp. 2-9.

sciences and finally, the formulation of philosophies of education by various scholars. It has to be remembered that after the Caliphates of *ar-Rāshidūn*, the government was never seen by scholars as the rightful establisher of education, especially with regards to the Islamic pedagogical sciences. Change in education did not always come from the government; at certain times alterations took place due to the scholars and the building of institutions from endowments. There are unfortunately no statistics that show the success rate of the *kuttāb*. However, it may be argued that the success of Arabic as a language which was read and written widely during this period is indirect evidence of the success of the *kuttāb*.

The Kuttāb *or* Maktab

The first institution to have come into existence after 'the period of the foundation of Islamic education' is most likely to have been the '*kuttāb*'.[50] It seems likely that the *kuttāb* already existed in the first century of Islam. The evidence often cited concerns Umm Sulaym bint Milḥān al-Anṣāriyyah ، mother of the Companion Anas ibn Mālik ، in Madīnah, who has been reported to have asked the school teacher of the *kuttāb* "to send her some boys to help her with wool carding."[51] In another source it is reported that Imam Mālik (710-795), who was born at the end of the first century of Islam in Madīnah, forbade that

---

[50] The root of the word *kuttāb* is *kataba* which means to write. One of the words used by Allah to describe the Qur'an is also from the same root as *kuttāb*, i.e. *kitāb* ['Book']. In the Qur'an, Allah says: "*Alif Lam Mim. That is the Book (kitāb), without any doubt. In it is guidance for the godfearing*" (Sūrat al-Baqarah 2:1-2). There is a controversy as to whether it or the word *maktab* is the right word for school. In the lexicon both are called schools, but al-Mubarrad and al-Fayruzabadi say that the term *kuttāb* is an error and that it literally means 'writers' i.e. 'the boys of a school' whereas ash-Shiʿab in his book *Sharḥ ash-Shifā* states that the *kuttāb* is not an error since this is how it was understood in the classical period and it should not be regarded as a post-classical word. For more information see: E. W. Lane, *Arabic-English Lexicon*, vol. II, (London: Islamic Texts Society Trust), 1984.

[51] Makdisi, op. cit., 1990, p. 48.

children be taught in the mosques because they might defile the place.[52] Thus, the *kuttāb* became an institution attached to the mosque but, at the same time, separate and independent.[53] However, the term *kuttāb* seems to have been used much earlier than the date of Imam Mālik's legal ruling. The Persian Companion Salmān al-Farsī ؓ is reported to have said that he had attended a Persian *kuttāb* in his childhood. When looking at Salmān al-Farsī's ؓ educational background, it is evident that he did indeed go to a Persian elementary school. According to *Encyclopaedia Iranica*, three terms for 'school' are indicated in Pahlavi texts, *frahangestān*, *dibīrestān* and *herbedestān,* where students were taught reading, writing, arithmetic and religion.[54] He grew up in a village called Jayyan in the area around Isfahan. His father was a rich man and also a *dhiqan*, a noble who was in charge of the village. Thus, Salmān ؓ was educated in the same way as were his peers: he learnt the arts of reading and writing, the religion of Zoroastrianism, arithmetic and military arts.[55]

Mosque education at the time of the Prophet ﷺ divided into two parts: the writing and reading stage where Muslim children were taught the art of literacy in relation to the Qur'an and the secondary stage where adults learnt Islam. There are other sources that speak of the existence of this *kuttāb* in the early period of Islam. It has been reported that the Companions Ibn 'Umar and Abū Usayd ؓ once passed by a *kuttāb* and attracted the attention of the pupils.[56] This early evolution of the *kuttāb* institute is supported by other historical sources, which point to a radical change in the terminology for elementary teachers in the second Islamic century.[57] In the early

---

[52]   Oadah, op. cit., p. 91.

[53]   Ibid., p. 91.

[54]   Ahmad Tafazzoli, (1997), *Education in the Parthian and Sasanian Periods*, http://www.iranicaonline.org/articles/education-ii, (accessed: 29/09/2011).

[55]   Abdul Wahid Hamid, *Companions of the Prophet*, (Leicester: MELS), 1995, p. 59.

[56]   Shalaby, op. cit., p. 19.

[57]   Oadah, op. cit., p. 94.

period the elementary school teacher seems to have been known by the term *muqri'*, indicating specifically the teaching of the reading of the Qur'an. Later when the *kuttāb* became more than a Qur'anic school and the curriculum consisted of more than the reading of the Qur'an, the elementary teacher came to be known as a *mu'allim* or 'teacher'.[58] This implies that in the early years of the Umayyads there were changes in both the curriculum and the establishment of a *kuttāb* that was independent from the mosque. By the middle of the eighth century CE it seems that a general system of elementary school education became adopted and at most times the *kuttāb* was semi-attached to the mosque.[59]

It is interesting to note that the confusion regarding the status of Islamic elementary school does not cease here. It seems from historical sources that there either existed two different elementary schools in the Islamic world, i.e. the *kuttāb* and the *maktab*, or that the terms were used simultaneously for the same establishment.[60] Nakosteen presumes that the *kuttāb* and the *maktab* are one kind of elementary school. However, he insists that they were places of learning to read and write and their origin was pre-Islamic, i.e. they originated from the Eastern Byzantine education system where pupils were taught in their teachers' homes.[61] Oadah also supports the claim of the *maktab* being a language teaching school stemming from Byzantine education. On the other hand, he avers that the *maktab* was not the same type of school as the *kuttāb*. He argues that the *maktab* was a secular school where literacy, poetry and grammar were taught whereas the *kuttāb* was the place where pupils learned the reading of the Qur'an.[62]

58 Oadah, op. cit., p. 94.

59 Bayard Dodge, *Muslim Education in Medieval Time*, (Washington: Middle East Institute), 1962, p. 3.

60 Makdisi, op. cit., 1981, p. 19.

61 Nakosteen, op. cit., p. 46.

62 Oadah, op. cit., p. 94.

It seems very clear from the historical sources that the *kuttāb* and *maktab* were both terms used for the elementary school, but what is not clear is whether or not both of them were used simultaneously.[63] The classical work *at-Tārīkh al-Baghdādī* seems to solve this problem by pointing out that evidently the word *kuttāb* was in use from the early period of Islam, whereas the term *maktab* was first used only in the year 895 CE in individual reports of scholars in Baghdad. There seems to have been a certain amount of controversy about the uses of the terms *kuttāb* and *maktab* for elementary schools in the third century AH.[64] There is no doubt that when the early Muslims came into contact with both Eastern Byzantium and Persia they came across very different educational systems. It is also a historical fact that while most of Persia became Muslim in a short time, most of the citizens of conquered Eastern Byzantium did not embrace Islam before the second century AH.

According to most sources, the school that was referred to as the *maktab* by the Muslims after the conquest of Eastern Byzantium, already existed in the Byzantine culture as a secondary school. It was a secondary school where pupils learnt the Greek language with prose, the literature of Homer and Greek grammar. This type of secondary education normally began at the age of twelve years, and its main aim was to Hellenise the child, to make him a proper citizen of Byzantium.[65] However, this Byzantine secondary school did not have a designated building; the *grammatikos* either rented a place or used his own house to teach the pupils.[66] The *grammatikos* continued to teach pupils in a similar way for at least the first century AH. This is supported by the Byzantine historian Cameron:

---

63 Ahmed, op. cit., p. 41.

64 Ibid.

65 Mango, op. cit., p. 125.

66 N. H. Baynes and L. B. Moss (eds.), *Byzantium: An Introduction to East Roman Civilisation*, (Oxford: Clarendon Press), 1949, p. 204.

> We have good evidence for the continued presence of the Greek population in Syria, Egypt and Palestine well after the Arab conquest and for social and economic continuity at least until the end of the seventh century...the sources indicate that the population of Syria, Palestine, Mesopotamia and Egypt, in less than two centuries, spoke broadly Arabic and all education started to be taught in the Arabic language.[67]

It is also accepted historically that the *kuttāb* arrived in East Byzantium with the building of the first mosques, since the *kuttāb* was attached to the mosque. It is therefore highly plausible that in countries such as Egypt, Syria and Palestine in the first and second century AH, the *grammatikos* were teaching Greek language and literature at the same time as teachers in the *kuttāb* began to teach the Qur'an. It has to be remembered that education in Byzantium was mostly available to a certain class who had Greek roots, and that the *kuttāb* was a revolutionary new school system where native Arabs and new Muslims of the former East Byzantium could learn to read and write the Arabic language and were taught the Qur'an and Arabic poetry irrespective of class and nationality.

It was inevitable that the Arabic language and the Islamic religion would take over the role of the Greek language and Christianity, thus, the Byzantine educational system went through a revolutionary change. According to the author of the book *Late Antiquity: A Guide to the Post-Classical World*, the Muslim population in the new Islamic realm (up to approximately 800 CE) was counted as a minority, around 5% of the whole. Accordingly, the rise of the Muslim population to become a majority in the Islamic realm is considered to have been reached

---

[67] Averil Cameron, *Changing Cultures in Early Byzantium*, (Aldershot: Variorum), 1996, p. 308.

around the late ninth century.[68] This is, of course, based on historical sources which inform us that the majority of the Arab Muslims in the early days were inhabitants of garrison towns with the native population living outside the walls. During this period the Greek language was seen as a valuable skill, as all administration was carried out in Greek and the majority of the administrators were Christians. By the ninth century, this started to change until even Christian scholars such as the Melkite Bishop Theodore Abū Qurra (d. ca. 830) and the orthodox Bishop Apamea Agapius of Manbij (d. 940) began to use Arabic in all their writings, including Christian theology.[69]

The *maktab's* teacher (*mukattib*) can be seen historically as the successor of the Byzantine *grammatikos.* These teachers could therefore not have been called *mukattib* until the beginning of the second century AH, when a large number of the population in Egypt, Syria and Jordan accepted Islam and started to speak Arabic as their first language. The starting point of the Arabic speaking *maktab* probably coincides with the Caliphal decree in the year 690 CE by the Caliph ʻAbd al-Malik ibn Marwān (r. 685-705) that all administration should be carried out in the Arabic language. However, the *maktab* seems only to have survived as an autonomous school for a short time; it soon semi-attached itself to the mosque and started to teach Qur'an with the other sciences.[70] The historical sources that do speak of the elementary school continually confuse the two terms *maktab* and *kuttāb.*

The Arabisation and Islamisation of the *maktab* led to a merger with the *kuttāb*, which meant that both schools united as one elementary school that was attached to the mosque. The *kuttāb* originally began as a school of Qur'an, whereas the *maktab* evolved from the Arabised Byzantine tradition of a school of grammar, language and science.

---

68 Bowersock, Brown and Grabar (eds.), *Late Antiquity: A Guide to the Post-Classical World*, (Cambridge: The Belknap Press), 1999, p. 517.

69 Ibid, p. 222.

70 Oadah, op. cit., p. 94.

When the majority of the population of this area became Muslims in the late ninth century, both schools were synchronised as one school of education, however, this merger led to the controversy regarding which name to use for the school in the third century AH (tenth century CE). Accordingly, looking at reports from *at-Tārīkh al-Baghdādī* on the ʻAbbasid period, it is evident that the educational school for children changed titles from one to the other. The first fifteen reports about schools in *at-Tārīkh al-Baghdādī* mention the *kuttāb*, whereas the use of the word *maktab* occurs in the year 895 CE when it replaces the term *kuttāb*. Abū Al-ʻAbbās Muḥammad ibn Yazīd al-Mubarrad (d. 898, Baghdad), the Arabic grammarian, wrote concerning the controversy regarding these two terms used for the elementary school. He believed that '*maktab*' was the only correct lexical term to be used for a school whereas the use of the term *kuttāb* was lexically incorrect.[71] It is still debatable as to which term is the correct one, either historically or lexically, but there is no doubt that both terms were used interchangeably in the late Islamic Caliphate of the Umayyads and the early ʻAbbasid period.

The school system in Persia was unlike the school system of Byzantine. Contrary to the Arabisation of the eastern parts of Byzantium, Persia accepted Islam *en masse,* but did not adopt Arab culture or Arabic as a spoken language. Under the ʻAbbasids, Persia developed its own language and Islamic traditions and played a leading role, together with the Arabs, in the spread of Islam. Thus, the first non-Arab language and culture to be seen as Islamic besides Arabic was the Persian.[72] Due to the differences between the Persian and the Arabic parts of the Caliphate there is reason to suspect that there were differences in the understanding of the two terms for the elementary school.[73] For example, the scholar Abū al-Ḥasan ʻAbd al-Ghāfir al-Fārisī

---

71 Ahmed, op. cit., p. 41.

72 Frye, op. cit., pp. 278-279.

73 Makdisi, op. cit., 1981, p. 19.

(d. 1134), seems to have attended the *maktab* at the age of five but then continued his education in the *kuttāb* at the age of ten, where he studied *adab* –literature.[74] It appears that the use of the terms *kuttāb* and *maktab* were highly fluid in their application not only in the Arab world, as Tibawi showed in his book *Islamic Education,* but also among the Persian-speaking population.[75]

The Desert and the Tutor System

The last type of elementary school to have been mentioned by historical sources is what historians have termed the '*palace kuttāb*'.[76] However, this title may be slightly too narrow in its meaning and perhaps it is better to label this elementary education 'private tuition', since not only did the tutor, '*al-mu'addib*', go to the palace to teach the children of the Caliphs, but he also taught the children of traders, sultans, military commanders and nobles at their homes.[77]

The origin of this tutor-based education by the *mu'addib* lies with the Umayyad dynasty, although this type of schooling may have existed in both Byzantine and Persian societies before the arrival of Islam. *Mu'addib*-based education was specifically for the wealthy, the royal court and for the nobles. Since the *Khulafā ar-Rāshidūn* were against the idea of teaching their children separately from other Muslim children, this institution could not have existed during their period. On the other hand, the earliest Umayyad Caliphs followed the Arab nomadic social ways and sent their children to stay in the Syrian Desert. Sources speak of the children of caliphs and nobles being sent to the desert where they learnt fluent Arabic, poetry and Arab genealogy. One example of an Umayyad noble going through this procedure was Yazīd ibn Mu'āwiyah. This style of education

74 Ibid.
75 A. L. Tibawi, *Islamic Education*, (London: Luzac and Company), 1972, p. 26.
76 Shalaby, op. cit., p.25.
77 Oadah, op. cit., p. 91.

was no different from the instruction of the children of Quraysh in the pre-Islamic period. The Prophet Muḥammad ﷺ himself had, in a similar fashion, been sent to the Hijaz desert at a young age so that he could achieve linguistic proficiency.[78] Mu'āwiyah ibn Abū Sufyān (602–680) ؓ is likely to have been educated in a similar way, since he was of the tribe of Quraysh and his father was a high standing figure in both pre-Islamic society and after the Opening of Makkah to Islam. After Yazīd, his son Mu'āwiyah II came to the throne, but died at a young age, thus ending the line of Mu'āwiyah ibn Abū Sufyān. The next Caliph to come to power was Marwān ibn al-Ḥakam (r. 684–685) of the Umayyad clan who was a cousin of Mu'āwiyah ibn Abū Sufyān, and it is again reasonable to assume that, like his cousin, Marwān was himself educated in the Hijaz desert.

The earliest sources to be found concerning the employment of a *mu'addib*, link this educational process to the Caliph 'Abd al-Malik ibn Marwān (r. 685-705). For example, it is reported that he instructed the *mu'addib* of his sons to teach them the manners and the etiquette of royal courts.[79] It is evident that at his time there was a change in the understanding of the tuition of royalty and the nobles. The Arab nomadic social ways came to an end; the Umayyads now emerged as kings who had to learn how to behave at royal courts and who required extensive education relating both to religion and literature. According to Nakosteen, the tutors were called *mu'addib* because their main objective was to teach their pupils *adab* (manners and etiquette), which is from the same root as the word *mu'addib.*[80] This is further demonstrated by the Caliph Hishām ibn 'Abd al-Malik (r. 724-743) when he is reported to have said to the *mu'addib* of his child, "Give him instruction first in the Noble Book, then in poetry and great oration, the knowledge of good and evil, accounts of famous wars and lastly

[78] See the first chapter of this book.
[79] Ahmed, op. cit., p. 46.
[80] Nakosteen, op. cit., p. 47.

the art of conversation."[81] The *mu'addib* seems to have been highly respected in society because of his connections with royalty and the wealthy and because they were also often well known scholars, which was the main reason that royalty and the rich approached them to teach their children.[82]

Although it seems to be accepted by historians that the *mu'addib* was more respected than the *mu'allim*, it is very important to understand that in early Islamic history various scholars refused to teach the children of the caliphs and the wealthy in their palaces or homes. Like the *Khulafā ar-Rāshidūn*, they believed that the children of caliphs and the wealthy should come to the *kuttāb* to learn. One example of such a teacher is Imam Mālik, who refused to leave the Prophet's mosque or teaching in his own home when he was asked by the 'Abbasid Caliph Hārūn ar-Rashīd (r. 786-809) to attend the court in order to teach his children. Imam Mālik's response, "*Amīr al-Mu'minīn*, one comes to knowledge, it does not come to one", impressed the Caliph to such an extent that he humbly sent his children to study with Imam Mālik during the Hajj period.[83]

The Rise of the Islamic Sciences

> Islamic sciences came into being from a wedding between the spirit that issued from the Qur'anic revelation and the existing sciences of various civilisations which Islam inherited.[84]

One of the first sciences to have been developed during this period was the science of the Arabic language, the language of the Qur'an;

---

81 Shalaby, op. cit., p. 25.

82 Ahmed, op. cit., p. 46.

83 Mawil Izzidien, *Islamic Law*, (Edinburgh: Edinburgh University press), 2004.

84 Seyyed Hossein Nasr, *Islamic Science*, (England: World of Islam Festival Publishing Company), 1976, p. 9.

it had its origins in the twin cities of Basra and Kufa specifically.[85] It was vital for the science of the Arabic language to be developed at this stage for a number of reasons: primarily, in order to understand the Qur'an; then to provide the Arabic language to non-Arab Muslims; fear of the corruption of the standard Arabic language also fuelled the advance; and finally, the need to bridge the gap between the classical Arabic of the Qur'an and everyday spoken colloquial Arabic.[86] All of these aspects were closely linked to the teaching and learning of the Arabic language, the reading of the Qur'an and the exegesis of the Qur'an via Arabic linguistics.[87] According to Ibn Khaldūn, the Arabic language consisted of four pillars that Muslims studied and developed: grammar, lexicography, syntax and style.[88] In the Umayyad period, it was the grammar that grew the most dramatically. It had been first focused upon by the Persian Abū al-Aswad ad-Du'alī (d. 688), who lived in the city of Basra. According to the scholar Ibn Khallikan (d. 1282) it was the Caliph 'Alī ﷺ who recommended ad-Du'alī to carry out this task when he noticed that linguistic mistakes were being made.[89] Ad-Du'alī was also responsible for devising the vocalisation signs.

During the first century, ad-Du'alī's work with regards to the organisation of signs to indicate the combination of two words or their partition, the doubling-up of a consonant and dots to distinguish between letters of the same shape was furthered. This helped the students who wanted to recite the Qur'an immensely, since prior to this development, it was only possible to read the Qur'an properly by knowing the Arabic language. Al-Ḥajjāj ibn Yūsuf (d. 714), the governor of Iraq and the eastern provinces during the Caliphate of 'Abd al-Malik ibn Marwān (r. 685-705), introduced the complete system of

85 Philip K. Hitti, *History of the Arabs*, (London: Macmillan and Co), 1968, p. 240.
86 Ibid.
87 All of these subjects were taught at various mosques in the Islamic world. For more information see Chapter 3.
88 Ibn Khaldun, op. cit., p. 319.
89 Ibid.

writing the Arabic script into the *muṣḥaf*, which had been produced in less than a century after the Qur'an was first revealed.[90] Another grammarian, 'Abd ar-Raḥmān ibn Hurmuz al-A'raj al-Madanī (d. 735), one of the students of ad-Du'alī, continued his work on grammar; he also taught grammar in Madīnah.[91] Another scholar from Basra who developed the sciences of philology and lexicography was al-Khalīl ibn Aḥmad (d. 791); he was the first to compile an Arabic dictionary, *Kitāb al-'Ayn,* and to deal with the principles of syntax.[92] Hence, the two cities of Kufa and Basra had developed into linguistic centres by the time the 'Abbasids came to power.

Throughout this period the demand for Arabic linguistic skills was so strong that a certain number of Bedouin decided to come to the new Muslim cities to earn money by teaching the Arabic language. The Bedouin Abū al-Baida ar-Rabāḥī came to Basra to teach Arabic language to children, as well as the well known Bedouin Abū Jamus Thawr ibn Yazīd who taught the famous Persian literary writer Ibn al-Muqaffa' (d. 756).[93] As mentioned earlier, royalty and the nobility used to send their children to the desert to acquire linguistic skills; however, with time they started to hire *mu'addibs* who were highly qualified in the Arabic language to teach their children at home. Some of the famous figures in the Umayyad and early 'Abbasid periods to have experienced desert education were the celebrated lexicographer al-Khalīl ibn Aḥmad (d. 791) and the famous Persian poet Bashar ibn Burd (d. 784).[94] Later teachers of grammar were Abū 'Ubaydah (d. 825) and al-Aṣma'ī (d. 828), who together represented the higher education of grammarians in the 'Abbasid period.[95]

---

90 Ismail R. al-Faruqi and Lois Lamya al-Faruqi, *The Cultural Atlas of Islam*, (New York: Macmillan Publishing), 1986, p. 233.

91 Makdisi, op. cit., 1990, p. 122.

92 Young and Serjeant (eds.), op. cit., p. 121.

93 Shalaby, op. cit., p. 45.

94 Ibid., p. 46.

95 Al-Faruqi and al-Faruqi, op. cit., p. 236.

In the very early days of Islamic history all types of literary studies began to be termed in educational circles as *adab* studies. These *adab* studies included subjects such as grammar, lexicography, poetry, prose, history, genealogy and many more.[96] In the Umayyad period, a scholar and successor to the Companions, Qatādah ibn Di'āmah (d. 735) became known as the foremost person to have mastered 'the science of the Arabians' (*'ilm al-'Arab*) which consisted of Arabic philology and the history and genealogy of the Arabs.[97] Hence, literature and poetry developed within the *adab* sciences, encouraged by the Umayyad government for its entertainment, political and educational benefits.[98] The creation of *dīwāns* in the Umayyad period led to the emergence of secretarial literature which laid down the rules of conduct and behaviour for various classes such as princes, court officers, secretaries and administrators of all types, and moreover, it supplied the professional skills required for the performance of their duties. These rules were written in various literary styles in the shape of poems, anecdotes and manuals. The two most famous writers of Arabic literature in the Umayyad period were 'Abd al-Ḥamīd al-Kātib (d. 750), who wrote the famous book *Risālah ila al-Kuttāb* ['Epistle to the Secretaries'] and Ibn Muqaffa' (d. 756) who wrote many books including *Adab al-Kātib* ['The Comprehensive Book of Rules of Conduct']. These books became the main textbooks for students who wanted to work in the administration of the government.[99]

Other sciences to have risen in this period in addition to the Law and the Arabic language were subjects closely related to the faith, the Qur'an and the *ḥadīth*. At the same time as linguistic, literary and legal studies were being encouraged, the development of the science of Qur'anic exegesis (*tafsīr*) had begun. Initially, in the early

96 Makdisi, op. cit., 1990, p. 52.
97 Ibid., p. 120.
98 Ahmed, op. cit., p. 34.
99 For more information, see section on Chancery schools below.

period of Islam there was no need for commentary on the Qur'an since the Companions understood the background of the revelation and had directly asked the Prophet ﷺ questions about it. However, by the time of the Umayyads the need for understanding the historical circumstances and the explanation of the verses led many scholars to study the traditions of the Prophet ﷺ and his Companions. The use of '*isnad*', a chain of names leading back to the Prophet ﷺ and his Companions, was used to prove the authority of the commentaries on the Qur'an. Numerous books were written on *tafsīr* during the Umayyad period. The oldest text available is attributed to Ibn 'Abbās (d. 687) ؓ who died in the Umayyad period. Other books of *tafsīr* in the Umayyad period include the works of successors such Zayd ibn 'Alī (d. 740) and Mujāhid (d. 722).[100] By the time the 'Abbasid era began, the science of the exegesis of the Qur'an had become highly developed and progressed to become one of the most respected sciences.[101] Another science that was taught within the context of the Qur'an was its readings, '*qirā'ah*', which is concerned with the pronunciation of the words of the Qur'an and its recitation. By the time the 'Abbasids came into power this science had become a complex subject matter.[102]

The importance of the study of *ḥadīth* was felt immediately after the death of the Prophet ﷺ. As has been mentioned in an earlier chapter, many *ḥadīth*s were collected in writing as early as the time of the Companions. However, it was at the request of the Caliph 'Umar ibn 'Abd al-'Azīz (r. 717-720) that the effort to collect the Sunnah and all the existing *ḥadīth*s commenced. The *raison d'être* behind this order seems to have been the Caliph's concern that the Sunnah and the traditions might be lost if they were not compiled in written form and

---

[100]   Ahmad Von Denfer, '*Ulum al-Qur'an*, (London: The Islamic Foundation), 1985, p. 137.
[101]   Dodge, op. cit., p. 43.
[102]   Ibid., p. 50.

that the traditions of the Prophet ﷺ could be misused for political and financial purposes if not scrupulously and authentically recorded. The first person to have compiled a collection of *ḥadīth*s was Ibn Jurayj, who lived at the time of the Umayyads.[103] During this period the science of *rijāl* 'narrators' developed, which was used to determine the soundness of a related *ḥadīth*. The science of *ḥadīth* involved the critical analysis of the character of the persons who transmitted the *ḥadīth*, such as their honesty and memory, which science was that of the *isnād*, and of the content (*matn*) of the *ḥadīth* to verify its conformity with the *āyāt* of the Qur'an, the Sunnah and existing well established *ḥadīth*s.[104] The science of *ḥadīth* took almost one hundred and fifty years to develop and all the major collections of *ḥadīth* were produced in the era of the 'Abbasids. However, it is generally recognised that while all the other literatures were developed with the patronage of the Caliphs, the scholars of *ḥadīth* and the science of *ḥadīth* were almost entirely ignored by the ruling élite, with the exception of the Caliph 'Umar ibn 'Abd al-'Azīz.[105,106]

Scientific subjects in the Umayyad period in comparison to literary and religious subjects were very basic and only began to be developed during the period of the 'Abbasids. In the early period of Islam there seem to be only two references to the physical sciences and both were linked to medicine. Primarily, there was the advice of the Prophet ﷺ concerning health, natural medicine and personal hygiene, which was later collected into the form of books known as *aṭ-Ṭibb an-Nabawī,* the Prophet's ﷺ medicine.[107] The importance of health in the Prophet's ﷺ

103 Ahmed, op. cit., p. 37.

104 Siddiqi, op. cit., pp. 36-40.

105 Ahmed, op. cit., p. 37.

106 In addition, the 'Abbasid Caliph Manṣūr commanded Imam Mālik to compile what was to become the *Muwaṭṭa'*, and some of his successors studied that work with Mālik. Many people regard the *Muwaṭṭa'* as the first *ṣaḥīḥ* work, and *ḥadīth* scholars after Mālik worked to document the *ḥadīth* for which he had not given a full *isnād* – Ed.

107 Young and Serjeant (eds.), op. cit., p. 342. Hitti, op. cit., p. 254.

mind is demonstrated by his statements in the *ḥadīth* narrated by 'Umar ⬢, "The Prophet ⬢ said, 'He for whom the doors of supplication are opened has the doors of mercy opened for him. And Allah is not asked for anything dearer to Him than asking Him for health,'"[108] and in the *ḥadīth* narrated by Abū Hurayrah ⬢, "The Prophet ⬢ said, 'There is no disease that Allah has created, except that He has also created its treatment.'"[109] The second reference to medicine was with respect to a Companion to whom the Prophet ⬢ used to refer people when dealing with medical problems: al-Ḥārith ibn Kaladah ⬢ of Ṭā'if (d. 634), who had studied medicine at Jundi-Shapur in Persia.[110] Hence, even as early as the Prophet's ⬢ time, the institute in Jundi-Shapur had an immense impact on the Muslims. However, the early Muslims did not pursue the field of medicine and during the first century of Islam most of the physicians were Jews, Christians or Zoroastrians. Only after the establishment of Arabic as a major medical language did a great number of Muslims enter this field.[111]

It was during the Umayyad period that Muslim rulers began to copy the medical institutions of Jundi-Shapur and Alexandria. The first translation of a medical text came about when Masarjawayh, a Jewish physician from Basra during the reign of the Caliph Marwān ibn al-Ḥakam (684–685), translated the *Pandectae Medicinae* of Ahron from Greek into Arabic. It was the Caliph al-Walīd ibn 'Abd al-Malik (r. 705-715) who built the first hospital (*bimaristan*) in the same tradition as the Jundi-Shapur institution in Damascus in 706 CE. Thus, Muslims came into contact with medicine and other natural sciences through

---

[108] Abu 'Isa Muhammad ibn 'Isa at-Tirmidhi, *Sunan at-Tirmidhī, Kitāb ad-Du'a*, Chapter 113, No. 3559, (Beirut: Dar al-Kutub al-Ilmiyyah), 1996.

[109] Muhammad bin Ismail bin al-Mughira al-Bukhari, Muhammad Muhsin Khan (tr.), *Ṣaḥīḥ al-Bukhārī – The translation of the meaning of Sahih al-Bukhari*, Book of Medicine, No. 582, Vol. 7, (New Delhi: Kitab Bhavan), 1984.

[110] Ibn Khaldun, op. cit., p. 3. Young and Serjeant (eds.), op. cit., p. 342. Hitti, op. cit., p. 254.

[111] Nasr, op. cit., 1976, p. 174.

Christian, Zoroastrian and Jewish scholars who had escaped from persecution elsewhere.

These physicians had established themselves in the buffer states between Persia and Byzantium.[112] The science of medicine at that time was mainly transmitted within certain families such as the Bukhtishu, Masawayh and Qurrah families. After the Muslim opening of Jundi-Shapur to Islam, many of these families developed into virtual dynasties of medical specialists and became the first medical teachers of the Muslims.

> Eventually many descendants and successors of these medical specialists moved to Damascus and then to Baghdad, when in turn these cities became the capitals of the Umayyad and 'Abbasid dynasties.[113]

It was to be during the 'Abbasid period that the translation of these sciences into Arabic and their further advancement was destined to begin. In the meantime the Umayyads granted various scientists the right to continue their individual work and teach Muslims in newly-made and existing hospitals. The only mention of translation work during the Umayyad period (except for work by Masarjawayh) is attributed to Khālid ibn Yazīd (d. 704), who sponsored the translation of Greek and foreign scripts regarding medicine and chemistry into Arabic.[114]

Higher Education in the Umayyad Period

It is customary to come across the three famous divisions of sciences described by the scholar Ibn Buṭlān (d. 1066): the revealed sciences,

---

[112] Al-Faruqi and al-Faruqi, op. cit., p. 46.

[113] Turner, op. cit., p. 132.

[114] According to Dimitri Gutas this report concerning Khālid ibn Yazīd may be a fabrication of a later date; for more information, see: Dimitri Gutas, *Greek Thought, Arabic Culture*, (London: Routledge), 1998, p. 24.

the literary sciences (*adab*) and the natural sciences,[115] which latter were also known as 'the sciences of the ancients'. The opinion of the majority of Western historians seems to be that because the literary sciences and the natural sciences were subservient to the revealed sciences in the Islamic world, they were either excluded from the regular courses or made subordinate to them in Muslim institutions of learning.[116] However, the whole *raison d'être* of the educational system of Islam is to understand the divine revelation and to live by it and therefore it makes perfect sense for the revealed sciences to be given a higher importance than the literary sciences and the natural sciences.[117] Furthermore, seeing how the *adab* sciences advanced in close parallel to the advance of the revealed sciences there is no doubt about their necessity for the study of the revealed sciences. In fact, most scholars expected their students to be substantially educated in various *adab* studies before advanced study of both the Qur'an and the *ḥadīth*. The natural sciences were not excluded from the regular courses for the plain reason that they were never a part of the regular courses in the mosques. The natural sciences were taught in other institutes of education.

It is important to recognise that even though natural sciences were taught largely in private institutions it does not diminish their importance.[118] The importance attached to all these sciences was eloquently demonstrated by the theologian and grammarian, al-Ḥasan al-Baṣrī (d. 728), who stated, "Learn the *sharī'ah*[119] for the benefit of

---

115 'Abd al-Wāḥid ibn 'Āshir reflects a slightly different threefold division of knowledge when he tangentially refers to: rational sciences such as mathematics, experiential/experimental sciences such as medicine, and revealed sciences. See: *The Practical Guidebook of Essential Islamic Sciences: A commentary on Ibn 'Āshir's al-Murshid al-Mu'īn* by Shaykh Ali Laraki al-Husaini – Ed.

116 Makdisi, op. cit., 1981, p. 75.

117 Dodge, op. cit., p. 43.

118 A. I. Sabra, *The World of Islam*, Bernard Lewis (ed.), (London: Thames and Hudson), 1980, p. 183.

119 This specifically includes Qur'an, *Ḥadīth*, *Fiqh* and Theology.

your religion; medicine[120] for the benefit of your body; and grammar[121] for the benefit of your tongue."[122] Accordingly, mathematics, one of the 'sciences of the ancients', was taught alongside both revealed and the literary sciences at the secondary stage in the 'finishing school' in the *kuttāb/maktab*.[123] This proves that all the sciences were taught in regular courses during elementary education. However, after this level, if the student desired to further develop his knowledge regarding the natural sciences or the literary sciences, he would proceed to the institution where general courses concerning these subjects were taught.

The Mosque

From the establishment of Madīnah, the first city-state of Islam, mosques were used as the main place of study. By the Umayyad period, the schools for children had been separated from the mosques, which left the mosque as the main place of higher education with the study circle (*ḥalaqah*) as the foundation of education.[124] During the Umayyad period a large number of mosques were built throughout the Muslim world in Basra, Kufa, Fusṭāṭ (Cairo), al-Mada'in, Damascus, al-Qayrawān and Jerusalem.[125] The mosques were not used only for worship and education but served also as political centres and courts of justice.[126]

However, a distinction was made between two types of mosques in the early days of Islam. It is reported that the Caliph 'Umar ibn al-Khaṭṭāb ﷺ requested his governors in Basra, Kufa, Syria and Egypt to

120 This includes sciences such as Chemistry and Mathematics.
121 This includes all the sciences linked to the Arabic language, i.e. *adab* sciences.
122 Makdisi, op. cit., 1990, p. 122.
123 Ibid., p. 49.
124 Shalaby, op. cit., p. 47.
125 Hitti, op. cit., pp. 256-267.
126 Shalaby, op. cit., p. 48.

establish a *Jāmi'* mosque so that the people of the city could gather for the Friday prayers.[127] The congregational mosque was termed *al-masjid al-Jāmi'* and the ordinary mosque was referred to as *al-masjid.* The *masjid* seems to have been built by the local community and was often named after the founder of the *masjid.*[128] Both kinds of mosques were used as teaching institutions for both the revealed sciences and the sciences of *adab*. The difference between these two styles of mosques became more apparent later in the late 'Abbasid period, when most local *masājid* were used for legal studies. Even as early as the Prophet's ﷺ time, the teaching of subjects such as the Qur'an was accompanied by the recitation and study of poetry by Ḥassān ibn Thābit (d. 674) ؓ in the mosque of Madīnah.[129] In the Umayyad period we find the scholar Abū Ja'far al-Madanī teaching in the Prophet's ﷺ mosque in Madīnah.[130] In *al-masjid al-Jāmi'* of Basra, Qur'an scholars and grammarians such as Ḥammād ibn Salamah and Abū 'Abd ar-Raḥmān Yūnus ibn Ḥabīb an-Naḥawī (d. 798) were seen to attend al-Ḥasan al-Baṣrī's *ḥalaqah* on grammar, theology and Islamic spirituality.[131] Similarly, 'Abdullāh ibn 'Abbās ؓ used to teach Qur'anic exegesis (*tafsīr*) beside the Ka'bah in Makkah on Thursdays, and Rabī'ah ibn Abī 'Abd ar-Raḥmān (d. 753) used to teach jurisprudence in the *Jāmi'* mosque of Madīnah.[132] Thus, every mosque had a number of study circles devoted to one subject each, and several study circles could be taking place at the same time. The names of various *ḥalaqāt* were sometimes attributed to the subject being studied and at times to the famous teacher. For example the study circle of grammar was called '*ḥalaqah an-naḥw*' in various mosques of the Muslim world, whereas

---

127 Ibid.
128 Makdisi, op. cit., 1981, p. 12.
129 Makdisi, op. cit., 1990, p. 52.
130 Makdisi, op. cit., 1981, p. 21.
131 Makdisi, op. cit., 1990, p. 50.
132 Shalaby, op. cit., p. 53.

the specific grammar study circle of Khalīl ibn Aḥmad in the Basra mosque was called the *ḥalaqah* of Khalīl an-Naḥawī.[133] Other *ḥalaqāt* in the mosques during the time of the Umayyads were devoted to the study of *fiqh, tafsīr, ḥadīth*, the science of Arabic, theology and the reading of the Qur'an and poetry.[134]

In this early education all the students were able to attend whatever subjects they required, or desired to learn. When either the teacher, or they themselves, believed their study was complete they would transfer to another teacher/subject.[135] Nakosteen states, "Students were mobile in circles, looking for the right teacher and leaving him when they could not find any further enlightenment."[136] Thus, there was no system of exams or a degree that was awarded upon completion of education. However, the *ḥalaqah* itself was highly disciplined and formulated once it started. There were pre-seated arrangements in the study circle; the most advanced students sat next to the teacher and the remainder of the students sat where they did depending on the level they had acquired with regards to that specific subject. In addition, there was always a pre-determined area in the study circle, which was reserved for visiting scholars or eminent figures. The teacher dealt with every part of the subject methodologically, first by making a general introduction to the subject, then he/she connected the day's lesson with previous lessons to develop a continuity and comprehension of the science taught.[137] This higher education was open for all who wanted to learn the Islamic revealed sciences or the literary sciences.

According to various historical sources the mosques of this period were bustling with crowds who came to learn and discuss various

---

133 Ahmed, op. cit., p. 54.
134 Ibid., pp. 50-55.
135 Dodge, op. cit., p. 13.
136 Nakosteen, op. cit., p. 45.
137 Ibid., pp. 45-46.

subjects. From this culture developed a literary-religious society which, by the 'Abbasid period (c. 750), led to the birth of various assemblies (*majālis*) in mosques and other educational places. These were either assemblies where teaching occurred (*majlis at-tadrīs*) or where discussion took place amongst scholars concerning all kinds of subjects. These exchanges and discussions brought into the 'Abbasid period an intellectual literary society openly displayed in the streets, in the mosques and even in the palaces of caliphs and sultans.[138]

The Chancery School

Makdisi termed the main educational institutions for *adab* sciences (besides the mosques) 'chancery schools'.[139] By the closing stages of the Umayyad period the governmental bureaucracy was already well formed with its organised departments (*dīwāns*), which were concerned with finance, official correspondence and the budget for the armed forces.[140] Thus, there was a need for training government secretaries and administrators (*kātib, pl. kuttāb*) at all levels; these needs were provided by the government chanceries. The training of these secretaries and administrators involved various subjects since they were to deal with finance, taxation, correspondence and the legal system. Hence, besides all the government departments' individual tasks, they required highly literate personnel with a wide range of knowledge. Chancery schools taught all their students mathematics, accounting skills, theology, legal studies and *adab* sciences specifically dealing with the Arabic language.[141] According to Makdisi, the students went through this school by attending on–the-job training. Consequently, they were employed in the government departments

---

138 Ahmed, op. cit., pp. 55-86.

139 Makdisi, op. cit., 1990, p. 64. "The chancery school would be labelled variously in Arabic: *dīwān ar-rasā'il*, *dīwān al-inshī'* and *dīwān al-mukātabāt*."

140 Young and Serjeant (eds.), op. cit., p. 342. Hitti, op. cit., p. 155.

141 Ibid., p. 155.

while they were given training and education in various subjects. The patronages of these training schools were caliphs, sultans, princes, *wazīrs*, chancery heads and other high functionaries of society.[142]

Certain administrators or secretaries became very successful by using their eloquence and linguistic expertise in the government chanceries or by providing poetry and witty repartee at court. Hence, the person who learnt the sciences of *adab* also became an *adīb,* a gentleman-scholar, whose education formed both his character and his intellect.[143] ʻAbd al-Ḥamīd ibn Yaḥyā al-Kātib (d. 750), the famous secretary of the Umayyad Caliph Marwān ibn Muḥammad ibn Marwān (r. 744-750), wrote down the curriculum the *kātib* should pursue:

> ....circle of secretaries, vie with one another in diverse kinds of knowledge and instruct yourselves in religion. Begin by knowing the book of Allah Almighty and the religious duties and then the Arabic language, for it sets your speech straight. Master calligraphy for it ornaments your correspondence and recite poetry, learning its obscurities and meanings. Learn about the *ayyām* of Arabs and non-Arabs, their tales and life histories, for this will help you to attain your ambition, and do not neglect arithmetic for it is the mainstay of tax officials.[144]

This curriculum demonstrates that the chancery schools took religion and its various sciences very seriously. There was no separation between religion and the rest of the education and it was in fact a prerequisite that a Muslim should have knowledge of the *dīn* before

142 Makdisi, op. cit., 1990, p. 64.

143 Tarif Khalidi, *Arabic Historical Thought in the Classical Period*, (Cambridge: Cambridge University Press), 1994, p. 83.

144 Ibid., p. 91.

he even set out to become an *adīb.* As has been stated earlier, apprenticeship was the basis of the training of a secretary, for example 'Abd al-Ḥamīd ibn Yaḥyā was trained by Sālim, the secretary of the Caliph Hishām ibn 'Abd al-Malik.[145] The continuity of these apprenticeships, even through changes in the political dynasty, highlights their importance to the government. 'Abd al-Ḥamīd ibn Yaḥyā, for example, was in turn the teacher of Ya'qūb ibn Dāwūd. The same Ya'qūb ibn Dāwūd then rose to became the *wazīr* of the 'Abbasid Caliph al-Mahdī from 775-785 CE.[146]

The Bimaristan *and the Library*

The Muslims came into contact with medical science and other natural sciences through Christian, Jewish, Zoroastrian and Sabaean scholars who lived in the lands newly opened to Islam, such as Alexandria in Egypt, Jundi-Shapur in Persia, Edessa in the Fertile Crescent, and Mosul and Nisibis in Northern Mesopotamia.[147] In the early days of Islam, the science of medicine was taught through apprenticeship. Very often the physician's apprentice would be his own son or nephew, but there were a few examples of apprentices unrelated to the physician. The most famous specialist medical families in the seventh and eight centuries were the Bukhtishu, the Masawayh and the Qurrah.[148] During their expeditions, the Muslims came across these families of medical specialists and their clinics.

Bimaristan or *maristan* is an ancient Persian word for hospital and literarily means 'the house/place of patients'. In ancient times it had two functions: first, a hospital and second, an educational medical institution.[149] The Christian physician, Ḥunayn ibn Isḥāq (d. 873),

---

145 Makdisi, op. cit., 1990, p. 64.

146 Ibid.

147 Dimitri Gutas, *Greek Thought, Arabic Culture*, (London: Routledge), 1998, p. 14.

148 Young and Serjeant (eds.), op. cit., p.342 and Hitti, op. cit., pp. 346-347.

149 Oadah, op. cit., p. 110.

describes the curriculum of the medical school of Alexandria in late antiquity comparing it with his own times:

> The members of the medical school in Alexandria would gather every day to read and study one leading text amongst those books by Galen, just as our contemporary Christian colleagues gather every day in places of teaching known as school for the study of a leading text by the ancients. As for the rest of the books, they used to read them individually – each one on their own; after having first practised with those books which I mentioned, just as our colleagues today read the commentaries of the books by the ancients.[150]

When the Muslims entered the Byzantine and Persian lands, they united them after centuries of conflict between their respective empires. Leading scholars and students of medicine and other sciences could continue their studies without fear of the officious 'orthodoxy' which had sometimes been prevalent under previous rulers. Numerous scholars of different backgrounds assembled in the new centres of the Muslim world to research and teach their respective fields actively. The most famous of these were Severus of Nisibis (d. 666/7), his student Jacob of Edessa (d. 708), Theophilus of Edessa (d. 785), Stephanus of Alexandria and Masha'Allah and Nawbaht, who were both of Persian origin.[151]

The main difference between the pre-Islamic medical clinics of Byzantium and the new Islamic hospitals is that it was in Islamic civilisation that the term 'hospital', as understood in the modern sense of the word, was first utilised. In these clinics the sick were treated scientifically and discharged upon conclusion of their treatment. It is argued that Byzantine medical clinics had not reached this stage of

150 Gutas, op. cit., p. 15.
151 Ibid.

specialisation nor were their clinics exclusively used for the sick.[152] Nevertheless, of all the medical centres inherited from the ancient world, the *bimaristan* in Jundi-Shapur (Persia) became the blueprint for the future *bimaristan* of the Muslim world. It was both a major medical institution where patients were given a certain amount of care and a place where physicians' apprentices were instructed extensively.[153] Makdisi says about this pre-Islamic hospital in the early Muslim era, "It is known that hospitals, *bimaristan,* were also schools of medicine."[154] Two hospitals were built during the Umayyad period: the first Muslim hospital in the capital Damascus was founded by the Caliph al-Walīd ibn 'Abd al-Malik (r. 705-715) in the years 706-707 CE and the other, reported by Ibn Duqmaq (d. 1406), was built in Cairo, but very little is known of this hospital. It was not until the 'Abbasid period that the main development of the *bimaristan* as an educational institution began.[155]

Another legacy of the Byzantine and the Persian Empires to the Islamic world was the institution of the library. As stated in an earlier chapter, when the Muslims came across the libraries in Persia and in cities like Alexandria they respected this medium of learning. During the Umayyad period, the ruling dynasty began to collect books of importance but these libraries included only a few dozen books. The library and the *bimaristan* remained dormant throughout the Umayyad period with regards to both the translation of ancient books and their utilisation as educational institutions. The question arises as to why the Umayyad dynasty was a period in which there was little development both with respect to the translation movement and to

152 Aydin Sayili, *Central Asian contributions to the earlier phases of hospital building – Activity in Islam*, p. 4, FSTC Limited, 2005, http://www.muslimheritage.com/uploads/Central%20Asian%20Hospital%20Building.pdf, (accessed: 22/07/10).

153 Nasr, op. cit., 1976, p. 155.

154 Makdisi, op. cit., 1981, p. 12.

155 Sayili, op. cit., (accessed: 22/07/10).

most of the sciences inherited from the ancients, when it was during this period that great numbers of Arab Muslims came to live amongst Persians, Greeks, and Hellenised Arabs.

According to Gutas, the answer lies with both the ruling government, i.e. the Umayyads, and the élite literary society in Syria-Palestine. The language was one obstacle, since Greek was spoken widely throughout the Umayyad period in the Syria-Palestine area. In addition, most of the work of administration in the Umayyad *dīwān* was done in the Greek language[156] and conducted in Byzantine style, at least until the reform of the Caliph ʿAbd al-Malik (r. 685-705). However, it seems the main reason for the lack of development was the 'orthodoxy' found amongst the Christian subjects of the Umayyads. In the early seventh century, the Church had attempted to alter the pagan outlook of Byzantine education by attempting to infuse it with Christian orthodoxy which eventually led to the rejection of the entire Hellenistic inheritance, and Hellenism was treated with contemptuous indifference. Hence, this stagnant religious intellectual climate could not sustain a *secular* Greek translation movement. The Umayyads might still have been able to commence a translation movement if they had promoted it aggressively in their domains, but this was lacking.[157] It is very interesting to note that the translation of various sciences of the ancients and their development began in the ʿAbbasid period. The translations and developments of the various ancient sciences were not only supported by the rulers but also by the *'ulamā'* as will be seen

---

156 The majority of the administrators were Greek or Greek-speaking Arabs, such as Sargun ibn Manṣūr ar-Rūmī. Even if Byzantium was separate from the Western Roman Empire, the Arabs, Persians and Turks have always known them as Rūmī, that is, 'Roman'. This was not a misconception, but the general understanding at that time since those belonging to the Byzantine Empire called themselves *Romaioi* or simply 'Christians'. Only those people living in Constantinople called themselves *Byzantios*, while Western Europeans at that time called them *Graeci*, meaning 'Greeks'.

157 Gutas, op. cit., p. 19.

in later chapters. This refutes those who state that Islam is inherently opposed to science; especially the essay written by Ignaz Goldziher, 'The Attitude of the Old Islamic Orthodoxy towards the Ancient Sciences.' The historian, Dimitri Gutas, who has extensively studied this subject, argues that this issue is simply a myth and that there is no historical evidence of an Islamic opposition to the Greek sciences.[158]

The Riḥlah

As we saw earlier, another institution of higher education prevalent during the Umayyad period was the *riḥlah,* 'the quest for knowledge'. It is no less important than other institutions and it can be argued that the *riḥlah* has had a deeper impact on Islamic civilisation than any other institution. The *riḥlah,* even though it has its roots in the Prophetic period, is in the strict sense of the word not an educational institution, but a method of gaining knowledge or education. Conversely, because of its impact on the sciences of the Sunnah[159] and *ḥadīth* and its influence on education from the beginning of Islam, there is a strong contention that we should include it as an institution, even though it is not a structurally organised one.

Certain Companions first embarked on *riḥlah,* seeking knowledge from the Prophet ﷺ himself. After the Prophet's ﷺ death, other individuals (normally referred to as the successors or the followers [*tābi'īn*]) searched out Sunnahs of the Prophet ﷺ by travelling and finding the Companions who knew them. By this time a number of the Companions had settled throughout the Muslim world. It was after

---

158 Gutas, op. cit., p. 166. For more information, see chapter three where the subject of 'The myth of Islamic opposition to the Greek sciences' is touched on in more detail.

159 We refer to Sunnah and *ḥadīth* since it is clear from the early community that they are not necessarily coterminous. For example, many people travelled to Imam Mālik to learn the Sunnah and *fiqh* from him without necessarily becoming *ḥadīth* scholars just as an equally large number went to him purely to learn his *ḥadīth.*

the death of most of the Companions that the successors became the first sources of knowledge. This 'quest for knowledge' was continued by generations of Muslim scholars, until most of the Sunnahs and the *ḥadīth* were compiled and categorised by individual scholars in the 'Abbasid period. The science of *ḥadīth* insisted that the chain of narration, '*isnad*', and the text, '*matn*', had to be critically analysed for authenticity. Thus, *riḥlah* from the early days came to be related primarily to the sciences of the Sunnah and the *ḥadīth*. According to Siddiqi, some of the Companions undertook long journeys to learn Sunnahs that they did not know from other Companions.

> Abū Ayyūb ﷺ, for instance, travelled from Madīnah to Egypt just for the sake of refreshing his memory on a *ḥadīth* which he together with 'Uqbah ibn 'Āmir ﷺ had learnt from the Prophet ﷺ himself.[160]

Makhūl (d. 730), a successor who lived during the Umayyad period, travelled through Egypt, Syria, Iraq and the Hijaz gathering the knowledge of the Prophet ﷺ from numerous Companions. Examples of those who studied and travelled in search of *ḥadīth* during the Umayyad period are: Ibrāhīm an-Nakha'ī (d. 715), Ibn Sīrīn (d. 728), 'Urwah ibn az-Zubayr (d. 712), az-Zuhrī (d. 741), Muḥammad ibn Isḥāq (d. 761), al-A'mash (d. 764) and al-Awzā'ī (d. 774).[161] *Ḥadīth* scholars of the first one hundred and fifty years of the Islamic civilisation did not intend to create a new science; they were simply preserving for the community a record of Muḥammad ﷺ and his Companions.[162]

Much of this preservation was undertaken by means of the *riḥlah*, which at this point was an education regarding the life and the practice of the Prophet ﷺ and his city, by travelling to those who possessed

[160] Siddiqi, op. cit., p. 40.
[161] Khalidi, op. cit., p. 83.
[162] Ibid., p. 25.

this knowledge. An example of someone who travelled for knowledge was 'Urwah ibn az-Zubayr who was of the tribe of Quraysh. His main teacher was 'Ā'ishah ⚘ (d. 678), 'Urwah's maternal aunt and the Prophet's ⚘ wife. 'Urwah came to be known as an expert on 'Ā'ishah's ḥadīth. He also obtained ḥadīth from other sources, and he became the teacher of az-Zuhrī. Az-Zuhrī is a well known expert on the Sunnah and the ḥadīth and possibly the earliest sīrah author. He was also the scholar assigned by the Caliph 'Umar ibn 'Abd al-'Azīz to compile the first collection of the Sunnah in writing. He continued to be an advisor to other Umayyad caliphs and a tutor to some of their children. Az-Zuhrī stated concerning the riḥlah, "I have been travelling from Hijaz to Syria and from Syria to Hijaz for forty-five years and have not come across a single ḥadīth that was new to me."[163]

By the end of the Umayyad period, the riḥlah had given rise to the writing of history by scholars who were influenced by the work of az-Zuhrī and 'Urwah. Muḥammad ibn Isḥāq (d. 761), a direct student of az-Zuhrī was labelled 'the Amīr al-Mu'minīn in ḥadīth' by some of his own generation.[164] He consummated the main work of the various ḥadīth scholars in the sīrah genre. He was the first Muslim to write a historical book concerning the genesis of creation, the life of the Prophet ⚘ and the military exploits of the early Muslims.

Scholars who travelled in search of knowledge also formulated rules and methods for the study of ḥadīth. The majority insisted that ḥadīth should only be studied after acquiring an extensive understanding of the Arabic language and its grammar. The main approaches to learning Sunnah and ḥadīth during the Umayyad period were basically samā' (listening), which was a procedure in which the student attended lessons of a teacher in the mosque, listened to his narration

---

[163]   Khalidi, op. cit., p. 33.
[164]   The title is used for a number of scholars among them Shu'bah, Sufyān ath-Thawrī, 'Alī ibn al-Madīnī, Mālik ibn Anas, al-Bukhārī and even among later scholars, Ibn Ḥajar al-'Asqalānī.

or teaching of the Sunnah and then either retained it through written dictation or memorisation. The second style after *samā'* was called *qirā'ah,* in which a student read out the teacher's written compilation to the teacher or what had been narrated to him/her, and other students compared that with their own memory or their own written copies.[165] The rigorous work of collecting the Sunnah and *ḥadīth* began during the early years of Islam and this endeavour bore fruit during the 'Abbasid period.

Students during the Umayyad period used *riḥlah* extensively and zealously to accumulate all of the Prophet's ﷺ teachings. It is difficult to differentiate the role of the *riḥlah* during the Umayyad and the 'Abbasid eras. Both periods were filled with students and teachers searching for knowledge, but whereas the earliest quest for knowledge was centred on the Sunnah and *ḥadīth*, later Muslims travelled to accumulate knowledge of sciences such as *tafsīr*, history and spiritual knowledge. An example can be given of the Spanish scholar, Ibn al-Faradi, who in 941/942 CE at the age of 14, went on a *riḥlah* that took him to Makkah, Madīnah, Jeddah, Sana' (Yemen), Fusṭāṭ (early Cairo), Jerusalem, Gaza, Damascus, Tripoli, Beirut, Caesarea, Ramla, Alexandria and Qulzum; this was not an uncommon route for those who went on a quest for knowledge. With the passing of time, due to their political and economic conditions, other newer cities became famous for knowledge, such as Baghdad and Nishapur in the tenth century, Cairo under the Fatimids and even remote places such as Bukhara in Central Asia.[166]

The Rise of Teaching Methods and their Theories

During the Umayyad period, various methods and theories were formulated to help teach students in both elementary and higher

---

165 Siddiqi, op. cit., p. 40.

166 Dale F. Eickelman and James Piscatori (eds.), *Muslim Travelers*, (Los Angeles: University of California Press), 1990, p. 55.

education. In the first century AH (seventh to eighth century CE), there were various opinions concerning what the exact age and ability of a student should be in order to commence education. Sufyān ibn 'Uyaynah (d. 813) said that, "Study is better at an early age because the student is clear headed at this stage and memorising is easy,"[167] and concerning the student's ability his statement was more abstract: "Knowledge suits only those whose character suits knowledge."[168] Other scholars set exact ages for the study of certain sciences, for example, scholars in Basra maintained that a child should be ten years or older to be able to commence the study of *ḥadīth*, whereas scholars from Kufa set the age for studying this subject at twenty years.[169] Since education was not controlled by central or local government, different regions in the Muslim world followed distinct local ideas of education. The scholar az-Zuhrī (d. 741), who lived in Damascus, was one of the first to introduce a distinction between primary subjects, which were to be taught in elementary schools, and advanced subjects, which were to be taught in higher education. According to him the primary subjects were reading, writing, arithmetic and the recitation and memorisation of the Qur'an; the advanced subjects included sciences such as *ḥadīth*, grammar and *tafsīr* etc.[170]

It is possible to surmise that since az-Zuhrī took up residence in Damascus, which used to be an ancient Byzantine city, his curriculum of primary subjects may have been influenced by the curriculum of the *grammatikos*, the secondary school teacher of Byzantium. As mentioned earlier, al-Ḥasan al-Baṣrī (d. 728) also developed a theory concerning the importance of certain subjects, "Learn the *sharī'ah* for the benefit of your religion, medicine for the benefit of your body; and grammar for the benefit of your tongue."[171] When az-Zuhrī used

[167] Oadah, op. cit., p. 31.
[168] Ibid.
[169] Oadah, op. cit., p. 32.
[170] Ibid., p. 33.
[171] Makdisi, op. cit., 1990, p. 122.

to teach in the mosque in Damascus, he would limit his lecture to an hour. He would then dismiss his students and explain his teaching method by stating, "Students lose interest after listening for a long period."[172]

The reasoning behind a pupil's desert education in the early Umayyad period was said to be that a pupil of the desert would emerge with a pure Arabic tongue, well versed in poetry, and imbued with qualities such as courage, endurance in the time of trouble, observance of the rights and obligations of neighbourliness, manliness, generosity, hospitality, regard for women and the fulfilment of solemn commitments. These virtues were greatly prized in Bedouin life.[173]

By the end of the Umayyad period, the education system comprised a number of styles and methods of teaching and learning. It is plausible that since the Umayyad capital was Byzantine Damascus, a certain amount of influence came from Byzantine society. The principal method of education in the Umayyad period was narration or '*riwāyah*' of the texts that were being taught. This was done either by one of the students narrating the text or the teacher himself narrating it to the students. It can be argued that early Muslims were already using this method of teaching with regards to the recitation of the Qur'an. Narration was also employed by the Greek *grammatikos*, who taught the main educational texts such as Homer's *Illiad* and *Odyssey* to his students; in Greek this method was called *aganosis*, which meant that the text had to be recited with proper intonation. However, whereas narration or recitation was the commencement of imparting knowledge in Islamic education, it was the second step in the Greek understanding. The first method of imparting knowledge by the *grammatikos* was the correction (*diorthosis*) of the text that was being studied; this was to ensure that the teacher and the student were in

172 Oadah, op. cit., p. 34.
173 Hitti, op. cit., p. 253.

possession of identical texts (since there was always a possibility of grammatical and spelling mistakes in the copies). This method would have been incorporated by Muslim students and teachers in the act of narration itself, since if the pupil read out something incorrect, the teacher would correct him and then the students would each correct any texts they had. Similarly, if the teacher read out from his own text, he would realise if there was a mistake and correct it and anyone who had a copy of the text would correct it. The main text was of course the Qur'an which had been collected at the command of the first Caliph Abū Bakr ﷺ and collated and published by the third Caliph 'Uthmān ﷺ.

The second step of the transmission of knowledge in the Muslim world was '*murāja'ah*' which is translated as 'review'. This process followed after the narration was over and the student had either memorised the text or written it down. The purpose behind this exercise was to see if the student had understood the *matn* (text) of the narration and had not made any mistakes regarding the *isnād* (chain of narration). Again, this can be compared to the method of exegesis in the Byzantine education system which comprised historical and linguistic explanation of the text.

The third method of learning, which had existed in essence in the first community of Madīnah and then became highly developed in the Muslim world during this period, was '*su'āl*' or 'question and answer'. The teacher encouraged this method so that by asking questions the students would learn more; moreover, any ideas or knowledge missed by other students during the lesson could be repeated. A comparison can be made regarding *su'āl* and the Greek education method called '*krisis*', which focused on the moral lesson of the text; in contrast, the Muslim students inquired with regards to the text.[174] Consequently, it has to be remembered that the Caliph 'Alī ﷺ had spoken of the methods

174 Mango, op. cit., p. 125.

of review and the question/answer session. He had emphasised the importance of discussion and review of the student's lessons, to ensure that the student had not forgotten or made a mistake in his/her understanding of the lecture. He is further reported to have said, "Knowledge is a treasure and its keys are the questions asked, so ask questions. As the question is rewarded by its answer, so is the person who asked the question, his teacher, the listener and the friend who stands by."[175]

The Muslims not only incorporated key elements of the education system of the Byzantines but also advanced it further with the wisdom gained from the revelation and subsequent experience. Islamic education became a social phenomenon that taught Muslims to use their reasoning within the framework of the Qur'an and Sunnah; this phenomenon reached a peak with the civilisation based in Baghdad in the ninth century.

During most of the Umayyad period education seemed to be synonymous with imparting knowledge and was not specifically linked with either spirituality or physical discipline. However, amongst the Companions of the Prophet ﷺ throughout the time of the first four Caliphs ؓ, there was always an emphasis on the spiritual elements of education such as teaching the spiritual importance of fasting and prayer.[176] In the early community, spirituality and law were both very much present in the example of the life of the Prophet ﷺ and his close Companions.

In the Umayyad period, however, with the complexification of civilisation, the emphasis started to shift towards the natural and legal sciences. Nevertheless, numerous individuals initiated the tradition of educating the masses regarding *taṣawwuf* (Islamic spirituality) in the main educational centres of Islam, i.e. the mosques. One of the

---

[175] Oadah, op. cit., pp. 37-38.
[176] J. Schacht and C. E. Bosworth (eds.), *The Legacy of Islam*, (Oxford: Oxford University Press), 1979, p. 368.

most imposing such figures was al-Ḥasan al-Baṣrī (d. 720), who taught Islamic spirituality as a part of the wider practice of Islam; it was possible to see him teaching the Arabic language, *'aqīdah* and Islamic spirituality in the *Jāmi'* mosque of Basra.[177]

By the 'Abbasid period, a number of *ḥalaqāt* concerning Islamic spirituality were organised in cities across the Caliphate, such as the *ḥalaqahs* of al-Ḥārith al-Muḥāsibī (d. 857) and of Junayd al-Baghdadi (d.910).[178]

[177] Shalaby, op. cit., p. 53.
[178] H. A. R. Gibb, *Shorter Encyclopaedia of Islam*, (Leiden: E. J. Brill), 1974, p. 580.

Chapter Three

The 'Golden Age' of Islamic Education

The 'Abbasids

The end of the Umayyad dynasty signalled not only the beginning of a new reign but also the end of an era. The Arabism that the Umayyads had appeared to champion was overwhelmed by various races, among them the Persians and the Turks, representing a more global picture of Islam.[1] The client policies of the Umayyads finally lapsed; the old Arab Muslims and the new Muslims from different races began to coalesce and shade into each other.[2] In hindsight, the 'Abbasid dynasty emerged at the right time and place in history to continue and advance the achievements of its predecessor. The 'Abbasids did not change the political institutions they found; instead there was continuity between the two dynasties even in the way the caliphs lived and ruled.[3]

The 'Abbasid period spans the years 750–1258 CE and comprises the reign of thirty-seven caliphs, although some of the caliphs did

1 Hitti, op. cit., p. 286.
2 Ibid., p. 287.
3 Frye, op. cit., p. 106.

not always rule directly.[4] The image normally drawn of a stable political empire that lasted for over five centuries is inaccurate, and the following is more correct. The political history of the 'Abbasid period can be divided into four main stages: the early period (750-833), generally distinguished as the age of the political power of independent caliphs; the middle period (833-945), the age when many of the caliphs were simply left as nominal rulers by viziers; the third period (945-1153), marked by the rule of various dynasties but still in the name of the caliph (such as the Shiite Buyid dynasty 934-1055 and the Sunni Seljuks 1055-1153); and the final period (1153-1258) when a number of caliphs regained direct control over Iraq, such as the Caliphs an-Nāṣir (r. 1180-1225) and al-Mustanṣir (r. 1226–1242). The Caliphate was effectively ended by the onslaught of the Mongols on Baghdad in 1258 except for a dynasty of 'Abbasids that claimed merely ceremonial importance under Mamlūk governance in Cairo until 1517.[5]

Nevertheless, neither the rule of the Umayyads nor the 'Abbasids checked the spread of Islam; the Prophet Muḥammad's ﷺ followers controlled a domain larger even than that of Rome at its peak. Stanton eloquently describes the way that Islam rose over political differences in his statement about the Muslim lands, "This vast area existed under one faith, one law, one language and loyalty to a theocratic state."[6] Hence, the literary and social aspects of 'Abbasid culture should be measured differently from its political features.

In the mid-eighth century, the Caliph al-Manṣūr (r. 754-775), the second 'Abbasid caliph, ordered the establishment of the new 'Abbasid capital, Baghdad. The 'city of peace' (*Madīnah as-Salām*), as it

---

4 Hitti, op. cit., p. 288.

5 Hasan, op. cit., p. 23.

6 Charles Michael Stanton, *Higher Learning in Islam*, (Maryland: Rowman and Littlefield), 1990, p. 4.

was also called, was situated on the west bank of the River Tigris and built in a circular form giving it its famous name of the 'Round City'. Within a few years, the capital grew to become a centre of commerce, government and literary accomplishments.[7] By the time of the Caliph Hārūn ar-Rashīd (r. 786–809) and his son the Caliph al-Ma'mūn (r. 813-831), the fifth and seventh caliphs of the 'Abbasid Caliphate, traders and commerce had arrived in Baghdad from all over the then-charted world such as Central Asia, India, Africa, China, Persia, Syria and Arabia. The bazaars and *sūqs* of the Muslim world were crowded with traders who bought and sold all kinds of craftwork and goods. Merchants became an influential social group in the new Caliphate.

The world of trade benefited greatly from the new *'pax Islamica'* but interestingly it was the world of agriculture that went through a major revolution. Prosperity derived from trade specifically favoured the merchant classes, whereas the new agricultural phenomena benefited everyone, all across the board. The opening of borders by the 'Abbasids, from India to Spain, saw the development of new agricultural techniques, a diffusion of the knowledge of farming and the importation of numerous plants, fruits and legumes across the Caliphate. A special aspect of the economic prosperity that all social strata experienced in the early centuries of 'Abbasid rule was provided not by trade as much as by agriculture.[8] This led to a high standard of living across all social strata in the new Caliphate, which in turn led to increased opportunities for the acquisition of education and for trade. The high standard of living was further supplemented by a factor that was to prove most important for the spread of knowledge and the advance of education in the 'Abbasid period, i.e. the introduction of paper-making technology into *Dār al-Islām* by Chinese prisoners of war in 751 CE.

---

7 Hitti, op. cit., pp. 288-293.

8 Gutas, op. cit., p. 12.

During the 'Abbasid period, numerous paper mills were established across the Muslim world. It is interesting to note that the various styles of paper that were developed in the early years of the 'Abbasids, bear the names of prominent patrons of the translation movement, such as the *Ja'farī* paper named after the 'Abbasid Vizier Ja'far ibn Yaḥyā al-Barmakī (767-803) and the *Ṭāhirī* paper named after the scholar Aḥmad ibn Abī Ṭāhir (819-893).[9] Furthermore, as time passed, the Muslims improved the paper inherited from the Chinese, by replacing materials such as wood and bamboo with linen fibres, thus creating a better-quality paper. This paper was then used across the lands of the *pax Islamica* by merchants for their trade, scholars and students for their books and by the government for its administration. For more than four hundred years before it arrived in Europe, paper was used exclusively by the Muslim world. In Baghdad, most paper mills were built after the year 793 CE, and from there the paper making industry spread to the rest of *Pax Islamica* and had reached Muslim Spain by the year 950 CE. The first paper mill in Europe was built by the Spanish Muslims of Xàtiva in Valencia.[10] Historical documents referring to the paper mill in Xàtiva in 1056 CE, shows it empoying twenty people and the historical evidence also refers to another paper mill in Toledo in 1085 CE.[11,12]

It is very important to understand the changes this made in the educational and literary worlds. Prior to this, the Muslim world had been using various materials such as leather and vellum, and pains-

---

9 Ibid., p. 13.

10 S. T. S. Al-Hassani, '1000 Years of Missing Industrial History', in Emilio Calvo Labarta (ed.), *A Shared Legacy: Islamic Science East and West: Homage to Professor J. M. Milas Vallicrosa*, (Barcelona: University of Barcelona), 2008, p. 67.

11 Even in 1238 CE, when Valencia was conqured by the Christians, the paper mills stayed in the hands of the Muslims (until the Christian conquest of all Spain in 1492 CE), but they were heavily taxed.

12 Leila Avrin, *Scribes, Script and Books*, (Chigago: ALA Editions), 2010, p. 287.

takingly taking time and effort to record various sciences in written form. The technology of paper made it possible for scholars to write books in large volumes and for students to have notebooks for their note-taking. Due to this and other developments, the early period of the 'Abbasids, from the year 750-850 CE, has been labelled the primary age and epoch of translation, with Baghdad at the core of this endeavour. In the first hundred years of the 'Abbasids, the Arabic-reading world came into possession of Greek philosophical works, Greek and Indian medical writings and Persian and Indian scientific masterpieces. These had been, in less than a century, translated and assimilated by the Muslim society.[13] With this movement came a rise in the number of physicians, lawyers, magistrates, teachers, writers and government administrators. The centuries of the 'Abbasid era that were to follow were full of creative activity:

> For the Muslims did not only assimilate the ancient lore of Persia and the classical heritage of Greece but adapted both to their own needs and ways of thinking.[14]

The Development of Islamic Education

The aim of Islamic education is the 'cultivation' of the individual so that he or she abides by and lives by the teachings of Islam. From an early period of its history, Islamic education began to grow into a dual (independent/government) form due to socio-political changes. While learning at the time of the Prophet ﷺ had started as basic education in the mosque for all Muslims, the first century and a half of Islamic history produced various kinds of educational institutions and sciences. Some of these, as mentioned earlier, originated from ancient cultures, while others began with the Prophet ﷺ and his Companions.

---

13 Ibid.

14 Hitti, op. cit., p. 363.

The elementary school, the *kuttāb* from the Prophetic period and the *maktab,* which was an Islamised Byzantine secondary school, evolved into one elementary school system. The second style of elementary education, where urban Arabs and later royalty sent their boys to the desert to be educated, grew into the tutor system, where the *mu'addib* was employed to teach at individual homes and in the palaces. This elementary education then led to further study at either the congregational (*jāmi'*) or local mosque (*masjid*), where various literary and religious studies were taught in an open learning environment. Thus, the mosques may, in a loose way, be compared to college education in the modern world. Mosques, however, were not the only higher education institutions in the early first century of Islam; the chancery schools also provided for students who wanted to become administrators and secretaries in the government. The third type of higher education institution, the *bimaristan,* was connected to the natural sciences; it was based upon apprenticeship, where the student learnt from medical and scientific teachers in their teachers' homes or in hospitals. Although often carried out separately, both governments and scholars simultaneously advanced all these institutions and sciences. The scholars undertook the transmission of knowledge whereas the various governments sponsored and helped develop many of the educational institutions.

The initial period of the 'Abbasid era was not any different in the sphere of education from that of the Umayyads. Then what made the 'Abbasid period such a fertile time for scholarship and learning? The translation movement literarily changed the world for the new Islamic Caliphate, for by it new ideas and fresh streams of thought came to pour into the cities of Basra, Kufa and Baghdad. In addition, the scholars acknowledged that the religion of Islam confirmed the unity of all knowledge; rather than early Muslims suppressing the declining Greek intellectual tradition, they instead sought out its sources and encouraged it.[15] Thus, all the early *'ulamā'* of Islam were polymaths, not simply experts in the religious arena or in one subject only, but rather, they linked mathematics, philosophy, art, law and any other science together in explaining the world of Islam.[16] Examples of such *'ulamā'* ranged from scholars such as al-Abari, historian and Qur'anic commentator; al-Kindī, philosopher, theologian and scientist; ar-Rāzī, physician and philosopher; al-Fārābī philosopher; al-Bīrūnī, geographer, historian, linguist and scientist; Ibn Sīnā, the physician and philosopher; al-Ghazālī, the theologian, mystic and lawyer; and Ibn Rushd, the physician, judge and philosopher. All of the elementary and higher education institutions mentioned above were advanced in the forthcoming centuries under the 'Abbasid rule in such a way that this era would be remembered as, *'The Golden Age'*.[17]

Elementary Education: The Kuttāb *or* Maktab

The *kuttāb* or *maktab* were more likely the same type of school, with the two terms used interchangeably throughout early Islamic history. This has been argued by many historians, beginning with the grammarian scholar al-Mubarrad (d. 898), who maintained that the word *maktab* was the only grammatically correct term for the elementary school and not *kuttāb*.[18] Shalaby described the elementary schools as a place where, "Learning the Qur'an preceded everything, next came religious instructions with some poetry, elementary grammar and arithmetic (with this) the primary course was closed."[19]

---

15 Sabra, op. cit., 1980, p. 183.

16 Stanton, op. cit., pp. 70-71.

17 Yusuf Waghid, 'Educational Institutions: Can the Heritage Be Sustained', *The American Journal of Islamic Sciences: Education*, Vol. 14, (and Kuala Lumpur: The International Institute of Islamic Thought), Winter 1997, pp. 35-51.

18 Shalaby, op. cit., p. 22.

19 Ibid.

After this description of the elementary school he notes that the curriculum obviously varied from one place to another by giving an example from the *Muqadima* of Ibn Khaldūn, however, he provides no evidence of any changes in this elementary education during the early centuries of Muslim history. There seems to be an assumption that elementary education did not change during the seven centuries that lay between the Prophet's ﷺ era and Ibn Khaldūn. For the reader it is already evident that education in all its forms did develop from the early period of Islamic history. The beginning of the *kuttāb* was a humble one; it was the teaching of reading, writing and the memorisation of the Qur'an in the mosque. However, by the end of the Umayyad period and the beginning of the 'Abbasid period this elementary institution, influenced by other various cultures, had advanced so much that it began to impart knowledge from a wide range of revealed sciences, *adab* sciences and the natural sciences.[20] Makdisi notes that by the Middle Ages this institution conveyed teaching at a much higher level than even contemporary elementary schools; it was *de facto* an institution that functioned as a 'finishing school' besides being an elementary school.[21] It is possible to find various statements littered throughout historical sources concerning the teachers and pupils of these schools. For example, the writer al-Katan during the eighth century noted the name of his *mu'allim* who was still alive when he was writing his book.[22] Aḥmad ibn Zauwal (1115-1190) spoke about his extensive studies in his *maktab* in the *adab* sciences which prepared him for further studies when he left at the age of fourteen to study grammar and lexicography under al-Jawaliqi.[23] An anonymous jurist in the late 'Abbasid period mentioned

20 Oadah, op. cit., pp. 93-95.
21 Makdisi, op. cit., 1990, pp. 48-49.
22 Ahmed, op. cit., p. 43.
23 Makdisi, op. cit., 1990, p. 49.

him and his classmate at the madrasah having been to same *maktab.*[24] All of these descriptions describe the *kuttāb/maktab* as an advanced finishing school that prepared them for future learning.

There are very few records that specify the exact age pupils commenced their elementary schools or when they left. The main reason for the lack of such information is more likely because the school system was not centrally organised by the state and since, all the elementary schools were independent and varied across the Muslim Caliphate, the age for the commencement of elementary education more likely varied widely. However, there are biographies of scholars that have helped shed light on the average age of pupils commencing and leaving their elementary schools. After studying the various biographical sources, it appears that most pupils seem to have entered the school at the age of five, seven or even ten; however, it has to be remembered that this did not apply universally.[25] For example, al-Bukhari (d. 869) is reported to have completed his study by the time he was ten. Other students were known to have written academic books while still at the *kuttāb.*[26] It is reasonable to imagine that most pupils by the 'Abbasid period spent their young age to adolescent years in the *kuttāb/maktab* until they proceeded to higher education or became apprenticed to various crafts. Sources seem to indicate that most children in the Islamic world in the 'Abbasid period could read, write and do basic mathematics. In addition, by the later period of the 'Abbasid rule, the elementary schools had become extremely sophisticated; Makdisi points out that the *maktab/kuttāb* imparted such excellent training that numerous students went into further study of *adab* sciences, law studies and into government administration apprenticeship. Furthermore, there is evidence that

24 Makdisi, op. cit., 1981, p. 19.
25 Ibid.
26 Ahmed, op. cit., p. 43.

pupils may have left one elementary school when they were finished and joined another school, for example Imam al-Bayhaqi (994-1066) a scholar of *fiqh* and *ḥadīth*, left his first *kuttāb/maktab* after he had memorised and studied eleven books concerning sciences such as grammar, lexicography and poetry. It is reasonable to assume from earlier evidence concerning the curriculum of schools that he also had extensive knowledge concerning the revealed sciences, mathematics and literacy skills. He then joined his second *kuttāb/maktab* at the age of fifteen years and continued his *adab* studies where he memorised and studied four more works in the field of grammar and lexicography. After two years he left this school at the age of sixteen; he did not finish his studies here, however, he continued to study at a higher level under various masters.[27]

Al-Mu'addib

By the beginning of the Umayyad dynasty, the desert education, which was a pre-Islamic elementary educational concept, was replaced by the tutor system. In contrast to the sources concerning the *kuttāb/maktab*, which are very few, the sources regarding the 'tutor system' are plentiful. The main group of tutors mentioned in the historical sources can be narrowed down to being the tutors of the royal and the wealthy families; these tutors had in-depth knowledge of both the religious and the *adab* sciences. This can be demonstrated by the following examples: the renowned grammarian and lexicographer al-Kisā'ī (d. 805) was the *mu'addib* of the Caliph Hārūn ar-Rashīd (763-809), and later on he was the *mu'addib* of his children, Amīn (787-813) and Ma'mūn (786-833). 'Ubaydah ibn al-Ḥamīd al-Kūfī, who was a well known scholar of Qur'an and *ḥadīth*, was also a tutor of Amīn, and Yaḥyā ibn al-Mubārak al-Yazdī was the *mu'addib* of Ma'mūn.[28]

27 Makdisi, op. cit., 1990, pp. 40-50.
28 Makdisi, op. cit., 1990, p. 273.

Other tutors of both Amīn and Ma'mūn were scholars such as Farra (d. 822), Abū 'Abd aṣ-Ṣamad and al-Aḥmar (d. 810). The scholar Ibn Bakkār taught the children of the Caliph Mutawakkil (821-861); Ibn Abī ad-Dunyā taught the Caliph al-Mu'taḍid (857-902) and Caliph Muktafī (d. 908), and *mu'addib* ad-Dabbi taught the son of Caliph al-Mu'tazz (861-908).[29]

The Caliph's family were not the only ones during the 'Abbasid Caliphate who employed tutors for their children; the élite in the government and trade also sought out tutors for their children. Hence, Thābit al-Khuza'ī, an élite member of the government, chose the scholar Abū 'Ubayd ibn Sallām to become his children's *mu'addib*.[30] The military commander, al-Qāsim ibn 'Īsā al-Injīl, employed Quṭrub and his son Ḥasan to tutor his sons; the Prime Minister 'Ubaydullāh ibn Sulaymān ibn Wahb employed Abū Isḥāq Ibrāhīm ibn Muḥammad az-Zajjāj (d. 923) to tutor his sons.[31]

Throughout the 'Abbasid period the employment of *mu'addib* to tutor the children of the élite was a common and well known practice. The tutors of that period can be divided into two types; the tutors who taught pupils of young age and the tutors who were known as an authority in their respective branches of knowledge, who taught the more advanced students. For example, Caliph Hārūn ar-Rashīd appointed Abū 'Abd aṣ-Ṣamad as the tutor for his young children, but when they grew up, he chose numerous specialists as mentioned above to educate his children.[32] The status of teaching the children of the élite was highly rewarded, sometimes with high pay or by material goods and sometimes even by becoming the confidant of the élite. There are many examples of such rewards; the tutor Aḥmar (d. 810) was originally a guard at the Caliph's palace who learnt his knowledge

---

29 Ahmed, op. cit., pp. 49-51.
30 Ibid., p. 46.
31 Makdisi, op. cit., 1990, p. 273.
32 Ahmed, op. cit., pp. 49-51.

from the famous tutor al-Kisā'ī while at work. When a need for a tutor's assistant became necessary, al-Kisā'ī chose Aḥmar to succeed him. When Aḥmar became a tutor he was provided with a furnished home and a good salary. Another illustration of the reward for the tutors from the élite can be seen in the example of the scholar Abū 'Ubaid ibn Sallam, who was the tutor of Thābit al-Khuzai; al-Khuzai appointed Ubaid ibn Sallam as the magistrate of the city when he became the governor of Tarsus.[33] The greatest influence of the tutors in the society on the other hand, lay in their network. The successful tutors were able to choose their own disciples as tutors; much of the time these disciples were family members, thus at some point during the period of the 'Abbasid era, there were dynasties of tutors who tutored for the same families of élites. Many tutors moved from being tutors to holding posts in the government and becoming confidants of the caliphs that they had educated, leaving behind their own family members as tutors for the next generation.[34]

Even if the statuses of the *mu'addib* (tutor) and the *mu'allim* (teacher) have been demonstrated as being distinct, there are some historical sources which reveal that a *mu'addib* could also be a *mu'allim* and vice versa. An example of this is the tutor Aḥmar, who tutored for the children of the Caliph and also taught *adab* sciences separately as a *mu'allim* at a *maktab.*[35] However, the titles were not interchangeable; when the preceptor performed a task at the school he was a *mu'allim* and in the role of a private tutor he was known as a *mu'addib.* It is also reasonable to assume that most specialist tutors would not have normally taught as *mu'allims* because they were scholars of various branches of knowledge and hence, normally taught in higher education.

33 Makdisi, op. cit., 1990, p. 273.
34 Makdisi, op. cit., 1990, pp. 273-275.
35 Makdisi, op. cit., 1990, p. 273.

Higher Education in the ‘Abbasid Period

The Mosque and the Khan

During the era of the early Islamic civilisation, the distinction between elementary education and higher education was very clear and the mosque was the main educational centre for higher education. The mosques were used as schools to teach adults Islam and literacy. By the Umayyad period two types of mosque emerged: ‘*al-masjid*’, the local mosque for the five daily prayers, and ‘*al-masjid al-jāmi*‘’ the major mosque at which the *Jumu‘ah* prayer was held. The mosque curriculum grew to teach the revealed sciences and *adab*. In the ‘Abbasid period, the majority of the local *masājid* began to be utilised for study circles concerned with law and jurisprudence.[36] In addition, during the early ‘Abbasid period, *adab* was taught extensively at the local mosques; the *masjid al-jāmi*‘ also included various study circles concerned mostly with jurisprudence but also *adab* studies.

The confirmation of the existence of such a higher education system is often found in various books written by later Muslim scholars concerning social issues, especially relating to the biographies of scholars or the categorisation of the sciences. In *at-Tārīkh al-Baghdādī,* the author, while writing the biographies of the scholars who lived or visited this city, also notes the importance of various mosques and their educational use in the new city of Baghdad. Although some mosques were well known for being educational centres for particular subjects, this did not mean that these mosques were not used for other sciences as well. As has been seen in earlier chapters, the first centre of Islamic education was the Prophetic city of Madīnah, followed by the cities of Basra, Kufa and Damascus. By the ‘Abbasid period, Baghdad had become

---

36 E. Ihsanoglu and F. Gunergun (eds.), *Science in Islamic civilisation*, (Turkey: IRCICA), 2000, p. 1.

37 Ibid., p. 24.

the main educational centre of the Muslim world. There were six main *jāmiʿ* mosques in the city of Baghdad during the ʿAbbasid period.[37] The first to be constructed was the *Jāmiʿ Madīnat al-Manṣūr* built between the years 762-766 CE and named after its founder, the second caliph of the ʿAbbasids. This mosque became well known as one of the greatest educational institutions during that epoch in the Muslim world. It is reported that around fifty *ḥalaqāt* were active when ash-Shāfiʿī, the famous Imām of jurisprudence, visited Baghdad half a century after the mosque's construction. The various *ḥalaqāt* contained recitation of the Qur'an, reporting and dictation of *ḥadīth*, poetry, *tafsīr* and even *kālām,* the science of *ʿaqīdah*, but this was rare. Although it is true that *fiqh* was later taught mostly at the local *masjid*, during the early period, throughout the third, fourth and the beginning of the fifth Islamic century, *fiqh* was taught continuously at the congregational mosques. Ash-Shāfiʿī himself taught *fiqh* in one of the *ḥalaqāt* at the *Jāmiʿ Madīnat al-Manṣūr* and the guild of Shāfiʿī scholars continued to teach at the mosque, however, this does not mean that the other guilds of law were excluded. The Ḥanbalī scholar Abū ʿAlī al-Hāshimī (d. 1037) taught *fiqh* and had a *ḥalaqah* for *fatwa* at the same mosque. The Ẓāhirī guild also had a few scholars teaching there, amongst them the founder of the guild, Dāwūd ibn ʿAlī aẓ-Ẓāhirī.[38] The *Jāmiʿ al-Ruṣafā*, the second *jāmiʿ* mosque in Baghdad, built by the Caliph al-Mahdī in 775 CE, was mostly used for teaching by *ḥadīth* scholars.

Most of the other mosques in Baghdad were also venues for specialised higher education. *Ḥadīth ḥalaqāt* were taught regularly by various scholars at local mosques, such as *Masjid al-Bazzāzūn* (the mosque of the fabric merchants), *Masjid Ibn Raghbān, Masjid ʿAffān, Masjid Ibn Shāhīn, Masjid al-Baghiyyīn* and *Masjid Abū Bakr al-Hudhalī al-Baṣrī*. Other local mosques, such as *Masjid ad-Dāraquṭnī, Masjid ar-Ruwaym ibn Yazīd, Masjid aṣ-Ṣaḥābah* and *Masjid Ibn Mujāhid*, where the famous Qur'an

[38] Ahmed, op. cit., pp. 115-120.

scholar Ibn Mujāhid taught his students the science of *qirā'ah* in the tenth century, functioned as educational institutions for the recitation of the Qur'an. Others, such as *Masjid 'Abdullāh ibn al-Mubārak,* were utilised for teaching Shāfi'ī *fiqh*, in this case by the well known Shāfi'ī scholar, 'Abd al-Majīd.

During the period of Baghdad's foundation, a number of Sufi scholars appeared on the scene of the world of education. They emphasised the importance of spirituality in Islam to a society that was becoming highly materialistic. Thus, numerous local mosques began to specialise in the teaching of the sciences of Sufism, such as, *Masjid al-Shunayziyah, Masjid Ma'rūf al-Karkhī, Masjid as-Sammāk* and *Masjid al-Bāb al-Kunas.*

Various local and congregational mosques taught a number of the *adab* sciences rather than the range of revealed sciences. These *ḥalaqāt* were taught by scholars such as the famous historian Abū Ja'far Muḥammad ibn Jarīr aṭ-Ṭabarī (838–923), who taught his students history and exegesis of the Qur'an at the *Masjid as-Sūq al-'Atīqah,*[39] Abū 'Abdullāh ibn 'Arafah Nifṭawayh (d. 935), who taught biography and history at the *Masjid al-Anbaryyīn,* and Abū Bakr al-Anbarī (d. 940) who taught his students lexicography, grammar, history, Qur'anic exegesis, and poetry at the same mosque.[40]

However, it was not only in Baghdad that mosques were widely used as educational institutions; throughout the 'Abbasid period, various congregational mosques and local mosques outside Iraq became famous for education. The Umayyad mosque in Damascus had study circles where sciences such as Qur'anic exegesis, grammar and law were taught. The *jāmi' masjid* of Basra had study circles on grammar, taught by grammarians such as Yūnus ibn Ḥabīb (d. 778-810), al-Kisā'ī (d. 805), and al-Farrā' (d. 822). Other famous mosques for higher

---

39 Ibid., pp. 120-134.

40 Makdisi, op. cit., 1990, pp. 50-52.

education in the Islamic world during this time were the old mosque of Cairo (Egypt), the congregational mosque in Cordoba (Spain), the congregational mosque of Aleppo (Syria), the congregational mosque of Alexandria (Egypt) and the mosque of Sinjar.[41]

Historians often speak about the sundry dynasties of both East and West at the time of the 'Abbasid caliphs as a political disaster for the power of the Caliphate. However, if looked at through a different lens, it becomes clear that it was largely due to the Sultans of these states that vast sums of money went into education, culture and art. The idea of statehood at that time always fluctuated, and the various borders of neighbouring states were quite fluid. Thus, by the early tenth century, after the rise and fall of various petty states, three rival caliphs in Baghdad, Cairo and Cordoba came to rule three separate Caliphates for a short period of time. This, of course, led to political rivalries and disunity but, at the same time, the three Caliphates ('Abbasid, Fatimid and the Cordoba Caliphate) vied to outdo each other in culture, education and art. Thus, centres of education and culture spread from Baghdad to numerous cities that became capitals of various states such as Cairo, Cordoba, Bukhara, Samarqand, Ghazna, Shiraz and Konya.[42]

Various sciences during the 'Abbasid period were taught or delivered differently simply because of the diversity of the sciences. An example of this is the core difference between the science of *taṣawwuf* and the science of *fiqh*. The latter is studied to understand the revealed law of Islam and the former is taught for the student to come spiritually closer to Allah. However, this does not mean that these sciences are fundamentally in opposition to each other. There are various historical sources that refer to scholars and students studying both *fiqh* and *taṣawwuf* and this is the case today in many

41 Ibid.

42 Makdisi, op. cit., 1990, pp. 50-52.

societies. One famous Sufi teacher who taught in Baghdad during the ninth century was the scholar al-Junayd. He taught his students to have a balanced spirituality in accordance with the *sharī'ah* (divine law) and the *ḥaqīqah* (the timeless spiritual truth).[43] The study of the above sciences was imparted differently because of their core structure and aims being poles apart, but the study of Qur'an reading and *ḥadīth* were conducted in a very similar way. The teaching of both Qur'an reading and *ḥadīth* reports was by definition an instruction. The methods that were employed in Qur'an instruction were *qirā'ah* (recitation), *tilāwah* (reading aloud) and *'arḍ* (submission to criticism).[44] The students first heard the recitation of the teacher and were then asked to read it back to the teacher for submission to criticism. The transmission of *ḥadīth*s was done through *samā'*: the teacher reported a *ḥadīth*, or the student or someone else read the *ḥadīth* out to the teacher, and the student memorised it and wrote it down in his notebook. It is interesting to note that whereas most other *ḥalaqāt* such as grammar, theology or *fiqh* were collectively called *majlis at-tadrīs* (translated as 'class of teaching'), the *ḥalaqāt* of *ḥadīth* were collectively called *majlis al-ḥadīth*.[45] This was done in order to emphasise that in the study circles where the *ḥadīth* were reported and collected, the emphasis was not on study but on gathering the various sayings of the Prophet ﷺ.

The scholars of various subjects such as the Qur'an, *ḥadīth*, grammar, theology, and *fiqh*, were famous as students for their memorisation of texts regarding their respective subjects. It is important, however, to recognise that this memorisation was accompanied by understanding and evaluation of the texts. The famous historian aṭ-Ṭabarī (d. 923)

43 Henry Corbin, *History of Islamic Philosophy*, (London: Kegan Paul International), 1993, p. 195.

44 Christopher Melchert, 'Ibn Mujahid and the Establishment of Seven Qur'anic Readings', *Studia Islamica*, 2000, p. 11.

45 Ahmed, op. cit., p. 59.

advised Muslim scholars and students alike not only to acquire knowledge, but also to understand it; he advised this because many of his followers had begun to limit themselves to memorisation and note-taking. The continuation of this methodology would be to create one's own work.[46] Al-Ghazālī (d. 1111) argued that education was ultimately about creating a moral person and that it involved all aspects of learning – intellectual, religious, moral and even physical. Al-Ghazālī further contended that imparting theoretical learning had to conclude with the practical since that would create a person who acted morally and ethically according to the faith.[47] The scholar Ibn Sīnā (d. 1037) divided higher education into theoretical instruction, which led to apprenticeship in crafts, and into theoretical education which, today may be referred to as 'academic'. He divided academic teaching in higher education into two types: the transmitted (*naqlī*) and the intellectual (*'aqlī*).[48]

The early 'Abbasid era is well known for its intellectual debates on the growing religious, scientific and humanistic studies. These exchanges seem to have been labelled *majlis al-munāẓarah* (exchange of views) and *majlis al-mudhākarah* (mutual reminder).[49] According to Makdisi, *munāẓarah* was used for disputation, and questions were encouraged because they were seen as the keys to knowledge.[50] The various styles of disputation varied in status, place and style so much that disputation and debate could occur in the markets and mosques as well as in the palaces of the caliphs. The first such exchanges were initiated by the early 'Abbasid caliphs and they became so

---

46 Makdisi, op. cit., 1981, p. 103.

47 Imam Ghazālī, H. M. Fazul ul-Karim (tr.), *Ihya Ulum ad-Din*, (New Delhi: Kitab Bhavan), Vol. 3, 1982, pp. 61-62.

48 Abd al-Rahman al Naqib, *Ibn Sīnā on Education*, http://www.muslimheritage.com/topics/default.cfm?ArticleID=1063#ftn55, (accessed: 26/06/10).

49 Ahmed, op. cit., p. 59.

50 Makdisi, op. cit., 1981, p. 103.

influential that soon the rich and the scholars commenced their own exchanges.[51]

There seem to have been two particular reasons why the caliphs established a *munāẓarah* in the palace. Primarily, it was politically showing leadership; for example, some historians have argued that through the establishment there of disputation by various scholars on issues of numerous sciences, the caliph could be the judge and create a status for himself as the principal source of leadership. There may be some truth to this argument because even the architectural structure of the Round City has been suggested to represent centralised power and to vividly assert the status of the caliph. The second reason for bringing scholars together for exchanges was in order to raise the awareness of Baghdad as an intellectual capital.

In many ways, both aims were successful; the exchanges which Caliph Hārūn ar-Rashīd (r. 786-809) and his son the Caliph al-Ma'mūn (r. 813-831) attended as judges have been immortalised in folktales about Baghdad and remembered for the wisdom of the Caliphs' verdicts. An example of this can be seen in the description given by the educational historian, Shalaby, regarding the Caliph Ma'mūn's period in Baghdad, to which he refers as the 'Augustan period' of Arabic sciences in which, "His court was crowned with men of science and letters, poets, physicians and philosophers from every part of the civilized world."[52] This type of disputation was copied by various governors and, later on, by sultans elsewhere to bolster their cities' and states' standing as intellectual centres.

The second type of *munāẓarah* was convened by scholars themselves in mosques or at their own homes. These exchanges were commenced by various teachers who encouraged their students to ask questions

51 Ahmed, op. cit., p. 59.
52 Shalaby, op. cit., p. 37.

and to discuss the questions and the answers with each other. Abū Ḥanīfah (d. 765) encouraged debates amongst his students which he supervised.[53] In many ways, this style of *munāẓarah* was a continuation of the education that students acquired in study circles. It created an intellectual atmosphere where the aim was to make the students understand conflicting ideas and listen to various teachers. This was pointed out by Ayyūb as-Sakhtiyānī (d. 748) when he stated, "A person will not know the mistakes of his teacher until he knows the conflicting ideas," and Khalīl ibn Aḥmad (d. 791) stated, "The sciences are padlocks and questions are the keys to them."[54]

The third type of *munāẓarah* is very similar to the one mentioned above, except that this type of disputation was not pre-arranged between the scholars; it was spontaneous and could even commence in the market. Moreover, this type of disputation was more frequent in contrast to the other styles of *munāẓarah* which were arranged and announced to the public.[55] These scholarly discussions were often conducted in places such as shops, city squares and gardens. According to writers of the 'Abbasid period such as Abū'l-Faraj Muḥammad ibn Isḥāq an-Nadīm (d. 998) and Yaqūt ibn 'Abdullāh ar-Rūmī al-Ḥamawī (d. 1229), the most famous discussions and debates were held in books dealers' markets where the proprietors were often themselves men of learning.[56] There is no doubt that the aim of all of these discussions and debates was sometimes simply to advance in knowledge, which consequently led many students to unhesitatingly challenge renowned scholars. Indirectly this created an intellectual environment where the teachers were constantly checked academically and had to prove

---

53 Ahmed, op. cit., p. 61.

54 Makdisi, op. cit., 1990, p. 210.

55 Ahmed, op. cit., p. 65.

56 Joel L. Kraemer, *Humanism in the Renaissance of Islam*, (New York: E. J. Brill), 1992, p. 57.

their worth at each step of their careers. It can also be argued that, whether arranged or spontaneous, these debates were a source of great entertainment for the general populace of the city and at the same time they provided an opportunity for scholars to educate them.

It is important to note that sometimes these debates were also misused by unscrupulous men who would try to humiliate their opponent by deception and obtain self-advancement through misguided praise of their own work. Nevertheless, there were scholars who continuously pointed out the need to be honest and maintain humility when debating. The Sufi scholar Ḥātim al-Aṣamm (d. 852) advised his fellow scholars concerning exchanges, by stating that the debater should be pleased when his opponent hits the mark, regretful when the adversary makes a blunder and should sincerely recognise his opponent's qualities.[57] The famous scholar and lecturer of the Nizamiyah Madrasah, al-Ghazālī (d. 1111), pointed out good and bad points of *munāẓarah* in his book *Iḥyā 'Ulūm ad-Dīn*. He said that only qualified people should be part of a debate, so that they do not need to refer to other scholars, but would have the ability themselves to cite crucial evidence. He pointed out the necessity of only debating actual cases or circumstances that could arise in the future and not future scenarios commonly accepted as being highly unlikely. He also advised that if the issue was a matter of right and wrong then it would be better that it was done in private since the debaters would put all their effort into dealing with the subject and not playing to the gallery. The debate should be carried out with two aims, primarily, to get to the truth and secondly, to learn from one's opponents who should in this role be seen as teachers. Thus both sides should be willing to accept their errors, accept the truth and be willing to lose the argu-

[57] Ibid, p. 69.

ment for its sake. In addition, al-Ghazālī warns against the damaging aspects of debating for personal gain which can lead to envy, pride, malice, backbiting, self-righteousness and hypocrisy.[58]

The *munāẓarah* included discussions on a wide range of topics, for example, *kalām, fiqh, adab,* and natural sciences, whereas it seems that the *mudhākarah* was used exclusively in *ḥadīth* studies. This kind of exchange seems to have originated with students who commenced informal exchange of *ḥadīth* in the mosques. They discussed matters such as:

> ....the different ways of transmission, the Companions who reported them, the authors of the *ḥadīth* collections, and the category of the soundness of *ḥadīth*.[59]

The majority of the scholars of *ḥadīth* attended and discussed in *mudhākarah* throughout the ʻAbbasid period. However, according to Makdisi, *mudhākarah* was also used in *adab* studies as instructive conversation; *mudhākarah* was famously used in the mosque of Basra, where Khalīl ibn Aḥmad (d. 791) used it in relation to grammar and poetry. It was later used for testing the knowledge of an applicant for a post. This happened specifically in the cases of tutors who wanted to obtain jobs at the palace; they were invited with other applicants and asked to debate in front of those who would hire them. The term *mudhākarah* seems to have been so synonymous with the term *munāẓarah* that in the ninth century when the Umayyad Prince of Spain, al-Mundhir ibn ʻAbd ar-Raḥmān (842-888), occasionally debated with his acquaintances regarding syntax, he called it *mudhākarah*.[60] Even the Sufi community began to use the term for *dhikr* gatherings, but in a sense closer to the root meaning: mutual reminder.

---

58 Ghazālī, op. cit., pp. 54-56.
59 Ahmed, op. cit., pp. 115-120.
60 Makdisi, op. cit., 1990, p. 210.

Financially, mosques were maintained through charitable foundations, governed by the law of *waqf.* Throughout Islamic history, philanthropists donated large sums of money to *waqf* properties, including mosques. There is also historical evidence that by the eighth century, *masjids* as higher education institutions, began to pay their staff salaries and were able to grant their students free tuition, i.e. students did not have to pay fees. However, as Makdisi points out, the mosques were not used as lodgings or for subsistence.[61] Hence, it can be argued that the financial requirements of students, especially those who were from out of town and the element of philanthropy were contributing factors to the evolution of the *masjid*-based education system.

It was Badr ibn Hasanwaih al-Kurdi (d. 1014), a governor appointed by the Shiite Buyid Sultan 'Aḍud ad-Dawlah (r. 978-983) in the tenth century, who triggered the advance of and long lasting effects on educational institutions across the Caliphate. He established three thousand *masjid-khan* complexes in a period of thirty years throughout all the provinces that he administered for the Buyid dynasty. These complexes were further education mosques with study circles and adjunct inns (*khan*), where students who did not have lodgings and subsistence were able to reside throughout their study.[62] This was the second stage of the evolution of further education in Islamic history. Although there is evidence that scattered student inns existed before the governor Badr al-Kurdi, it is he who stands out as the cornerstone of the *masjid-khan* complex initiative. The *khan* that existed before the tenth century only served as a simple inn or a hotel for travellers, situated in the town, at the roadside or in the desert.[63] Higher education

61 Makdisi, op. cit., 1981, p. 29.

62 Khalil I. Seemaan (ed.), *Islam and the Medieval West*, (Albany: State University of New York Press), 1980, p. 32.

63 Oadah, op. cit., p. 109.

was provided at the *khan* adjunct to the mosques, whereas it is evident that other *khans* continued to be utilised as inns as was customary for travellers. Hence, the evolution of the mosque into the *masjid-khan* complex during the Buyid period (934-1055) of the 'Abbasid Caliphate foreshadowed the development of the madrasah.

The Madrasah

In 1055 the Seljuk Sultan Toghril Beg (r. 1038-1063), who was from a Turco-Persian background, restored Baghdad to rule according to the Sunnah,[64] keeping the 'Abbasid caliph as the titular head of the Islamic community. Although, Sultan Toghril Beg and his descendants only ruled Baghdad and the surrounding areas until 1157 CE, the Seljuks continued to rule parts of Central Asia and the Middle East including Anatolia until the fourteenth century. It was during the early period of Seljuk rule in Baghdad that the madrasah was instituted by the minister Abū 'Alī al-Ḥasan aṭ-Ṭūsī Nizam al-Mulk (d. 1092).[65] Nizam al-Mulk entered the service of the Seljuk Sultan Alp Arslan (r. 1063-1072), the conqueror of Anatolia, in the year 1063 and by 1065 CE he had founded the *Nizamiyyah* madrasah of Baghdad. However, he not only established that madrasah but in addition numerous other madrasahs that were named after him throughout the 'Abbasid Caliphate in cities such as Nishapur, Balkh, Herat and Isfahan.[66] After Nizam al-Mulk,

---

64 Here the term Sunnah refers to what is popularly known in English as Sunni or Sunnism. In Arabic the overwhelming majority of the Muslims, i.e.Sunnis have been known as *Ahlus Sunnah wa Al-Jamā'ah* (أهل السنة والجماعة) meaning *People of the Prophetic way and the majority of Scholars.* This title historically emerged as a response to the sectarianism of the first and second centuries of Muslim history but the title is based upon a prophetic tradition. See: T. J. Winter (ed.), *The Cambridge Companion to Classical Islamic Theology*, (Cambridge: Cambridge Press), 2008, p. 39 and Ṭaḥāwī, Aḥmad ibn Muḥammad, Yusuf, Hamza (tr.), *The Creed of Imam al-Tahawi*, (USA: Zaytuna Institute), 2007, p. 112.

65 Shalaby, op. cit., p. 57.

66 Z. H. Faruqi, 'Madrasa Nizamiya of Baghdad', *Studies in Islam*, Vol. 17, 1980, pp. 1-2.

the pace of madrasah building accelerated throughout the Muslim world; rulers such as Nūr ad-Dīn of Damascus (r. 1146-1174) and the Ayyūbid dynasty of Egypt and Syria (1174-1250) founded numerous other madrasahs in the areas they ruled in the name of the 'Abbasid Caliph.[67]

The Spanish Muslim traveller of Valencia, Ibn Jubayr (d. 1217), described the Nizamiyyah madrasahs in Baghdad as:

> ....There are approximately thirty madrasahs, all of which are on the East Side [of Baghdad], and there is not a single one of them but that a magnificent palace falls short of it in magnificence. The greatest and most famous among them is the Nizamiyyah, which is the one built by Nizam al-Mulk and reconstructed in the year 504 AH (1110 CE). The madrasahs have considerable endowments and landed property tied up inalienably, the proceeds of which go to the professors of law who teach there, who in turn grant scholarship from it to the students for their subsistence. Great honor and perpetual glory devolve upon this city because of these madrasahs and hospitals. May God be merciful towards the first of the founders and those who subsequently followed this pious practice.[68]

A number of reasons for the establishment of the madrasah have been advanced by contemporary historians. Makdisi and Nakosteen have both noted financial, religious and political motives behind the establishment of such an institution. The religio-political motives according to them stem from events that occurred in the century

---

67 Shalaby, op. cit., pp. 57-69.

68 Cited from Ibn Jubair's 'Rihla' in George Makdisi, 'The Madrasa in Spain: some remarks', *Revue de l'Occident Musulman et de la Méditerranée*, Vol. 15, No. 15-16, 1973, pp. 153-158.

preceding the establishment of the madrasah. From the mid-tenth and early eleventh century, the Twelver Shiite Buyid dynasty ruled most of Persia and Iraq in the name of the 'Abbasid Caliphate and all of North Africa had been subjugated under the Ismaili Shiite Fatimid Caliphate (909-1171). During this period of time, it may have appeared to the average Muslim that the Shiites had at last taken control of most of the Muslim lands. It was within this political landscape that the Seljuk dynasty arose as defenders of the Sunnah and took their opportunity in the late tenth century to come to power. According to some contemporary Western historians, in this political drama the madrasah was a religio-political tool to educate the masses in the doctrines of the Sunnah and to combat Shi'ism.[69]

The English term 'university' is derived from the Latin, '*universitas magistrorum et scholarium*', translated as, 'community of teachers and scholars'. According to Hugh Goddard, the Western university is an Islamic innovation in that the Islamic world was the first civilisation to introduce an institution of learning that centred on various faculties, as opposed to the learning of antiquity that centred on specific individual teachers.[70] Historically, the first higher education institution in the Islamic world was al-Qayrawiyyīn in Fez founded in 899 CE by the Tunisian woman, Fāṭimah al-Fihrī.[71] The higher education institute of al-Azhar in Cairo was second in 969 CE, established by the Ismaili Shi'ite dynasty.[72] Al-Azhar did not become a fully fledged madrasah of the Sunnah until the eleventh century when Sultan Ṣalāḥ ad-Dīn Yūsuf ibn Ayyūb (1138-1193) conquered Egypt from the Fatimid Caliphate.

---

69 Nakosteen, op. cit., p. 38.

70 Ibid.

71 John Esposito, *The Oxford Dictionary of Islam*, (Oxford: Oxford University Press), 2003, p. 328.

72 Hugh Goddard, *A History of Christian-Muslim Relations*, (Edinburgh: Edinburgh University press), 2000, p. 99.

According to Makdisi, there is also a financial reason for the establishment of the madrasah. The legal status of the mosque as a *waqf* property is that it belongs to Allah because of His words, "*The mosques belong to Allah*" (Sūrat al-Jinn 72:18); it can neither be sold, rented or put to private use. Taqī ad-Dīn as-Subkī (d. 1355) described the *waqf* of the mosque as:

> ....it was as though the mosque was a manumitted slave, just as the master, in freeing his slave no longer has any right over him, so also the founder of a mosque, once the mosque is instituted as *waqf*, the founder no longer retains any right over his property.[73]

On the other hand, the *waqf* deed for a madrasah means that the founders of the madrasah can stipulate staff in the foundation deed and there is the possibility of carrying out a certain amount of long-term planning and thus benefitting academically from an exclusive higher education institution.[74] The madrasah, nevertheless, did not bring educational activity in the mosques abruptly to an end; instead they existed side by side for centuries, with teaching going on in both congregational and local mosques.

The effect of the madrasah on the general population can be seen clearly in various historical sources. One of the main positive effects of the madrasah was upon financial benefits for the students. The *waqf* of a madrasah would provide salaries for staff and a large amount of scholarships for students.[75] The students of the madrasah, in addition to the scholarship, were also provided with board and lodgings, a continuation of the *masjid-khan* tradition. According to Stanton, this

---

73 Makdisi, op. cit., 1981, p. 33.

74 Ibid., p. 32.

75 George Makdisi, 'Muslim Institutions of Learning in the 11th Century', *Bulletin of the SOAS Studies*, Vol. 24, 1961, p. 51.

aspect of the madrasah is the historical origin of the residential colleges at Bologna, Paris, Oxford and Cambridge and also of the scholarships for impoverished scholars during the medieval period in Europe.[76] Another positive aspect of the madrasah was the incorporation of a library within the main structure of lecture halls and dormitories. It gave the students the opportunity to have firsthand experience of numerous works and the different views of the scholars.[77] The impact of the Nizamiyyah madrasah was so great that Nizam al-Mulk founded further madrasahs also named Nizamiyyah in Balkh, Nishapur, Herat, Isfahan, Basra, Merw, Amul and Mosul. The impact and success of the madrasah movement did not stop here, but spread throughout the Muslim world. In Egypt, Sultan Ṣalāh ad-Dīn founded five madrasahs in Cairo; by the twelfth century madrasahs had spread throughout Iran, Iraq, Egypt, Palestine, Syria, and Central Asia.[78]

The madrasahs founded by philanthropists became primarily colleges of law, which highlights Islam's focus on orthopraxy, 'right action', responding to the call of Allah through deeds. *Sharī'ah* has historically been the main focus of Muslim scholarship; the need for Islamic jurisprudence, which guides Muslim behaviour throughout life, has predominantly superseded the theoretical dedication to Muslim theology. Since the eleventh century, the teaching of jurisprudence in the mosques had mainly been identified with one of the four *madhāhib*. Hence, when the madrasahs came along, they followed in the same tradition; the madrasahs established by Nizam al-Mulk were all instituted with an accompanying endowment, which established them for the teaching of the Shāfi'ī *madhhab*. In contrast, the Sarakshī madrasah and the madrasah of Abū Ḥanīfah in Baghdad exclusively taught the Ḥanafī *madhhab*. The madrasah of Abū Sa'd al-Mukharrimī,

---

76 Stanton, op. cit., p. 38.
77 Ibid.
78 Shalaby, op. cit., pp. 57-64.

later renamed after one of its most famous students, 'Abd al-Qādir al-Jīlānī, and the madrasah of Ibn al-Abradī were endowed to teach the Ḥanbalī *madhhab*.[79] On the other hand, according to the understanding (*fiqh*) of the Mālikī *madhhab*, the *waqf* did not allow the benefactor to influence the appointment of the lecturer, his successors or the appointment of a trustee. The consequence was that such appointments were very different in the higher education of Muslim Spain.[80]

The final stage of the madrasah's development in the 'Abbasid period occurred in the year 1234 CE when the 'Abbasid Caliph al-Mustanṣir (r. 1226-1242) established the Mustanṣiriyyah madrasah.[81] In contrast to many of the early madrasahs, which followed the tradition of the local mosques with regards to exclusively teaching only one *madhhab*, the Mustanṣiriyyah like the *masjid al-jāmi'* before it, began to teach all the *madhāhib*. Thus, each *madhhab* had an academic chair in the institution.[82] In addition, the *adab* sciences and other religious sciences were also taught there.[83] The new higher education institution was a large two-storied structure, oblong in shape, with a great open court in the centre. This madrasah had a classroom (*īwān*) for each guild of law, which was based on the study circle with three walls opening onto the courtyard where there were rooms allocated to teachers and students. The *masjid* was a central feature of the madrasah, and there was a fountain of water in the middle of the courtyard. In addition to the kitchen, the madrasah housed a considerable library for all kinds of sciences, which was run by a librarian and his assistants.

79 Ibid., pp. 17-29.

80 This had deep impact on Western education. This style of education from Spain migrated to Sicily and then to the Italian peninsula where it carved out the model for the establishment of higher education for the study of Roman and Canon law, the most important facility of the medieval university in Southern Europe. See Stanton, op. cit., p. 39.

81 Stanton, op. cit., p. 41.

82 Makdisi, op. cit., Vol. 24, 1961, p. 55.

83 Oadah, op. cit., pp. 249-261.

The madrasah also had a *ḥamām* (public bath) and was attached to a hospital. The Mustanṣiriyyah has also become well known for its famous clock, set in a design of the heavens, with twelve doors one for each hour, each opening to announce the hour. According to Bernard Dodge, the Mustanṣiriyyah type of madrasah is what most closely resembles our contemporary university.[84]

The *waqf* deed of the Mustanṣiriyyah madrasah makes it clear that it was more highly advanced than its predecessors. It includes all aspects of a modern university administration, such as a Chancellor *(wāṣī)*, Vice Chancellor *(nāẓir)*, Bursar *(kātib)*, school officers *(dīwān)*, Treasurer *(mushrif)*, administrative staff, porters, librarians, bath manager, domestic servants and kitchen staff. Facilities such as a library, kitchen and public bath were clearly an advance over earlier madrasahs of the eleventh century.[85] In addition, at the request of the Caliph al-Mustanṣir, the new madrasah included a medical faculty where a doctor was appointed to lecture on medicine, pharmacy and natural sciences to a number of students who were offered stipends.[86] One of the main features that distinguished the mosque from the madrasah during this period was that the madrasah was in some way directed by ministers and rulers of the state such as the Vizier Nizam al-Mulk and the Caliph al-Mustanṣir.

Ibn Baṭūṭah (d. 1369), the famous North African traveller, in the year 1327 CE described the Mustanṣiriyyah madrasah in Baghdad, which was then a century old:

> In the centre of this bazaar [the Tuesday Bazaar] is the wonderful Nizamiyyah College, the splendour of which is commemorated in a number of proverbial phrases, and at

---

84 Dodge, op. cit., pp. 23-24.
85 Oadah, op. cit., p. 300.
86 Shalaby, op. cit., p. 57.

> the end of it is the Mustanṣiriyyah College...All four schools are included in it, each school having a separate *īwān*, with its own mosque and lecture room. The teacher takes his place under a small wooden canopy, on a chair covered with rugs; he sits [on this] in a grave and quiet attitude, wearing robes of black and his [black turban], and with two assistants on his right and left, who repeat everything that he dictates. This same system is followed in every formal lecture of all four sections. Inside this college there is a bath-house for the students and a chamber for ablution.[87]

Al-Ghazālī (1058-1111), a close friend of the Vizier Nizam al-Mulk, was offered a lectureship at the Nizamiyyah madrasah at the age of thirty-three. He noted that the period he lived in was experiencing an impediment to social change that was due to a misunderstanding involving the true purpose of education.[88] He continually indicated in the *Iḥyā' 'Ulūm ad-Dīn* that there is no true learning without putting it into practice and using it for the betterment of society. He believed that society's aim is to apply the *sharī'ah* so that it can be possible to have a just and positive society. The aim of education is to nurture the human being so that he or she lives by the teachings of Islam, individually and socially, and at the same time is aware that human beings are ultimately created for the hereafter so that this is what they ultimately aspire to.[89] Hence, to reach this goal al-Ghazālī integrated *taṣawwuf* and *sharī'ah* in his scholarship, so that the spirit of *sharī'ah*

---

87 Cited from Ibn Baṭūṭah's 'Rihla' in George Makdisi, 'The Madrasa in Spain: some remarks', *Revue de l'Occident Musulman et de la Méditerranée*, Vol. 15, No. 15-16, 1973, pp. 153-158.

88 W. Montgomery Watt, *Muslim Intellectual: A Study of Al-Ghazālī*, (Edinburgh: Edinburgh University Press), 1963, p. 163.

89 'Abdullāh al-Fahad, *Classical Educational Thought, Curriculum and Methods of Teaching in Islam*, (PhD: Cardiff), 1998, p. 72.

would be understood; he introduced the temporal modal logic to *kalām* to explain the faith and applied reasoning by analogy, deductive logic, and inductive logic within jurisprudence. Scholars who came after him such as Fakhr ad-Dīn ar-Rāzī (1149-1209) and Ibn Taymiyyah (1263-1328), also applied inductive logic to Islamic *sharī'ah* law.[90] Both Gutas and Savage-Smith in their respective writings have demonstrated the successful impact of al-Ghazālī's scholarship on logic, philosophy and medicine in the Islamic world between the eleventh and fourteenth centuries and its legacy.[91]

This brings us to the potent question as to whether there was a decline in the intellectual life of the Muslims after al-Ghazālī's period? Many Western scholars have argued that from the eleventh and twelfth century onwards there was a decline in Islamic civilisation and many have spoken about the closing of the doors of *ijtihād.* However, later chapters in this book demonstrate instead that there was a continuing and creative intellectual tradition, not only in the heartlands of the 'Abbasids, but further west towards Egypt, Anatolia and Spain. It is clear that the Mongol onslaught caused horrific destruction of Islamic civilisation in 1258 CE in the eastern part of the Caliphate, but it was only half a century later that the same Mongols became Muslim champions of art and science in the Islamic world. However, the devastated regions in Iraq and Central Asia never reached the same intellectual level as they had once achieved. Nevertheless, other regions of the Islamic world would have spectacular accomplishments in not only the intellectual world but

[90] Wael B. Hallaq, 'The Logic of Legal Reasoning in Religious and Non-Religious Cultures: The Case of Islamic Law and the Common Law', *Cleveland State Law Review*, Vol. 34, 1985-1986, pp. 79-96.

[91] Emilie Savage-Smith, 'Attitudes toward dissection in medieval Islam', *Journal of the History of Medicine and Allied Sciences*, Vol. 50, 1995, http://jhmas.oxfordjournals.org/cgi/reprint/50/1/67, pp. 67–110, (accessed 09/07/2010). Gutas, op. cit., pp. 28-53.

also in the arenas of trade and politics. Although Europe commenced its rise from its 'Dark Ages' around the twelfth century, influenced strongly by Islamic civilisation, with the building of colleges in Bologna, Oxford, Cambridge and Paris, the majority of its population were still illiterate for centuries to come.[92]

William H. McNeil and Marilyn Robinson Waldman in their book, *The Islamic World,* argue that Islamic civilisation continued to be amongst the major players in world history in the intellectual, political and military arenas until the eighteenth century, when the continuing impact of intellectual stagnation from within and colonisation from without brought 'Islamdom' to a standstill.[93] During the late Middle Ages, Western civilisation slowly advanced from their 'Dark Ages' following four centuries of antagonistic clashes between Church and State reaching a position where, in most European countries, Church and State were separated. After the Peace Treaty of Westphalia in 1648, European civilisation moved towards the so-called 'Age of Enlightenment', where reason was advocated as the primary source of legitimacy and authority. In this intellectual amphitheatre, European nations such as Spain, Italy, Portugal, England and France moved towards aggressive economical, political and military expansion.

Medical Clinics, Hospitals and Medical Madrasahs

Even at the height of activity in the Islamic sciences, there is little doubt that in the domain of the *'aqlī* sciences, the natural and mathematical sciences except for logic and philosophy were taught to a large extent outside the madrasah. This seems at least to be the conclusion when one reflects upon the curricula that have survived from the earlier

---

92 Williams Boyd, *The History of Western Education*, (Edinburgh: Black), 1966.

93 William H. McNeil and Marilyn Robinson Waldman, *The Islamic World*, (New York: Oxford University Press), 1973, pp. vi-vii.

period. As far as the *'aqlī* sciences are concerned, the activity of the madrasah in traditional Islamic society was complemented and augmented by two other types of body: scientific institutions and private circles.[94]

Even though it has been verified historically that the natural sciences were typically taught in institutions outside the mosques and madrasahs, it does not mean that these sciences were subsidiary to the religious and *adab* sciences. The natural or 'ancient' sciences (*'aqlī* sciences) being taught in private institutions outside the mosque and madrasah tradition did not diminish the importance they had in the Islamic society of the time.[95] However, many Orientalists have maintained that the natural sciences in Islamic civilisation were considered marginal and subsidiary,[96] but contrary to their position, the historical evidence regarding the rise and the development of institutions such as hospitals, the vast libraries and private study circles, demonstrates the importance of the natural sciences in relation to the education of that time. It is a known fact that the majority of innovation in the physical sciences during this period of time was accomplished in the Islamic world.

In the year 938 CE, the scholar Abū'l-Faraj Muḥammad ibn Isḥāq an-Nadīm (d. 998), wrote a comprehensive index of the curricula of Islamic institutions called the '*Fihrist*' (Index of the sciences); another encyclopaedia on the same subject was compiled by the Sufi fraternity, '*the Brethren*', in Basra during the second half of the tenth century.[97] Both of these encyclopaedic works were further developed by later Muslim scholars who wanted to elucidate the hierocracy of the various sciences and harmonise the relationship between reason

94 Nasr, op. cit., 1987, p. 127.
95 Sabra, op. cit., 1980, p. 183.
96 Ibid., p. 183.
97 Stanton, op. cit., 1990, p. 45.

and revelation. Abū Naṣr al-Fārābī (d. 950/951) was able to classify all the Islamic sciences available in the higher institutes of the Islamic world. According to his work, *Iḥṣā' al-'ulūm* ['The Enumeration of the Sciences'], these were the recognised sciences:

- The science of language and its branches: The elements pertaining to all languages such as grammar, dictation, recitation and prosody.
- Logic and its branches: The Categories, On Interpretation (*Peri Hermenias*), Prior Analytics, Posterior Analytics, Topics, Sophistic Rhetoric, and Poetics.[98,99]
- Propaedeutic (introductory) sciences and their branches: Arithmetic, Geometry, Optics, Astronomy, Music, the Science of weights, and Mechanical Devices.[100]
- Natural sciences: Principles of natural philosophy, Study of simple bodies, Generation and Corruption, Accidents pertaining to elements, Minerals, Plants and Animals.
- Metaphysical sciences: Science of being qua being, principles of the sciences and discussion of non-material bodies.
- The science of society and its branches: Jurisprudence and Theology.[101]

---

98 The Peripatetic students of Aristotle collected his works on logic in six books: *Categories, On Interpretation, Prior Analytics, Posterior Analytics, Topics, and Sophistical Refutations.*

99 The sciences of language and logic composed, along with rhetoric which is here included with logic, the three elements of the mediaeval Trivium, which are not so much subjects as tools for learning. See Dorothy Sayers' essay, "The Lost Tools of Learning" (recovered from: http://www.muslimsofnorwich.org.uk/?p=792 on 28/11/11) – Ed.

100 After study of the Trivium, the mediaeval scholar advanced to the study of the Quadrivium, which comprised the Propaedeutic sciences of Arithmetic, Geometry, Music and Astronomy – Ed.

101 Nasr, op. cit., 1976, p. 15.

All of the sciences enumerated by al-Fārābī were taught in their own specific centres, and this was also true for medicine and the sciences associated with it. When Islam came into contact with Persia and the Byzantium, Muslims inherited the institution of the hospital; the hospitals that existed in Persia and in Syria were rapidly integrated into the Muslim world. This is where Muslims learnt about medicine and the natural sciences associated with it. According to Shalaby, the majority of medical studies in the classical age were conducted in hospitals. Thus, the *bimaristan* was both a medical practice as well as an institution where students learnt medicine from practising physicians.[102] In addition, the hospitals established in the Muslim world did not restrict admittance to people of the Muslim faith. According to Savage-Smith, the Islamic faith makes it a moral requirement for the physician to treat all the sick regardless of financial status, whether male or female, civilian or military, adult or child, rich or poor or Muslim or non-Muslim.[103]

The first mention of a physician in the history of Baghdad was sixteen years after the city was built. It was in the year 766 CE that the Caliph al-Manṣūr (r. 754-775) appointed Jurjis ibn Bukhtishu (d. 679), the Dean of the medical school of Jundi-Shapur, Court-Physician in Baghdad.[104] It was during his son, the Caliph Mahdi's reign (r. 775-785) that the first *bimaristan* was founded in Baghdad. It was named the Barmakid (*Barmakī*) hospital after its patron Khālid Barmak (d. 781/782), who belonged to the famous Barmak vizier dynasty; its director was the Indian scholar Ibn Dahn al-Hindī. Both the Indian scholars Mankah al-Hindī and Ibn Dahn al-Hindī enjoyed the patronage of the Caliph

---

102 Shalaby, op. cit., p. 64.

103 Emilie Savage-Smith, http://www.nlm.nih.gov/exhibition/islamic_medical/islamic_00.html#toc, *Islamic Culture and the Medical Arts*, (Maryland: National Library of Medicine), 1994, (accessed: 20/10/03).

104 Nasr, op. cit., 1976, p. 175.

to translate the medical opus *Susruta*. The third hospital in Islamic civilisation was founded by the fifth Caliph Hārūn al-Rashīd (r. 786-809); he appointed Ibn Bukhtishu's grandson, Jibrā'īl (d. 828/829), Chief Physician of the Baghdad *bimaristan*. Jibrā'īl Bukhtishu is also known to have written many manuals on medicine and to have initiated the training of future physicians at the same medical clinic.[105] During this time other prominent medical families such as the *Masawayh* and the *Qurrah* immigrated from Syria and Jundi-Shapur to Baghdad, thus making Baghdad the medical centre of the world.[106] Continuing the tradition of founding hospitals, the Caliph Muqtadir (r. 908-932) built two hospitals in Baghdad in 918 CE. The first, which he named as-Sayyidah *bimaristan* after his mother, was located on the east side of the city and the other, which he named al-Muqtadirī *bimaristan* after himself, was on the west. It was at the time of the Caliph Muqtadir that a qualifying examination was instituted specifically for physicians. According to the doctor and historian al-Qifṭī, this occurred due to a case of malpractice brought to the notice of the Caliph because of which he passed a decree that none should practise medicine in Baghdad unless tested by the then Chief Physician Sinān ibn Thābit (d. 943) with regards to his competence in the profession. This may be the earliest examining board in history to regulate the medical profession. The eight hundred and sixty physicians working in Baghdad at that time were all screened according to the new regulations and only those who qualified continued to practise medicine. This process was not limited to Baghdad; the Caliph ordered that the same edict apply in cities such as Damascus and Madīnah.[107]

---

105 Aydin Sayili, *Central Asian Contributions to the Earlier Phases of Hospital Building - Activity in Islam*, pp. 10-11, FSTC Limited, 2005, http://www.muslimheritage.com/uploads/ Central%20Asian%20Hospital%20Building.pdf, (accessed: 22/07/10).

106 Nasr, op. cit., 1976, p. 175.

107 Young and Serjeant (eds.), op. cit., p. 347.

During the same century, Muḥammad ibn Zakariyā ar-Rāzī (d. 925) became the Dean of the Baghdad *bimaristan* where he used his immense clinical experience to compose works concerning philosophy, psychology, alchemy and medicine; in the tradition of his predecessors he trained numerous future physicians.[108] According to some letters found in Cairo concerning medical practice at that time, it was not easy to obtain the status of a physician. It was an absolute prerequisite that the students obtain letters of recommendation from an authority such as a governor or a judge. In addition, a person who wanted to achieve the role of a physician (*ḥakīm*) in an Islamic society had to be of good character, because it was recognised that he was a person who was responsible for the well-being of the society. Thus, every student of medicine had to obtain a certificate of good character from the Chief of Police so as to prove himself a reliable person.[109] In the years following the establishment of Caliph Hārūn al-Rashīd's hospital in Baghdad, numerous hospitals were founded throughout the Muslim world by amirs and sultans. Amir Ziyādat Allah I ibn Ibrāhīm (r. 817-838) of the Aghlabid dynasty in Tunisia, constructed the al-Qayrawān hospital in the district of ad-Dimnah. Since this was such a renowned hospital in the Amirate of Ifriqiya, all future hospitals in Tunisia were called ad-Dimnah instead of the Persian equivalent *bimaristan.* In Egypt, Sultan Aḥmad ibn Ṭūlūn (r. 868-884) constructed the Fusṭāṭ *bimaristan* in the year 872 CE in the city of al-Fusṭāṭ, which is on the outskirts of present-day Cairo. One of the most renowned *bimaristans* to be built in Baghdad was the 'Aḍudī *bimaristan* built in the year 981 CE by Sultan 'Aḍud ad-Dawlah (r. 978-983). In Damascus, Sultan Nūr ad-Dīn az-Zangī (r. 1146-1174) established an-Nūrī *bimaristan* in 1156 CE. The physician Ibn Abī 'Uṣaybi'ah (1203-1270) described the daily

[108] Nasr, op. cit., 1976, p. 177.

[109] Young and Serjeant (eds.), op. cit., p. 347.

routine of the first director and physician of an-Nūrī hospital in his book, *Sources of Information on the Classes of Physicians*:

> When Nūr ad-Dīn built the Grand bimaristan, he appointed Abu'l-Majd al-Bahilli as the director. This physician went regularly to the hospital to care for the patients, to examine them and to give the necessary orders to the attendants and servants who worked under his direction. After that, this physician went to the citadel to examine the dignitaries and the noblemen that were ill. This task completed, he returned to the hospital, sat in the *liwan* (vestibule hall) richly furnished, and commenced his lectures.[110]

In Jerusalem, European Christians followed the Muslims' tradition and built the Saint John Hospital in 1055 CE. Sultan Ṣalāḥ ad-Dīn Yūsuf ibn Ayyūb (r. 1171-1193) renamed the same hospital aṣ-Ṣalāḥānī *bimaristan* after the liberation of Jerusalem in 1187 CE. In North Africa, Amir al-Manṣūr Ya'qūb ibn Yūsuf (r. 1188-1199) of the Almohad dynasty established the Marrakech *bimaristan* in the capital city of Marrakech in the year 1190 CE. During his travels, Ibn Baṭūṭah wrote eloquently of the al-Manṣūrī *bimaristan* in Cairo established in 1284 CE by the Mamlūk Sultan al-Manṣūr Qalāwūn (r. 1279-1290). All of the above hospitals were also medical schools and the majority of them had grants of libraries and lecture-halls where the physicians taught their students.[111]

At this juncture our objective is to ascertain the way scholars and students were educated in the medical sciences. Looking at various biographies of famous scholars of medicine in the classical Islamic

---

110 The an-Nūrī Hospital, http://www.muslimheritage.com/topics/default.cfm?ArticleID=325, (accessed 10/07/2010).

111 Young and Serjeant (eds.), op. cit., p. 347.

world, it is evident that the majority of them learnt their sciences in private study circles before entering practical experience in the *bimaristan.* It is important to acknowledge the contribution of these scholars to the translation movement and to scholarly advancement. At the beginning of the ʻAbbasid period most of the education of various natural sciences seems to have been imparted by various oriental Jewish and Christian families, who had practised medicine for generations before the arrival of Islam. During the early centuries of the Islamic era, medicine was dominated by these non-Muslim families.[112] In the twelfth century, Ibn Abī Uṣaybiʻah, in the first chapters of his book *Sources of Information on the Classes of Physicians*, wrote biographies of one hundred and forty-one physicians, who practised during the early era of Islam, one hundred and thirty of whom were Christians, three Jews, three pagans and five Muslims. He described how in the following two centuries the number of Muslim physicians rose to become the majority. Leiser explains that this phenomenon was due primarily to a large number of conversions to Islam from amongst the physicians during the early ʻAbbasid period.[113]

During the early history of medicine in Islam, it is clear that Muslims and non-Muslims taught and studied with each other and their relationship was not problematic from a religious point of view. According to early historical sources, one of the ways of educating yourself to be a physician during the early period of Islam was to be taught by a member of a family who was traditionally in the profession. The Persian Nestorian Christian Bukhtishu family is a good example of this, since they were physicians in Jundi-Shapur long before the arrival of Islam.[114] Thus, sons and, in rare cases, daughters learnt the

112 Gary Leiser, 'Medical Education in Islamic Lands from the Seventh to the Fourteenth Century', *Journal of the History of Medicine and Allied Science*, (Ankara), Vol. 38, 1983, p. 48.

113 Ibid.

114 Nasr, op. cit., 1976, p. 15.

medical profession from fathers and uncles. As noted earlier, Jurjis ibn Bukhtishu was the first physician to be employed by al-Manṣūr as a court physician, and he had been taught by his father. The Bukhtishu family continued to provide physicians to the 'Abbasid court for generations to come.[115] Yūḥannā ibn Māsawayh (777-857) also came from a long tradition of physicians in his family; he came to Baghdad and gained fame as an ophthalmologist. In the West he is called Mesue Senior and is well known as the first to write independent medical texts in the Arabic language.[116] Ḥunayn ibn Isḥāq (d. 873), a Nestorian Christian from Hira, was one of his students. Yūḥannā ibn Māsawayh's teaching Ḥunayn ibn Isḥāq demonstrates that the members of famous medical families did teach outside their families. Ḥunayn then taught medicine to his two sons Dāwūd and Isḥāq, and his nephew Ḥubaysh ibn al-Ḥasan (d. 900). To make education easier for them, he was possibly one of the first physicians to write texts on medical instruction for his students. The well known medical instruction texts were the *Questions on the Eye*, and the *Questions on Medicine*, (which Ḥubaysh completed after him).[117] Another famous physician was Thābit ibn Qurrah (d. 901), who instructed his son Sinān (d. tenth century), and who, following in the footsteps of Ḥunayn ibn Isḥāq, wrote an instructional medical text for him known as *The Treasure of the Science of Medicine*. Sinān in turn passed his knowledge to his son Thābit ibn Sinān (d. 976).[118] During the eleventh century, one of the earliest teachers of medicine was the Christian Physician 'Īsā ibn Yaḥyā, who taught the famous Muslim physician Ibn Sīnā (980-1037).[119]

---

115 Ibid.

116 Nasr, op. cit., 1976, p. 175.

117 M. Meyerhof, *Studies in Medieval Arabic Medicine*, (London: Variorum Reprints), 1984, pp. 686-724.

118 Gary Leiser, 'Medical Education in Islamic Lands from the Seventh to the Fourteenth Century', *Journal of the History of Medicine and Allied Science*, (Ankara), Vol. 38, 1983, p. 50.

119 Young and Serjeant (eds.), op. cit., p. 390.

Major study of and research in medicine commenced in earnest after the majority of the classical foreign medical and scientific works had been translated into Arabic. Muslim physicians instigated the writing of commentaries and original works. Ibn Sīnā is the best example of a student who had teachers, was also an autodidact and who practised in the *bimaristan*. He was introduced to medicine by 'Īsā ibn Yaḥyā; he taught himself the scientific encyclopaedia of the Ikhwān aṣ-Ṣafā, and practised medicine in numerous hospitals.[120] The study circles of physicians were conducted in private houses, mosques, bookshops and hospitals. The system of education around medicine and allied sciences was very flexible and could combine a number of teaching and learning styles.

It has been noted that in Islamic history a few medical madrasahs did emerge at the beginning of the thirteenth century, but these never became widely used for clinical instruction. The first such medical madrasah, a combination of a hospital and medical school, was built in Anatolia in Kayseri during the reign of the Seljuk Sultan Ghiyāth ad-Dīn Kaykhusraw ibn Qilij Arslān (d. 1211). The hospital was founded in 1205 CE by his sister Gevher Nesibe Sultan, and the madrasah adjacent to it was founded by the Sultan himself. The two buildings have been referred to as the Ghīyāthiyyah and the Shifā'iyyah madrasahs. The next medical madrasah seems to have been built by the governor of Basra, Shams ad-Dīn Abū Muẓaffar (r. 1210-1211), during the reign of the 'Abbasid Caliph an-Nāṣir (r. 1180-1225). As mentioned earlier, medicine and pharmacy were also taught at the famous Mustanṣiriyyah Madrasah in Baghdad, which was built in 1234 CE by the 'Abbasid Caliph al-Mustanṣir (r. 1226–1242). Another medical madrasah was established in Damascus, the Dikhwāriyyah Madrasah, which was founded in 1225 CE by the physician and bibliophile, Muhadhdhab ad-Dīn 'Abd al-Mun'im ibn 'Alī ibn Ḥāmid ad-Dikhwār (d. 1230), who taught in the

[120] Ibid.

madrasah.[121] There are many examples of the existence of such medical madrasahs in the Mamlūk era, nevertheless from historical sources it is obvious that most medical teaching was carried out at hospitals or privately rather than at the medical madrasahs described here.

Certain factors contributed in making this medical education Islamic; for example, the *ḥakīm* was never only a physician, but also a philosopher and a master of various religious sciences. In addition, the theory of Islamic medicine was linked to the theories of philosophy, cosmology and Islamic metaphysics. All Muslim and non-Muslim physicians were in perfect harmony in viewing the body as related to the soul, thus accepting the inter-relatedness of the well-being of the spirit and the physical well-being of the body. Nasr notes that the only reason Muslims were able to assimilate Greek medicine was its traditional nature and its harmony with the Islamic conception of the universe.[122] Thus, medical science was seen as just another endeavour, one more Islamic discipline within Islamic cosmology. In addition to the science becoming Islamised, the majority of the physicians of this period not only practised medicine and philosophy but produced literary as well as medical compositions. ʻAlī ibn Rabbān aṭ-Ṭabarī (838-870), Yaʻqūb ibn Isḥāq al-Kindī (800-873), Muḥammad ibn Zakariyā ar-Rāzī (864-930), Abū al-Qāsim Khalaf ibn al-ʻAbbās az-Zahrāwī (936-1013), Ibn Sīnā (980-1037), Abū'l-Walīd Muḥammad ibn Aḥmad ibn Muḥammad Ibn Rushd (1128-1198), Ibn Maymūn (Maimonides, 1135-1204) and Ibn an-Nafīs (1213-1288), can be included amongst the most famous physicians.[123]

---

121 Aydin Sayili, *Certain Aspects of Medical Instruction in Medieval Islam and its Influences on Europe*, http://www.muslimheritage.com/topics/default.cfm?Taxonomy Type ID=11andTaxonomySubTypeID=57andTaxonomyThirdLevelID=1andArticleID=1005#ftn4, (accessed: 26/06/10).

122 Nasr, op. cit., pp. 154-159.

123 For further information on these physicians, see: Young and Serjeant (eds.), op. cit., p. 390.

Libraries, State Chancery and Private Circles

In the era when Europe had no knowledge of paper-making and the few books available were found in scattered monasteries and royal libraries, the Islamic world produced the first ever wide-ranging book publishing industry. During the middle of the eighth century, almost a thousand years before the West began its own book industry, books on all types of sciences were being produced in both quality and quantity. These books found their homes in palace, mosque, madrasah and hospital libraries, in the private collections of scholars and students and in the hands of the book-dealers, who were at times also publishers employing a corps of copyists.[124]

Scholars of all the sciences utilised these libraries. The library was an institution which provided books, was a place for discussion and for study. In rare cases it also operated as a classroom. The origin of the Muslim library is closely connected to the study circles and the bookshop. Due to the introduction of paper in the year 751 CE, the translation movement and the rise of sciences, books started to flood cities such as Baghdad, Damascus, Merv, Mosul, Basra, Cairo, Cordoba, Fez and Qayrawān. Hence, the bookshops began to develop the first discussion circles, in which scholars of various sciences came together for debates and discussions. Primarily, it was the ruling families, the nobility and the wealthy who first established their own private libraries which became grand state libraries; these were followed by public and other private libraries.[125] Throughout the medieval period, the library was designated by seven different labels in Arabic, which were used interchangeably or even anachronistically, these were: *bayt al-ḥikmah, khizānat al-ḥikmah, dār al-ḥikmah, dār al-kutub, khizānat al-kutub*

[124] *Knowledge, Learning Institutions and Libraries in Islam: Book Publishing and Paper Making*, http://www.muslimheritage.com/topics/default.cfm?articleID=642, (accessed 12/07/10).

[125] Stanton, op. cit., p. 128.

and *bayt al-kutub.*[126] According to Makdisi, there were many activities such as reading, copying, debates, discussions and disputation taking place at the various libraries, but the teaching of official courses was not a central function of the library. However, he points out that according to some sources there were rare exceptions where the library was utilised as a classroom, for example, the geographer Muḥammad ibn Aḥmad Shams ad-Dīn al-Muqaddasi (d. 1000), mentions that in the Basra library, *kalām* was taught by a professor. It seems more likely that teaching was an added feature of the library that was available on request, but that it was an exceptional practice.[127] On the other hand, the use of the library for private study and research was common. For example, the Ibn Ṭūlūn Mosque in Cairo housed a library that contained some of the most celebrated works on medicine, which the students of medicine utilised.[128] Ibn Sīnā used the Samanid library at Bukhara for his own research during the reign of Amir Nūḥ ibn Manṣūr (r. 976-997). He described it thus:

> I entered a *bait* with many chambers, in each chamber were coffers of books...in one chamber were Arabic books and poetry, in another, books of law and so on, in each chamber books on one of the sciences.[129]

The library became a major part of the Islamic education milieu. Large collections of books could be found right across Muslim society. The Buyid Sultan 'Aḍud ad-Dawlah (r. 978-983) founded a well known library in Shiraz, Persia, which the geographer al-Muqaddasi (d. 1000) during his travels visited and described as:

---

[126] Makdisi, op. cit., 1981, p. 25.

[127] Ibid, p. 27.

[128] Jonathan Berkey, *The Transmission of Knowledge in Medieval Cairo,* (Princeton: Princeton University Press), 1992, p. 52.

[129] Shalaby, op. cit., p. 80.

> A complex of buildings surrounded by gardens with lakes and waterways, the buildings were topped with domes, and comprised an upper and a lower storey with a total, according to the chief official, of 360 rooms....In each department, catalogues were placed on a shelf....the rooms were furnished with carpets....[130]

All major cities throughout the Caliphate, such as Cairo, Aleppo, Bukhara, Qayrawān and Damascus, boasted libraries. The Caliphal city of Baghdad had the astonishing number of thirty-six libraries and over a hundred book dealers by the thirteenth century. During the same century, the city of Merv in eastern Persia housed ten libraries, two in the *jāmiʿ* mosques there and eight in the madrasahs.[131] It is in this literary atmosphere that treasured manuscripts were illuminated and bound with leather, fragrant woods and inlaid with silver and gold. Many of the mosque and madrasah libraries were bequeathed private collections. The Abū Ḥanīfah Mosque in Baghdad benefited from a library that housed volumes bequeathed by the physician Yaḥyā ibn Jazlah (d. 1099) and the historian az-Zamakhsharī (d. 1143). The Sufiya Library in the Umayyad Mosque in Aleppo contained a book collection of which ten thousand volumes had been bequeathed by the ruler of northern Syria, Amir Sayf ad-Dawlah Abū al-Ḥasan ibn Ḥamdān (r. 945-967) of the Arab Hamdanid dynasty. The famous library in the Qayrawān Mosque and the library housed in the Zaytuna Mosque were both built by the Aghlabid dynasty (800-909) and could boast a scientific, religious and literary book collection.[132] By the tenth

130 Shams al-Din Muhammad ibn Ahmad al-Muqaddasi, *Kitab Ahsan al-taqasim fi ma'rifat al-aqalim*, M.J. de Goeje (ed.), 1877, 2nd edition, 1906, p. 449. http://www.muslimheritage.com/topics/default.cfm?articleID=642, (accessed: 12/07/10).

131 J. Pedersen, *The Arabic Book*, (Princeton: Princeton University Press), 1984, p. 128.

132 Shalaby, op. cit., p. 100.

century, Cordoba, the capital of Umayyad Spain had numerous public libraries and the court library of Cordoba is recorded to have had over 400,000 titles.[133]

Scholars and students were well known to visit these libraries and even take the opportunity to reside in the mosques and madrasahs for a short period of time while studying and researching. Both al-Baghdādī (d. 1071) and al-Ghazālī (d. 1111) resided in the accommodation provided by the Umayyad *jāmi'* in Damascus; the scientist Abū 'Alī al-Ḥasan ibn al-Ḥasan ibn al-Haytham (d. 1039) resided in the accommodation provided by al-Azhar Mosque, where he carried out his research at the library. One of the most famous scholars to have studied at the Zaytuna Mosque who was also well known to have used the Abdaliyah Library was Ibn Khaldūn (d. 1406).[134]

To understand the scope of the libraries and bookshops during this period, Abū'l-Faraj Muḥammad ibn Isḥāq an-Nadīm's (d. 998) catalogue of books is important. He published the masterpiece, *Kitāb al-Fihrist*, in the year 938 CE, and in it he provides a detailed bibliography of more than sixty thousand titles, relating to all types of subjects, found in bookshops and libraries across the Caliphate. The first part of the first chapter of *al-Fihrist* is devoted to a variety of styles of writing (including Chinese), qualities of paper, penmanship and the pre-eminence of the book. He specifically categorised all the titles under subheadings such as:

> Language, calligraphy, Christian and Jewish scriptures, the Qur'an and commentaries on the Qur'an, linguistic works, histories and genealogies, official government works, court accounts, pre-Islamic and Islamic poetry, works by various

133 Sonn, op. cit., p. 53.

134 *Knowledge, Learning Institutions and Libraries in Islam: Book Publishing and Paper Making*, http://www.muslimheritage.com/topics/default.cfm?articleID=642, (accessed 12/07/10).

> schools of Muslim thought, biographies of numerous men of learning, Greek and Islamic philosophy, mathematics, astronomy, Greek and Islamic medicine, literature, popular fiction, travel (India, China, Indochina), magic, miscellaneous subjects and fables.[135]

Only two centuries after the death of the Prophet ﷺ, Islamic civilisation had gathered together the knowledge of the ancients, advanced the sciences and created a literary society such as had rarely been seen before. The evidence of this highly literate and educated population could be seen from the bookshops, the palace libraries, public libraries, the abundant authors, translators, copiers, illuminators, librarians, booksellers, collectors and all those connected to the books that were being produced and read on a large scale across the Caliphate.

The State Chancery

Connected to this literary society was the state chancery; it was a state department for the secretaries who were employed by a vast range of professions, such as those working for the élite of the state – the Secretary of the Land Tax, Secretary of the Chancery, Secretary of the Judiciary, Secretary of the Army, Secretary of the Police – down to the average copyist and calligrapher who worked as secretaries. Similar to the library, this institution also had various aspects; the chancery functioned both as an educational institution and a department of government. The education of the chancery school took place at the state chancery, which was variously called *dīwān ar-rasā'il, dīwān al-inshā'* and *dīwān al-mukātabāt.*[136] Since the fall of the Umayyad period, the state chancery had advanced and had come to contain numerous

[135] Ibid.

[136] Makdisi, op. cit., 1990, pp. 283-284.

government departments (*dīwān*), such as the postal department, the water department and the intelligence department.[137]

It is interesting to note here that the Latin word *secretarius* originated from an Arabic sage saying, regarding the office of secretary, "The first requisite of a *kātib* (secretary) is his ability to keep a *secret*." Thus, the Arabic term for state secretaries who worked as 'recorders of secrets' or 'keepers of secrets' (*kātib as-sirr)* influenced the Latin West to derive its term for the *kātib* from the Latin word *secretum*, meaning secret, i.e. secretary.[138] During the Umayyad period, 'Abd al-Ḥamīd wrote many epistles concerning the curriculum that students of the chancery school should pursue. Ibn Qutaybah (d. 889), the litterateur and philologist, continued the work by writing regarding the correct grammatical and linguistic usage for the *kātib* in his book, *Adab al-Kātib.* But it was Ibn Yaḥyā as-Sūlī (d. 946) who concentrated on the practicalities of the *dīwān* official in his book, *Adab al-Kuttāb*. His book included the use of preliminaries in correspondence, expressive titles for persons of rank, the various sizes of papers used for writing letters and the appropriate script to use in different situations.[139] The educational system of the chancery school continued well into the declining years of the 'Abbasids.

However, there were scholars (*'ulamā'*) of various physical sciences who were not dependant on an institution, but learnt and taught in private circles. Abū Mūsā Jābir ibn Ḥayyān (ca. 721-815), the polymath scholar, known as the 'father of chemistry', instructed his students concerning the correct conduct of the scientist:

> The first essential is that you should conduct experiments. For he who does not conduct experiments will never attain to the least degree of mastery. It must be taken as an

137 Young and Serjeant (eds.), op. cit., pp. 155-167.

138 Makdisi, op. cit., 1990, p. 279.

139 Young and Serjeant (eds.), op. cit., pp. 155-167.

> absolutely rigorous principle that any proposition which is not supported by proofs is nothing more than an assertion which may be true or may be false.[140]

Abū 'Alī al-Ḥasan ibn al-Ḥasan ibn al-Haytham (ca. 965-1039), known as the 'father of modern optics', wrote an influential book on optics, which once translated into Latin, opened up the study of physical phenomena for European scholars such as Grosseteste, Wittlo and Galileo. The most famous mathematician that this age produced was Muḥammad ibn Mūsā al-Khwārizmī (d. 863). He was one of the first Muslims to work on algebra (the term is derived from the title of his book, *Ḥisāb al-Jabr wa'l-Muqābalah*) and then other Islamic mathematicians further developed this art until it became the foundation for that which we know today. Another scholar known for his mathematical work was the famous Persian poet 'Umar Khayyām (1050-1123). Again it has to be remembered that most of these scholars were polymaths, as was Nāṣir ad-Dīn aṭ-Ṭūsī (1201-1274), who lived during the Mongol invasion. He was most known for his astronomical work, establishing under Mongol rule the most sophisticated observatory and scientific institution at Magarah for that time. Another famous polymath of the time was Abū Rayḥān Muḥammad ibn Aḥmad al-Bīrūnī (d. 1038), who performed revolutionary work in physics, mathematics, geography and mineralogy.[141]

The question that comes to mind is: what makes the above literary and scientific figures specifically Islamic? Is it simply that the majority of them were Muslims who lived in a culturally Muslim world? This is not the complete answer, although it is partly true. The sciences of the age were integrated into the Islamic worldview by these scholars and scientists; they applied the moral, ethical and legal rules of the

---

140 Stanton, op. cit., p. 100.
141 Ibid., pp. 100-119.

dīn to their subjects as much as to themselves. In certain cases the sciences were studied and presented in order directly and practically to support the *dīn*, such as the study of astronomy which helped the Muslims establish calendars, find the direction of Makkah and set the times for the required prayers. Other sciences indirectly supported the *'aqīdah*, such as mathematics, which leads to belief in unity that is central to Islam and whose rigour encourages clear thinking. Other practical sciences such as medicine, architecture, engineering, animal husbandry and agriculture were considered worth pursuing as they benefited the human being to live in harmony with the plan of Allah for the cosmos. Most importantly, Muslim society in general never thought of the physical universe and *īmān* as separate.

> Commanded by the Koran to seek knowledge and read nature for signs of the Creator, and inspired by a treasure trove of Ancient Greek learning, Muslims created a society that in the Middle Ages was the scientific centre of the world. The Arabic language was synonymous with learning and science for five hundred years, a golden age that can count among its credits the precursors to modern universities, algebra, and names of the stars and even the notion of science as an empirical inquiry.[142]

The Translation Movement

How much effect did the translation movement have on the progress of Islamic education? As we saw in earlier chapters, the Arabs of the peninsula brought with them no other literary work than the Qur'an. This same book was, however, the basis of Muslim scholars' assimilation

[142] Dennis Overbye, 'How Islam Won, and Lost, the Lead in Science', *New York Times*, Oct. 30, 2001. See http://www.jonathantan.org/handouts/Islam/Islam-H111af-sciences.pdf, (accessed: 20/07/2010).

of all other sciences. They wanted to understand the world around them in terms of the Islamic faith and they commenced this mission by translating works from Persia, Egypt, China, Greece and India.[143] The next step for many of the scholars in the 'Abbasid period was to learn and then contribute to Hellenistic dialect and logic in order to advance theological and legal studies; builders and engineers used and advanced mathematics and mechanics; geographers commenced to study the *Geographike Hyphegesis* of Ptolemy and a similar interest was aroused in sciences such as astronomy, astrology, alchemy and medicine.[144]

Given the prestige of the *dīn* in Islamic society, it is not surprising that it was the basic motive for seeking all kinds of knowledge and applying them. Some relevant sciences, such as the study of medicine, were counted as communal religious duties (*farḍ kifāyah*) by al-Ghazālī.[145] Another element that was crucial in both the motivation and in financial support for the translation movement was the political arena. When the caliphal seat moved to Baghdad, the second Caliph of the 'Abbasid dynasty, al-Manṣūr (r. 754-775), understood that he needed to reconcile his previous rivals and various interest groups. As is evident, from a political and ideological point of view, the translation movement brought in the majority of the non-Arab élite that the Caliph needed to bring close in order to maintain control of his Caliphate. The Persian population was one of the major constituencies of the new 'Abbasid Empire and by promoting Persian and Greek translations, Manṣūr was making the point that the Persians were important in the new Caliphate (the Sassanian empire had for centuries been known for translating Persian, Indian and Greek works). This

[143] Sabra, op. cit., 1980, p. 183.
[144] Manfred Ullman, *Islamic Medicine*, (Edinburgh: Edinburgh University Press), 1978, p. 8.
[145] Sonn, op. cit., p. 57.

duly proved true during the Caliphate of Mahdi, when the whole 'Abbasid administration was under Persian families such as the Barmakids and Nawbahts.[146] Whatever the motives behind the translation movement, it was without a doubt a breath of freedom for the society, especially for Islamic education. The main success of Islamic education during this period was the creation of the polymath scholar and the advance of all the sciences and thus of the society.

The work of the translation movement *per se* did not end in the ninth century, but rather it transformed into research and innovation. Following the earliest translation work on various sciences carried out by Christian, Jewish, Zoroastrian and Muslim scholars at places such as *Bayt al-Ḥikmah* in Baghdad, Muslim scholars of the ninth, tenth and eleventh centuries advanced the sciences further. In the tenth and eleventh centuries, al-Kindī, Abū 'Abdullāh al-Khwārizmī and al-Ghazālī continued to develop a system of thought that demonstrated that Islam encompasses religion, politics and all the sciences including the rational and physical sciences.[147] Although there were variations in different systems of classification regarding the sciences, all scholars agreed upon the supremacy of the Divine Revelation.[148] Abū 'Abdullāh al-Khwārizmī demonstrated the peak of this era in education by compiling the encyclopaedia *The Keys of the Sciences* in 977 CE, which specified all the sciences that existed at that time. In it, Islamic education was presented as including the religious sciences, *adab* sciences (humanities) and other sciences, such as the mathematics and philosophy which had been acquired from various civilisations.[149] As Stanton points out, "[the book] '*The Keys of the Sciences*' provides us

[146] Gutas, op. cit., pp. 28-53.

[147] Howard R. Turner, *Science in Medieval Islam*, (Austin: University of Texas Press), 1997.

[148] Ibid.

[149] Stanton, op. cit., pp. 137-141.

with a unique view of the breadth and depth of knowledge expected of an educated person in the Islamic society."[150]

The Persian physician ar-Rāzī (d. 925), a translator of many ancient manuscripts, advanced the work of the translation movement by producing his masterpiece, *Kitāb al-Asrār*, which became the foundation for chemistry and was translated into Latin three centuries later. Ibn Sīnā (d. 1037) wrote numerous commentaries on Aristotle, which again became primary sources when translated into Latin, but it was his masterpiece, *al-Qānūn fi'ṭ-Ṭibb*, published in 1025 CE, which became the main medical text in the Islamic world and was used as the standard medical textbook by physicians in Europe until the 1700s. The translation movement also led to major technical development across the Caliphate. Technicians developed magnifying and refracting lenses for work at telescopic and microscopic levels. Navigational technology for travel, such as the sextant and the astrolabe were produced. The Banū Mūsā brothers of the ninth century and al-Jazarī (d. 1206) in the thirteenth century became popular for their treatises on mechanics, producing mechanical devices such as a sophisticated water-raising machine, a water supply system driven by gears and hydropower, and conical valves for engineering.[151] It was during the translation era that the Arabic numerals – known as *Hindi* because they originated in India – were adopted and then further advanced in mathematics by Muḥammad ibn Mūsā al-Khwārizmī (d. 863) by the addition of the cipher (zero), which in Arabic is *ṣifr*. These Arabic numerals were later adopted in Europe where they replaced the Roman letter system that had been used for calculation. Al-Bīrūnī (d. 1050), working in Ghazna in Afghanistan, with his linguistic skills in Persian, Arabic, Hebrew, Turkish, Syriac and Sanskrit, wrote

[150] Ibid.

[151] Donald Routledge Hill, *The Book of Ingenious Devices by the Banu Mūsā ibn Shakir*, (Dordrecht, Holland: D. Reidel Publishing Company), 1979.

widely on subjects such as geography, mathematics, religions and astronomy.[152]

During the early era of the translation movement, one of the main works translated into the Arabic language was Ptolemy's work on astronomy entitled, 'The Great Work' or *Almagest*, from the Arabic *al-Majisṭī* itself a transliteration of the Greek μεγίστη. This work, which was based on the belief that all the heavenly bodies circled the earth, became the basis of cosmology in the Islamic civilisation although it was not considered a theological position in Islam as it was in Christianity, and Muslims later adopted the heliocentric model of the solar system without difficulty.[153] The scholar al-Bīrūnī furthered this work through his writings on astronomy, and in the light of his work it is apparent that Islamic civilisation of the eleventh century thought of the earth as being a sphere rather than flat, as was the common belief in Europe at the time. He also advanced this knowledge of astronomy by calculating longitudes and latitudes of the earth as accurately as was possible for his time.[154]

It is due to this massive advance in both the religious and non-religious sciences that this era is recognised as a 'Golden Age'.

> In less than four centuries after the first Islamic conquest, philosophers, mathematicians, botanists, physicians, geographers, alchemists and their peers in other scientific disciplines, at work throughout the wide reaches of the Islamic empire, had accomplished the remarkable feat of unwrapping the vast intellectual legacy received from past

---

152 Sonn, op. cit., p. 59.

153 Overbye, op. cit., pp. 3-4. The concept of heliocentrism rather than geocentrism being the correct notion was put forward by theologians as early as Fakhr ad-Dīn ar-Rāzī (d. 1149), az-Zamakhsharī (d. 1144) and Molla Ebu's-Su'ud (Abū as-Su'ūd) Effendi (d. 1574) without any major resistance.

154 Sonn, op. cit., p. 59.

civilisations, analyzing it in relentless detail, fussing with it, testing and retesting its hypotheses and answers, evolving new ones and further revising, discarding and reformulating many of those...In sum, a new concept of the universe was put together...from macrocosmic to microcosmic element, this Islamic universe appeared orderly, functional and workable.[155]

[155] Turner, op. cit., p. 33.

Chapter Four

Islamic Education during the Mamlūk Period

The Mamlūks

In the year 1218 CE the Mongols, united under Genghis Khan, first began to invade Muslim lands in Central Asia.[1] By the year 1221 CE, both the great cities of Bukhara and Samarqand (in present-day Uzbekistan) were destroyed by Ghengis Khan. Upon the death of Genghis Khan in 1227 CE, his son Ogadai became the Great Khan, but the Mongol territory was divided amongst his four sons. Ogadai inherited Western Mongolia, Chaghtai inherited Central Asia, Jochi inherited Russia and Toulai inherited Eastern Mongolia. It was Hulagu Khan, son of Toulai, who later descended upon Baghdad with his army and burnt it to the ground. The libraries, madrasahs, mosques, *kuttābs*, hospitals and the entire heritage accumulated over five centuries disappeared on that fateful day in Baghdad.[2] Thereafter, the Mongols continued their march through the Muslim lands conquering all of

1 Masud ul Hasan, *History of Islam Vol. 2,* (Lahore: Islamic Publications), 1998, pp. 1-20.

2 Sonn, op. cit., p. 86.

Iraq and Iran. The two lands became known as the Il-Khan dominion and were ruled by Hulagu Khan. However, the people of Iran and Iraq continued to be Muslims under this foreign rule. At its highest peak, the Il-Khanate (1256-1353) included modern-day Iran, Iraq, Afghanistan, Turkmenistan, Armenia, Azerbaijan, Georgia, certain parts of Turkey and western Pakistan. Two years after the fall of Baghdad, the Mongols began their march towards Syria, where they destroyed the city of Aleppo and occupied Damascus. In 1260 CE, the Mongols began their march towards Egypt.[3]

Prior to the fall of Baghdad, Egypt had been politically and culturally passive during the early centuries of Islamic rule, simply following the developments of the Islamic East. When the Fatimids took over Egypt in the tenth century, the link to Eastern Islamic power was broken due to the Fatimids being Ismaili Shiites. With regards to education, the Fatimids can be credited for having established one of the first higher education institutes, al-Azhar, in 972 CE, before even the madrasah in Nishapur. Al-Azhar became the main higher educational institution and the main propaganda tool for the Shiite élite in Egypt. It was only when the Ayyūbids re-conquered Egypt in the name of Islam that Egypt started to be an Islamic political power in the Islamic world.[4] However, due to the status of al-Azhar in the Fatimids' reign, the institute was supplanted by numerous other madrasahs established by the Ayyūbids. They reacted against al-Azhar due to its origins and Sultan Ṣalāḥ ad-Dīn Yūsuf ibn Ayyūb (1138-1193) transferred the Friday *khuṭbah* to the al-Ḥakīmī mosque. Although Muslim scholars continued to teach at al-Azhar during the Ayyūbid period, the institute was neglected to a great extent, and thus commencing its decline.[5]

---

3 Hasan, op. cit., p. 14.

4 C. F. Petry (ed.), *The Cambridge History of Egypt Vol. I,* (Cambridge: University Press), 1998, p. 377.

5 Bosworth, Bearman, Bianquis, Van Donzel and Heinrichs (eds.), op. cit., Vol. 1, p. 814.

It was the military slave dynasty (the Mamlūks) of the Ayyūbids that changed the face of al-Azhar and of Egypt in 1250 CE. At the death of Sultan aṣ-Ṣāliḥ Ayyūb (r. 1240-49) of the Ayyūbid dynasty, his widow Shajar ad-Durr became the Sultana of Egypt for a short period. She married the first Mamlūk Sultan ʿIzz ad-Dīn Aybak (r. 1250-1257) and eight years later when Baghdad fell, the Mamlūk capital of Cairo had became the metropolitan centre of Islamic civilisation. Due to the Mongol invasion in the east, numerous scholars, artisans and other refugees had flocked to the new centre of Muslim power in Cairo.[6] The buildings of al-Azhar were renovated and continuously built up throughout the Mamlūk period and Sultan aẓ-Ẓāhir Rukn ad-Dīn Baibars al-Bunduqdārī (r. 1260-1277) allowed the Friday *khuṭbah* to be read there again.[7] The Mamlūks as military slaves of the Ayyūbid dynasty were of humble origin; they were captured mostly in campaigns against Caucasian, Turcoman, Mongol and Turkish tribes. The Mamlūk reign can be divided into two parts: the *Bahris*, who provided the leadership from 1250–1382 CE; they were ethnically Turks and Mongols; and the *Burjis*, who were Circassians (a north Caucasian ethnic group), who ruled from 1382–1517 CE. It is important to note at this point that the slave system in the Islamic lands during this time cannot be compared with the later Trans-Atlantic slave trade of the United States or the slavery practised in antiquity. In the Islamic lands this practice did not lead to the forced labour and inhumanity of the latter instances, rather it often resulted in the emancipation of the slaves. In addition, being an ex-slave did not keep an individual from acquiring a high government position, or in the case of certain Turkish Mamlūks, even sultans of their ex-owners' respective municipalities.

---

6 J. Bloom and S. Blair, *Islam: A Thousand Years of Faith and Power,* (London: Yale University Press), 2002, p. 172.

7 Bosworth, Bearman, Bianquis, Van Donzel and Heinrichs (eds.), op. cit., Vol. 1, p. 814.

Amidst growing tensions, the slave sultans of Egypt removed the remnant of the last Crusaders from the Syrian and Egyptian domains, thereby bringing an end to the advance of Hulagu Khan's Mongol hordes in 1260 CE. The Mongols sustained their first defeat at the Battle of Ayn Jalut near Nazareth. The Mamlūks did not achieve this victory alone; they were supported by an unlikely ally called Berke Khan (d. 1266). Berke Khan was the grandson of Genghis Khan and the son of Jochi. Prior to the attack on Baghdad, Berke Khan had accepted Islam through a meeting with some people from Bukhara; in 1257 CE he became the ruler of the western Khanate of the Mongol Empire in Russia, better known as the Golden Horde. In 1260 CE, Berke Khan allied himself with Sultan al-Muẓaffar Sayf ad-Dīn Qutuz (r. 1259-1260) and later, Sultan Baibars (r. 1260-1277) to defeat Hulagu Khan. Due to the alliance between the Mamlūks and the Golden Horde, Egypt was saved from the devastation that befell both Syria and Iraq.[8] In the year 1270 CE, the Mongol Chaghtai ruler in Central Asia, Borak Khan, also accepted Islam and began a war against the Il-Khan. An Il-Khan ruler, Aḥmad Taguder Khan (r. 1282-1284), grandson of Hulagu Khan, also became a Muslim, although his rule was very brief. It was, however, at the time of Mahmud Ghazan (r. 1295–1304), the seventh ruler of the Il-Khan, that Islam became the main faith of Mongol rulers throughout the Muslim lands.

In less than half a century after the fall of Baghdad, the Mongols across the Muslim lands had accepted Islam *en masse*. However, they were divided into numerous factions and they continued to wage wars against each other until the Il-Khan totally disappeared in 1353 CE. Thus, it was the Mamlūks that stood out as the main power in the Middle East from 1260 CE.[9]

---

8 Hitti, op. cit., p. 671.

9 Hasan, op. cit., p. 16 and p. 98.

The Mamlūks ruled Egypt, Syria, western Arabia and parts of Anatolia from Cairo, from 1258 to 1517 CE. During the Mongol ransacking of Baghdad and the killing of the Caliph al-Musta'ṣim (r. 1242–1258) and his family, an uncle of the Caliph survived and fled to Cairo. The Mamlūk Sultan Baibars (r. 1260-1277) provided the much needed legitimacy for his dynasty by installing this surviving uncle Aḥmad ibn Muḥammad known as al-Mustanṣir II (r. 1261-1262), as the legitimate 'Abbasid Caliph.[10] However, the caliphs were mere figureheads during this time; their caliphal line of eighteen caliphs functioning simply to provide legitimacy for the Mamlūk regime for more than two centuries, until the Ottomans took over. By 1517 CE, the Ottoman Sultan Salīm had conquered both Egypt and Syria; his son Sulaymān announced himself Caliph, following the death of the last 'Abbasid Caliph al-Mutawakkil III of Cairo (d. 1543) in Istanbul.[11]

Education and Society

Mamlūk society was divided in two: the élite foreign military rulers and the native peoples they ruled. The Mamlūks themselves were a warrior people, thus it can be assumed that their main education would naturally have been geared towards a military education. Originally the Mamlūks lived separately from the local population, for example, in the city of Cairo the young Mamlūks (who were captured during various wars), were placed in the twelve *tibak* (military quarters); an equal number of individuals in each *tibak*. These *tibak* contained military training schools for Mamlūk students.[12] The students' education consisted of two main parts, i.e. learning the elements of Islam and military training; due to the young men being largely of

10 P. M. Holt, 'Some Observations on the 'Abbāsid Caliphate of Cairo', *Bulletin of the School of Oriental and African Studies*, University of London, Vol. 47, No. 3, 1984, pp. 501-507.

11 N. Robinson, *A Concise Introduction to Islam*, (Surrey: Curzon Press), 1999, pp. 33-35.

12 Bosworth, op. cit., Vol. VI, p. 317.

non-Muslim origin it was believed that they should first be brought up as Muslims, thus allowing them to feel like insiders in contrast to just being 'mercenaries', before they received any military training.[13] According to the contemporary historian, Taqī ad-Dīn Aḥmad ibn 'Alī ibn 'Abd al-Qādir ibn Muḥammad al-Maqrīzī (1364-1442), the philosophy behind this style of education was to create in the Mamlūks a strong Muslim identity and a proficiency in the art of war. Hence the Mamlūk would have a strong loyalty to the Islamic community in view of his having 'being brought out of darkness and into the light'. This is how Ibn Khaldūn (d. 1406), a Mālikī jurist and contemporary historian-sociologist, described the career of the Mamlūks:

> They place them [Mamlūks] in government barracks where they give them good and fair treatment, educate them, have them taught Qur'an and kept at their religious studies until they have a firm grasp of it. Then they train them in archery, fencing, horsemanship, hippodromes, and thrusting with the lance and striking with the sword.... Often they use them in the services of the state, appoint them to high state offices and some of them are chosen to sit on the thrones of sultans....[14]

All the students were manumitted at the end of their military school, ready to serve as soldiers in the Mamlūk army. Instead, a significant number of these Mamlūks continued to engage in study at higher educational institutes.[15] By this route it was possible for them to rise

---

13 André Raymond, *Cairo – City of History*, (Egypt: American University in Cairo Press), 2000, p. 112.

14 Carl F. Petri (ed.), *The Cambridge History of Egypt Vol. 1*, (Cambridge: Cambridge University Press), 1998, pp. 242-243.

15 Thomas Philipp and Ulrisch Haarmann, *The Mamlūks in Egyptian Politics and Society*, (Cambridge: Cambridge University Press), 1998, p. 164.

in rank and even become members of the aristocracy.[16] In comparison to Europe at this time, where nobility was based upon bloodline and a person from humble origins could never rise in society, in Mamlūk society an individual with humble beginnings could even become the Sultan. For example, Aḥmad ibn Ṭūlūn (r. 868-905) was the earliest Mamlūk to rule Egypt as Sultan, which he did in the name of the ʻAbbasid Caliph.

During their training the Mamlūks were instructed in the religious sciences; this was then complemented with training in the military arts or *furūsiyyah.*[17] The rational sciences were not a major part of their education, although this route was open to them during higher education. Throughout the Mamlūk period (1250-1517), Islamic education was widely available to all citizens. The question that comes to mind is: what type of social structure existed at this time to allow integration between the natives and the Mamlūks, especially regarding Islamic education? In general, Mamlūk society was politically constructed in such a way that Mamlūks did not normally succeed to their fathers' offices or positions. This meant that most Mamlūks either remained soldiers until they retired or they married and worked within the local community. There are many examples of Mamlūks marrying within the religious élite amongst the civilians. Those who married into the civilian society were totally integrated within the space of one generation. Thus, the local population continued to have an influx of new people in their midst. At the same time, the arrival of Mamlūks from abroad continued to increase due to the constant need for soldiers to protect the country and for continuous expansion. As a result, this cycle seems to have continued for several generations.

The majority of the society during this time had wide ranging links to education; very familiar to the modern educational phenomenon in

---

16 Bosworth, op. cit., Vol. VI, p. 317.

17 Michael W. Dols, *The Black Death in the Middle East,* (Princeton: Princeton University Press), 1977, p. 145.

our society. The population was always aware of the physical presence of Islamic education around them. The general Muslim population of Mamlūk cities such as Cairo felt the presence of academia because of the vast number of students and *'ulamā'* who dominated the urban scene. Madrasahs such as that of Sultan Nāṣir ad-Dīn al-Ḥasan (r. 1347–1351 and 1354-1361) dominated the physical landscape of the town and schools were clustered into one large group. Men and women of various occupations passed by schools and academies everyday and even dealt with them through trade and work. Businesses, stalls and other enterprises relied heavily on both scholars and students for their success in trade. As Berkey states, "The life of the academic world blended thoroughly into that of the urban metropolis around it."[18] The cities were filled with both 'home' scholars and students and there was an influx of foreign students and scholars, making cities such as Cairo and Damascus urban metropolises. Other than their educational service, madrasahs, *khanqahs* and mosques were also meeting places for judges, where food and help for the poor were collected, marriage contracts were established, and even teaching as 'open learning' (to use a 'current' usage) for the common people was prominent. Numerous madrasahs provided the service of collecting and giving food and income to the needy in the local area. Certain madrasahs in the cities were used for the sittings of judges so they could hear pleas and render judgments. In addition, there are various examples of the local community being continuously in direct contact with academia, for example, until the year 1388 CE, postal couriers arriving from Syria and elsewhere stayed exclusively at the Shamsiyyah al-Qarasunquriyyah madrasah.[19]

For everyday purposes, educational institutions provided focal points for the prayer, worship and other pious deeds of those who were neither students, teachers nor involved in academic institutions.

---

[18] Berkey, op. cit., 1992, p. 189.

[19] Ibid.

In fact, the madrasahs became such public places that by the end of the thirteenth century, the students' rooms, which were usually situated in their interiors, were relocated on the outside so as to give students space away from the very busy courtyards where prayers and other activities were taking place. Further evidence of increased interaction between the world of academia and the general population was the statement of the jurist Badr ad-Dīn Muḥammad ibn Jamā'ah (d. 1333) that he was concerned because students from the madrasahs meeting and mixing with the general non-academic population was not a good influence on their studies.[20]

The madrasahs provided ample work opportunity for the local population. Higher education institutions needed a substantial number of people to fill non-academic positions. For example, the Mu'ayyadiyyah mosque, where the famous polymath scholar Jalāl ad-Dīn Muḥammad ibn Aḥmad al-Maḥallī (d. 1459) taught jurisprudence, employed more than a hundred and fifty non-academic staff.[21] In addition, during the earlier time of Sultan Baibars, Qādis commenced to be state appointed from each of the legal guilds (*madhāhib*), contrary to the practice during the Ayyūbid dynasty when the Qādi could only be appointed from the Shāfi'ī guild. In this way the Mamlūks patronised all four legal *madhāhib* and the educated religious élite had a common set of values. The Mamlūks also took advantage of the long-lived Islamic tradition of *waqf* endowments and became patrons of numerous institutions. The Mamlūk Sultans and the wealthy endowed institutions such as the madrasah, the *bimaristan* and the growing number of Sufi institutions such as the *khanqah,* the *ribāṭ* and the *zāwiyah.* Upon completing their studies, students of religious sciences graduated to receive appointments in the Mamlūk judiciary, to secretarial posts and in the religious establishment.[22]

---

20 Berkey, op. cit., 1992, pp. 190-191.

21 Ibid., p. 193.

22 Philipp and Haarmann, op. cit., p. 164.

Educational Institutions in the Mamlūk Period

The madrasah and its history during the 'Abbasid period has been sufficiently described in the earlier chapters. The definition of the classical madrasah was that of an institution of higher education devoted to religious and literary sciences, providing salaries for teachers, stipends for students and accommodation for staff and students. However, during the Mamlūk period it seems that the madrasah went through a further development. According to Berkey, a significant number of madrasahs in the later Mamlūk period were not exclusively or even principally higher educational centres.[23]

During the whole of the Mamlūk period more than sixty educational institutions were founded by Mamlūk Sultans, government officials and army officers. The greater educational centres were endowed by sultans and their immediate family members.[24] Just before the fall of Baghdad, a renowned madrasah for women was established in Damascus by Khātūn, the daughter of Amir Ashraf Mūsā of Damascus (r. 1229-1237). In the year 1354 CE, Oghl Khātūn, the daughter of Shams ad-Dīn Muḥammad ibn Sayf ad-Dīn of Baghdad, endowed the Khātūniyyah Madrasah.[25] However, the best known madrasah of this period was the Grand Madrasah of Sultan Ḥasan (r. 1347-1351 and 1354-1361), established during the second half of the fourteenth century. The mathematician and writer Aḥmad 'Abdullāh al-Qalqashandī (d. 1418) described it as Cairo's 'greatest madrasah'. There were four halls assigned to the four *madhāhib*, a small mosque for each *madhhab* and a tomb specifically designated for the Sultan and his children. The majority of its students studied the law, but there were also separate courses for Qur'anic exegesis, *ḥadīth*, Qur'anic readings, *fiqh*, Arabic

23 Berkey, op. cit., 1992, p. 62.
24 Ibid.
25 Salah Zaimeche, *Aleppo*, http://www.muslimheritage.com/uploads/aleppo.pdf, FSTC Limited, 2005, p. 6., (accessed: 27/07/10).

language, medicine and even the science needed to determine prayer times.[26]

Another madrasah that dominated the educational scene in Cairo was the Ashrafiyyah. There is a lot of information about this madrasah, which was founded by Sultan al-Ashraf Sayf ad-Dīn Barsbay (r. 1422-1437) in approximately 1422 CE. Architecturally it was based on a cruciform plan with four *īwānāt* (halls) surrounding the central courtyard. In each *īwān* there was accommodation for students, in addition to instruction in the sciences of the *dīn* from the perspective of the four *madhāhib*.[27] It also included a place to pray with paid *imām*, *khaṭīb* and Qur'an readers. However, here the similarities with the classical madrasah end, since during the Mamlūk period, it became common to link primary/secondary schools (*kuttāb*) with the madrasah. The Ashrafiyyah not only had a *kuttāb* but also a multi-storey structure that contained a public fountain.[28] The Mamlūk historian Muḥammad ibn Īyās (d. 1522) reported that not only did this highly complex madrasah include the aforementioned but it was also a *khanqah*. According to an inscription on the building itself, the institution included both a madrasah and a Sufi convent with provisions for sixty-five Sufis.[29] However, what makes the institution's status more obscure is that its *waqf* deeds referred to it as a *jāmi'* mosque. It is obvious from the historical evidence cited above that the institution of the madrasah was going through a further development in the mid-fifteenth century. However, what of the earlier Mamlūk madrasahs during the thirteenth and fourteenth centuries in Cairo?

"Sultan Barsbay's institutions were constructed and endowed in the early fifteenth century, more than one hundred and fifty years after

26 Berkey, op. cit., 1992, pp. 67-69.

27 Ibid, p. 46.

28 Leonor Fernandes, *The Evolution of a Sufi Institution in Mamluk Egypt: The Khanqah*, (Berlin: Klaus Shwarz Verlag), 1988, pp. 83-85.

29 Berkey, op. cit., 1992, p. 48.

the founding of the Mamlūk state."[30] During the early Mamlūk period, the madrasahs were places mostly for the teaching of religious and literary sciences. Following the classical model they were institutions that paid salary to staff and stipends to students. Two of the most famous madrasahs of this type were the madrasah of Sultan aẓ-Ẓāhir Baibars (r. 1260-1277) with its courses in Islamic jurisprudence, *ḥadīth* and Qur'anic reading and the madrasah of Sultan Sayf ad-Dīn Qalawūn (r. 1279-1290) with classes in the four *madhāhib, ḥadīth* and Qur'anic exegesis.

During the same period a number of hospitals, medical madrasahs and libraries were founded across the Muslim world. During the thirteen century, three medical madrasahs were established in Damascus. The Dikhwāriyyah madrasah was founded in 1225 CE by the physician Muhadhdhab ad-Dīn 'Abd al-Mun'im ibn 'Alī ibn Ḥamīd ad-Dikhwār (d. 1230). In 1265 CE, during Sultan Baibars' reign in Egypt and Syria, the Labūdiyyah medical madrasah was founded in Damascus by the physician Najm ad-Dīn Yaḥyā ibn Muhammed ibn al-Labūdī. The third medical madrasah in Damascus was founded by the physician 'Imād ad-Dīn Abū 'Abdullāh Muḥammad ibn 'Abbās ibn Aḥmad ar-Rabi ad-Dunaysirī (d. 1287).[31] During his reign the Mamlūk Sultan Ḥusām ad-Dīn Lāchīn al-Manṣūr (r. 1297-1299) restored the Ibn Ṭūlūn mosque in Cairo; in addition to paying salaries to the professors and stipends to the students, he also provided for the physician Sharaf ad-Dīn Muḥammad ibn al-Ḥawāfīr to lecture on medicine.[32] Further west in Fez, new libraries were built in the mosques and higher education institutions, such as al-Qarawiyyīn, the oldest higher education

30 Ibid.

31 Aydin Sayili, *Certain Aspects of Medical Instruction in Medieval Islam and its Influences on Europe*, FSTC Limited, 2005, http://www.muslimheritage.com/topics/default.cfm?TaxonomyTypeID=11andTaxonomySubTypeID=57andTaxonomyThirdLevelID=-1andArticleID=1005#ftn6, (accessed: 28/07/10).

32 Berkey, op. cit., 1992, pp. 52-4.

institution in the Muslim world, founded in 899 CE by Fāṭimah al-Fihrī of Tunisia.[33] The most recent library in al-Qarawiyyīn was founded by the Maranid Sultan Abū 'Inān Fāris al-Mutawakkil of Morocco (r. 1348-1358) in 1349; it contained books on the religious, literary and natural sciences.[34] In 1476 CE in Herat, in Afghanistan, the Turkish poet 'Alī Shir Nawā'ī built a *bimaristan* together with a madrasah where medicine was taught. During the same era in the Ottoman lands, Sultan Bayezid II (r. 1481-1511) built a madrasah hospital complex in Edirne between the years 1484 and 1488 CE. One and a half centuries later, the traveller Evliya Celebi (b. 1611), described the madrasah hospital complex as both a place for medical practice by physicians and a place where students studied medical works.[35]

There was also extensive work undertaken across the Muslim world in natural sciences such as mathematics, medicine and astronomy. After stability was restored in Mongol-dominated Muslim lands in the thirteenth and fourteenth century, Islamic society continued to be creative and prosperous. Under the patronage of Hulagu Khan (r. 1256-1265), the Persian mathematician and astronomer aṭ-Ṭūṣī (d. 1274), built the great observatory at Magarah in present-day Azerbaijan and developed an accurate scientific table of planetary motion at the same observatory.[36] The astronomer Mu'ayyid ad-Dīn al-'Urḍī (d. 1266) of Aleppo worked at the same observatory, building astronomical instruments and creating the first planetary models. He wrote very important scientific works such as *The Instruments of the Observatory of Magarah*, *Kitāb al-Hay'ah* ['Book on Astronomy'], *Construction of the Perfect Sphere* and *On the Determination of the Distance between the Sun*

---

33 Esposito, op. cit., p. 328.

34 Josef W. Meri and Jere L. Bacharach , *Medieval Islamic Civilisation: L-Z, index,* (New York: Routledge), 2006, p. 450.

35 Sayili, op. cit., 2005, p. 1.

36 Sonn, op. cit., pp. 108-112.

and the Apogee. In 1325 CE, the astronomer Ibn Sarrāj devised two types of astrolabes in the city of Aleppo. One of the famous astronomers in the late Mamlūk period was Aḥmad al-Ḥalabī (d. 1455) of Aleppo; he wrote the book *Aims of students on operations with the quadrant of Astrolabe*. Salah Zaimeche below eloquently describes the zenith of the science of astronomy by Muslim scholars during the thirteenth and fourteenth centuries.

> Islamic astronomy reached its zenith, at least from the Western perspective, in the thirteenth and fourteenth centuries, when al-Tusi and his successors pushed against the limits of the Ptolemaic world view that had ruled for a millennium. According to the philosophers, celestial bodies were supposed to move in circles at uniform speeds. But the beauty of Ptolemy's attempt to explain the very un-uniform motions of planets and the Sun as seen from Earth was marred by corrections like orbits within orbits, known as epicycles, and geometrical modifications. Al-Tusi found a way to restore most of the symmetry to Ptolemy's model by adding pairs of cleverly designed epicycles to each orbit. Following in al-Tusi's footsteps, the fourteenth century astronomer Ala ad-Din Abul-Hasan ibn al-Shatir had managed to go further and construct a completely symmetrical model.[37]

In medicine, scholars such as Ibn al-Labūdī (d. after 1267) continued to push the subject's boundaries forward in Syria and Egypt. He wrote widely on the subjects of psychology, medicine and mathematics. The thirteenth century physician, Khalīfah ibn Abī al-Maḥāsin of Aleppo, wrote widely on the subject of medicine; he is well known for

---

[37] Overbye, op. cit., p. 3.

his work on surgical instruments and eye surgery.[38] In North Africa the sociologist and historian Ibn Khaldūn (d. 1406) wrote extensively on understanding political, social and historical processes. His work *al-Muqaddimah* is regarded as the first work of historiography and a cornerstone of modern disciplines such as anthropology, sociology, economics and political science. His greatest contribution to the Islamic civilisation was the cyclical *'aṣabiyyah* theory, which describes and analyses the ever changing bonds between human communities. His conclusion was that the cycle applied to all civilisations at all levels, leading to both their rise and fall due to psychological, sociological, economic and political factors.[39]

During this period the famous Chinese Muslim Admiral Zheng (1371-1433) began his hitherto unprecedented seven naval expeditions for the Emperor of China, more than half a century before Vasco da Gama (1469-1524) and more than a century and a half before Columbus (1451-1506). Three of the Admiral's seven voyages, which started with the amazing number of three hundred and seventeen ships, were described eloquently by another Chinese Muslim, Ma Huan, who accompanied him on them. The first three voyages (1405-1411) took the Chinese fleet to Vietnam, Malaysia, Indonesia, Sri Lanka and India. The fourth (1413-1415) took the Admiral to Arabia and the Persian Gulf. The last three voyages (1416-1422 and 1430-1433) took them as far as East Africa.[40] More than half a century earlier the North African traveller, Abū 'Abdullāh Muḥammad Ibn Baṭūṭah (1304-1369) began his famous travels in 1325 CE. He visited all of the Middle East, Africa,

---

38 Salah Zaimeche, *Aleppo,* http://www.muslimheritage.com/uploads/aleppo.pdf, FSTC Limited, 2005, pp. 11-14, (accessed: 28/07/10). For more detail, see: Francois Charette, *Mathematical Instrumentation in Fourteenth-century Egypt and Syria: The Illustrated Treatise of Najm Al-Din Al-Misri,* (Leiden: Koninklijke), 2003.

39 Zaimeche, op. cit., p. 14.

40 See Patricia Buckley Ebrey, Anne Walthall and James B. Palais, *East Asia: A Cultural, Social and Political History,* (USA: Houghton Mifflin Company), 2008, p. 226.

Constantinople (Istanbul), Afghanistan, India, Central Asia, Malaysia, Sri Lanka, Cambodia and finally China.[41] This period, although undergoing major changes, was stable, creative and prosperous enough to produce two of the greatest travellers in history to have travelled the then Muslim world and beyond.

It is clear from the above description that the Mamlūk period was very successful educationally, politically and socially across the Muslim world. However, there were changes that occurred with regards to education, especially by the third decade of the fourteenth century, when the madrasah in Mamlūk lands began to undergo further change. According to Berkey, the functional distinctions that existed in the early Islamic period between the madrasahs, mosques and *khanqahs* had commenced to break down by the fourteenth century. The three different terms began either to be used for the same institution by various contemporary authors or the term's original functions seem to have been entirely erased.[42] It appears that authors of chronicles contemporary with these institutions were themselves not sure as to how a particular institution should be labelled. Al-Maqrīzī (d. 1442) labelled the institution founded by Amir Aslam an-Nāṣirī in 1345/46 CE a *jāmi'*, whereas in the same period, the contemporary historian Yūsuf Abū al-Maḥāsin ibn Taghrī Birdī (d. 1470) described it as a madrasah. During this period a large number of Sufi buildings were used to teach religious sciences and a great number of mosques or madrasahs seemed to be endowed to support Sufis, with no provision for educational activities. For example, the *khanqah* of Mughultay al-Jamālī, established in 1329 CE, was a place for Sufi students to learn the Ḥanafī *madhhab*; the *khanqah* of Zayn ad-Dīn Sidqa taught Sufi students the Shāfi'ī *madhhab*, whereas, the madrasah and mosque founded by

---

41 See Ross, E. Dunn, *Adventures of Ibn Battuta: A Muslim Traveler of the 14th Century*, (LA: University of California Press), 1986.

42 Jonathan, op. cit., 1992, p. 49.

Sultan al-Ashraf Qansuh al-Ghawrī (r. 1501-1516), did not make any provisions for teachers or students but rather for Sufis, their Shaykh, *ḥadīth* and Qur'an readers and other non-educational staff.[43]

It seems that educational institutions were going through drastic changes; the question arises: what caused these changes and how can the results of such changes be characterised? The later years of the Mamlūk era have been described as an era of Islamic history in which social, political, cultural, religious practices and institutions were in a state of flux. Scores of historians consider political instability and the coming of the Black Death as the reasons behind this flux.[44] It has been estimated that from Sultan Ṣalāḥ ad-Dīn's period (1138-1193), until the coming of the Black Death in the middle of the fourteenth century, the population of Egypt arose from 2.4 million to 4 million.[45] According to various historical sources the population of Egypt as a whole appears to have risen from the end of the twelfth century. This substantiates the historical statement that Cairo became a major city of intellectual life and trade during the decline and fall of Baghdad from the beginning of the thirteenth century to its destruction in 1258 CE.

During the reign of Sultan an-Nāṣir from 1294-1340 CE, there was strong political stability in Egypt, and education flourished. During this period there was a widespread custom of intermarriage between Mamlūks and native Egyptians and, in addition to social stability, there was a general upturn in trade. However, a few years after Sultan an-Nāṣir's reign, in approximately 1348 CE, the Black Death reached the centre of the Mamlūk world.[46] Due to the Black Death and unstable government, the economy of the Mamlūk Sultanate began to decline.

---

43 Berkey, op. cit., 1992, pp. 67-69.
44 Philipp and Haarmann, op. cit., p. 168.
45 Raymond, op. cit., p. 138.
46 Dols, op. cit., pp. 143-154.

By 1382 CE, the Burji dynasty of the Mamlūks took over through a revolt that had begun in 1377 CE. Continuous political intrigues at court, corruption in the upper echelons, the effect of the Black Death and of war with the expanding empire of Timur Lane (r. 1370-1405) led to the downfall of Mamlūk society. By 1463 CE, in their expansion, the rising Ottoman *dawlah* began to incorporate Egypt.

The great decline in population due to the plague and harsher taxation created further social decline in Mamlūk society. Due to financial limitations, wealthier individuals in society could no longer endow educational institutions. According to historical sources, madrasahs and mosques that were already established dispensed with teaching staff and stipends in order to economise. Another reason may also be that, due to the rise of religious expression in such a milieu, the responsibility of wealthy individuals moved towards providing the essential requirements of religious expression and not the common guaranteed income for teachers and students.[47] In the face of such tribulations, the population moved towards popular preachers for solace rather than recognised scholars. Berkey describes the situation thus:

> ....on the one hand, the omnipresence of death left Muslims with a renewed commitment to Islam, and on the other hand, it carved a deeper niche for mysticism, magic, and other expressions of popular religion.[48]

According to Shoshan, this period reintroduced the old association of religion with magic due to the popular psychology of the masses which is always drawn to the supernatural and superstition.[49] Scholars such as Taqī ad-Dīn Aḥmad ibn Taymiyyah (d. 1328) and Ibn Baydakin

---

47 Berkey, op. cit., 1992, p. 19.

48 Philipp and Haarmann, op. cit., p. 168.

49 Boaz Shoshan, *Popular Culture in Medieval Cairo,* (Cambridge: University of Cambridge Press), 1993, p. 11.

al-Turkumani (fl. late fourteenth century) wrote numerous treatises against this kind of innovation by popular preachers and the superstitious customs and belief (popular religion) of the masses.[50]

Sufism and 'Popular Religion'

Mamlūk society was established in a Sunni and Sufi religious environment.[51] Unfortunately in later years, Mamlūk society embraced not only Sunnism and Sufism in all their forms, but also the branches that sprouted from it and have been labelled 'popular Islam' or 'popular religion' by scholars such as Berkey and Shoshan.

In the classical age, at least until the twelfth century, the idea of *taṣawwuf* (the Arabic term for Sufism) was based upon individual piety and spirituality. Primarily, it began simply as a personal, individual spiritual quest. The science of *taṣawwuf* therefore generally denotes the inner and spiritual dimension of Islam.

> Theologically, Sufism emphasizes the personal and intense relationship between a Merciful and Caring God and a believer in the process of spiritual ascent. The believer expresses this relationship through practices such as meditation and *dhikr* (the constant remembrance of God), which can be recited individually or in groups.[52]

Accordingly, one of the earliest of those known particularly for their cultivation of the inner dimension and spirituality of Islam was Rābi'ah al-'Adawiyyah (713/714- 801). She lived in Basra and preached *zuhd* (doing without what one does not need) and spirituality in order to draw closer to Allah. One of her famous sayings was:

---

50 Ibid.

51 Carl F. Petry (ed.), *The Cambridge History of Egypt Vol. 1*, (Cambridge: Cambridge University Press), 1998, p. 266.

52 Ninian Smart, *Atlas of the World's Religions*, (Oxford: Oxford University Press), 1999, p. 178.

> I have not served God from fear of Hell, for I should be but a wretched hireling if I did it from fear, nor from love of paradise, for I should be such a bad servant, if I served for the sake of what was given me, but I have served him only for the love of Him and desire of Him.[53]

Another early adherent of the science of *taṣawwuf* was the scholar al-Muḥāsibī (d. 857), who taught in one of the numerous mosques of Baghdad in the ninth century.[54] The science of *taṣawwuf* divided into two styles in the late ninth century, which some historians of Sufism have labelled the 'sober' style and the 'drunken' style.[55] Abū al-Qāsim al-Junayd of Baghdad (d. 910) is regarded by the majority of scholars as the Imam of the Sufis and often carries the title of *shaykh aṭ-ṭā'ifah*, i.e. 'Shaykh of the Order'. He believed that all quest for spirituality needs to follow the rule and conduct laid down by the *sharī'ah*, i.e. a 'sober' type of Sufism.[56] On the other hand, Abū Yazīd al-Bisṭāmī (d. 874), who lived and taught in Baghdad, was very well known for ecstatic utterances which caused continual disagreement about his 'drunken' type of Sufism among the jurists of that period. There were many confrontations which led to some verdicts of heresy against Sufis such as the famous case of al-Ḥallāj.[57] It should not be thought that either al-Bisṭāmī or al-Ḥallāj espoused flaunting the *sharī'ah*, but sometimes their incautious statements caused doubts about their *'aqīdah*.

Ibn Khaldūn described these confrontations against the minority 'drunken' type of Sufis in these words:

[53] Gibb and Kramers, *Shorter Encyclopedia of Islam*, (Leiden: E. J. Brill), 1974, p. 462.

[54] Julian Baldick, *Mystical Islam*, (London: I. B. Tauris), 1992, pp. 33-34.

[55] Seyyed Hossein Nasr (ed.), *Islamic Spirituality: Foundations*, (London: Routledge and Kegan Paul), 1987, p. 256.

[56] John L. Esposito, *The Oxford Encyclopedia of the Modern Islamic World*, (Oxford: Oxford University Press), 1995, p. 107.

[57] Nasr, op. cit., 1987, p. 256.

> Finally, there are the suspect expressions which the Sufis call 'ecstatic utterances' (*shaṭaḥāt*) and which provoke the censure of the orthodox Muslims. As to them, it should be known that the attitude that would be fair to the (Sufis) is to (observe) that they are people who are removed from sense perception. Inspiration grips them. Eventually they say things about their inspiration that they do not intend to say....This was the experience of Abū Yazid al-Bistami and others like him. However, (Sufis) whose excellence is not well known deserve censure for utterances of this kind; since the data that might cause us to interpret their statement so as to remove any suspicion attached to them are not clear to us. Furthermore, any Sufis who are not removed from sense perception and are not in the grip of a state when they make utterances of this kind also deserve censure. Therefore the Jurists and the great Sufis decided that al-Ḥallāj was to be executed because he spoke ecstatically while not removed from sense but in control of his state. And God knows best.[58]

During the eleventh century, the idea that the inner dimension of Islam is to be found clearly in the Book and the Sunnah and is reconcilable with the *sharī'ah*[59] reached the peak of its intellectual development in the writings of al-Ghazālī (d. 1111), and *taṣawwuf* took its rightful place in mainstream Islam.[60] However, the formalisation

---

58 Ibn Khaldun, op. cit., pp. 101-102.

59 Al-Ghazālī's thesis was that the inner and outer dimensions of Islam are to be found in the Book and the Sunnah but had become separated and he laboured to re-unite them. The Mālikī scholars of north and west Africa and Andalusia took the position that in their tradition the inner and outer had never been separated, and that thus there was no need to re-unite them. Nevertheless, in the main, al-Ghazālī's work became highly influential here too - Ed.

60 Nasr, op. cit., 1987, pp. 261-264.

of Sufi orders did not appear until the twelfth century, reportedly in Khurasan. By the end of the century, the institutionalisation of Sufism as Sufi orders was underway.[61] During the twelfth and thirteenth century, Sufi orders or, as they are called in Arabic *ṭuruq* (sing. *ṭarīqah*), became major social organisations across the Muslim world, especially in the Caliphal capital, Cairo.[62] All of the Sufi orders traced their spiritual lineage back to the Prophet Muḥammad ﷺ through his cousin and son-in-law, ʻAlī ibn Abī Ṭālib ؓ, or through his Companion Abū Bakr ؓ. Historians find it impossible to verify these lineages since there are few primary historical documents covering this issue directly. The Sufis with their chains claim Abū Bakr or ʻAlī ؓ as the foremost spiritual students of the Prophet Muḥammad ﷺ, who then transmitted the inner teachings to future generations.

Although it is true that Sufism existed in Egypt hundreds of years before, by the thirteenth century Sufism was no longer simply an individual private quest with regards to the inner dimension of Islam; it had, on the contrary, become a part of community life.[63] This, according to some sources, came about as a result of Sufism being theologically accepted within mainstream Islam. Accordingly, the majority of Sufi orders primarily based themselves on two styles of rites: on daily devotional exercises such as recitation of a *wird* usually composed of *āyāt* of the Noble Qur'an, *dhikr* of Allah, asking for blessings on the Messenger of Allah ﷺ, and *du'ā*, meditation and retreat and secondly, on regular group events focused on *dhikr* and the recitation of prayers. The main elements of Sufism during this period were the establishment of various orders and the status quo of their followers. "As *ṭurūq* formalized, a period of apprenticeships became customary before followers could become full members of the

61 Adam Sabra, *Poverty and Charity in Medieval Islam: Mamlūk Egypt, 1250-1517,* (Cambridge: Cambridge University Press), 2000.

62 Smart, op. cit., p. 178.

63 Shoshan, op. cit., p. 11.

order."[64] The hierarchical organisation of the Sufi orders positioned a Shaykh at the top and the orders were based upon the master-disciple relationship, which may be reminiscent of the relationship between 'Īsā (Jesus) ﷺ and his *ḥawāriyyīn* (disciples) but indeed may also be just as suggestive of the relationship between the Messenger of Allah ﷺ and his Companions.

Although the establishment and development of Sufism may be complex, the definition of what has been labelled 'popular religion' is simply perplexing. It is challenging to define 'popular religion' in the Islamic historical setting. Looking at various sources, it appears that it can be loosely defined as the 'culture of the masses' in contrast to a scriptural or a 'high' cultural tradition.[65] The title of one author's work, *The Arab Medieval Culture is an Élite Culture*, sums up the general character of works written in the field of Islamic history during the twentieth century. It has been argued that historians, in contrast to anthropologists, wrote 'from above' with regards to history and not 'from below', since they relied heavily on scholarly texts.[66] There were, however, examples of works by historians who did write 'from below' with regards to the culture, such as *The Cult of Saints* by Ignaz Goldziher, Bosworth's study of the medieval Islamic 'underworld' and Memon's *Investigation of Ibn Taymiyyah's Critique of Popular Islam.*[67] However, it could be argued that there is no classical Arabic word for 'popular religion' and instead at both ends of the spectrum, words such as heresy were used constantly to draw a distinction. So, how can we define 'popular religion' in the Middle Period? According to both Berkey and Shoshan, it is clear that 'popular religion' was never identical to Sufism, but it was (and still is) closely identified with it.

---

64 Smart, op. cit., p. 178.

65 Jonathan P. Berkey, *Popular Preaching and Religious Authority in the Medieval Islamic Near East,* (USA: University of Washington Press), 2001, p. 4.

66 Shoshan, op. cit., p. ix.

67 Ibid.

The rise of Sufism and its development as shown above made various practices associated with Sufism popular amongst the population. It has been argued that with Sufi orders came what is loosely called 'pseudo Sufism' which had no links with the *ṭuruq* nor were its people adherents to the 'inner dimension of Islam' holding strongly to the *sharī'ah*.

It was during this period that much of the populace began to take to *zāwiyahs*[68] established by shaykhs who were not attached to any Sufi order. In many villages and towns this kind of shaykh became the only source of religious knowledge; he led the prayers, delivered the sermons and performed *dhikr* and meditation.[69] This corresponds with the characteristics of the religious experience and expectations of common people, since 'popular religion' was based mostly on reverence for one person. This person may have either been known to be saintly or renowned for great knowledge. Some of these scholars did happen to be genuine and respectable scholars. Both Ibn Taymiyyah (d. 1328) and as-Suyūṭī (d. 1505) had significant followings among ordinary people. However, there were other figures who were followed by the masses and who were not always so legitimate. According to sources, it appears that numerous Egyptians began to actively join Sufi orders; for example, it is known that Abū al-'Abbās al-Ḥārithī (d. 1538) initiated ten thousand disciples.[70] This number in itself, even though possibly inflated, demonstrates that such a following may not have been easily trained.

Fake shaykhs may also have played the role of 'holy men'. It was in this period that ordinary people may have become devoted to only asking for intercession with Allah through 'holy men'. Even though there are various verses in the Qur'an that have been interpreted

---

68 See below for definition.

69 Jonathan P. Berkey, *The Formation of Islam: Religion and Society in the Near East 600-1800*, (Cambridge: Cambridge University Press), 2003, p. 249.

70 Shoshan, op. cit., p. 12.

to reject such a possibility (for example, 2:48) by those who took a stance against it, this belief became so strong that it was inculcated as ordinary Muslim piety. Primarily, this desire for intercession seems to have been focused upon the Prophet ﷺ respecting whose intercession, numerous sound *ḥadīth* are narrated, but very rapidly, belief in a more local intercession began to take root. The common practice of going to tombs of saints and holy men for help with sick children, cure for an illness or even alleviation of debt commenced. In addition, living learned men and saints were asked for the same favours.[71] This increased the demand for popular preachers who may not have undergone any education; many of them were simply charismatic and alleged that their preaching had been validated by dreams. A story of such a man may be of interest:

> Some time in 1343, a man called Shu'ayb claimed that he had a dream where a vision told him that a recently unearthed alleged old mosque in Cairo was in fact an ancient grave of one of the Companions of the Prophet. He began to preach to the people, and due to him being so charismatic, people flocked to him. The success of his preaching made Shu'ayb commence to give guided tours for fees. Later on, the shrine he claimed had healing powers that could give sight to the blind and heal all the sick. With time Shu'ayb himself appeared to have gained supernatural powers. This began to alarm the authorities who sent their judge to see what was happening. The people who now were adherents of Shu'ayb threw stones and pelted him away from the shrine. At last, extra enforcement was used to disperse the crowd; meanwhile, Shu'ayb had disappeared with a large sum of money given to him by his adherents.[72]

71 Berkey, op. cit., 2003, p. 250.
72 Shoshan, op. cit., p. 9.

Although eventually the public did discover that Shu'ayb was a charlatan, such events only increased in subsequent centuries. Even sultans and other leading amirs found themselves following such ambiguous shaykhs. In many ways these shaykhs may remind the Western reader of the infamous Russian Orthodox Christian preacher Rasputin in the twentieth century. He was a man who had achieved royal favour with the Tsar but in the end, turned out to be an impostor and charlatan.

As mentioned earlier, magic and miracles became everyday in tales about various popular preachers, and in later centuries, the blame for such beliefs was to be laid at the door of Sufism. Various shaykhs began either to claim or be renowned for actions that ordinary mortals are ordinarily unable to perform. Extraordinary powers such as miraculous healing, telepathy and tales of flying from Delhi to Makkah[73] were some of the things ascribed to them. Musallam al-Barqī al-Badawī (d. 1274) was one of the shaykhs described thus. He was visited continuously by the masses for his blessings. It is been reported that during the time of the Prophet Muhammad ﷺ, the Companions ؓ would compete for anything they could treasure of the Messenger of Allah ﷺ.[74] Similarly, it seems that throughout history the masses

---

[73] Such feats are not deemed impossible according to Islamic Theology. However, these have also been the kind of feats that many charlatans in the past (and to-day) have ascribed to themselves.

[74] When Quraysh sent 'Urwah ibn Mas'ūd to the Messenger of Allah ﷺ in the year of al-Ḥudaybiyyah, he saw the unparalleled respect which his Companions displayed towards him. Whenever he did wuḍū' they ran to get his leftover wuḍū' water and very nearly fought over it. If he spat they took it with their hands and wiped it on their faces and bodies. If a hair of his fell they ran to get it. If he commanded them to do something, they ran to do his command. If he spoke, they lowered their voices in his presence. They did not stare at him due to their respect for him. When he returned to Quraysh, he said, "People of Quraysh! I have been to Chosroes in his kingdom, and Caesar in his kingdom and the Negus in his kingdom, but by Allah, I have not seen any king among his people treated anything like the way Muḥammad is treated by his Companions." (Al-Bukhārī, kitāb ash-shurūṭ, bāb ash-shurūṭ fī al-jihād).

have sometimes gone to great lengths in treasuring similar items left behind by noted scholars in the same spirit as the Companions, for example, when the scholar Shams ad-Dīn al-Ḥanafī (d. 1443/44) came to the public bath to cut his hair, people would quarrel for a single lock of hair. However, the question arose as to its value only when the people then went on to make these into talismans (at the same time ignoring Qur'an and Sunnah in which the definition of a talisman clearly excludes relics) or even worse, when the masses began to do this while following men and women who were charlatans posing as scholars.[75]

Scholars such as Ibn Taymiyyah (d. 1328) wrote treatises on various rites that they considered incorrect. Ibn Taymiyyah believed that rituals such as visiting the tombs of saints in such a manner and the exaggerated supernatural belief in intercession by local saints should be prohibited, since they harmed the integrity of the religion. As-Suyūṭī (d. 1505) also disapproved of excessive visiting to saints' graves and requesting their intercession, but on the other hand, he approved of the celebration of the birthday of the Prophet ﷺ as a commendable innovation, something a significant number of scholars of that era disagreed with.[76] When looking at various scholarly treatises from the Mamlūk period, it becomes obvious that there was a perplexing problem for the scholars to define what legitimate spiritual knowledge is and how to regulate it. There were increasing numbers of debates and confrontations between scholars and popular preachers throughout the Middle Period. According to Berkey, both groups hotly debated what constitutes authentic Islam and what defines the *'ulamā'*.[77] However, Berkey describes this confrontation as being between Jurists and Sufis, whereas the more probable scenario is that it was

[75] Ibid., pp. 18-19.

[76] Shoshan, op. cit., pp. 68-69.

[77] Berkey, op. cit., 2001, p. 4.

scholars confronting popular preachers who were impostors, such as the aforementioned man Shuʿayb. Seen from this viewpoint, it is easy to understand how the scholars of law and the scholars of Sufism were trying to bridge the gap, in contrast to the anonymous popular preachers who misused their powers to control the populace.

It is in this context that Ibn Taymiyyah became known as a stern critic of what he identified as *Ṣūfiyyat ar-Rasm* (cultural Sufis), although he defended individual Sufi inspiration, such as that of the shaykh of the Shādhiliyyah *ṭarīqah*, ʿAlī ibn Wafā' (d. 1363) as juristically acceptable testimony. Although both Ibn Taymiyyah and, even earlier, Ibn Jawzī (d. 1200), were stern critics of popular religion, they were nevertheless members of Sufi orders.[78] Thus, the main problem with regards to authentic learning during the Middle Period was that of defining the parameters of Sufism, which had never been formulated, hence leaving a gap between legalised Sufism and popular religion, or what Ibn Taymiyyah labelled *Ṣūfiyyat al-Arzāq* (salaried Sufis) and *Ṣūfiyyat ar-Rasm* (cultural Sufis). Historically, the majority of scholars have agreed that Sufism is a part of Islam, but what seems to have been continuously disputed is the difference between acceptable and unacceptable behaviour, or in more modern terms, the difference between Sufism and popular religion.

Looking at the impact of Sufism and 'popular religion' on Islamic education during this period, it is important first to closely examine the institutions and organisations that were utilised during this period to educate and instruct the populace. Three institutions were very important in relation to education and *taṣawwuf*; these were the *khanqah*, the *ribāṭ* and the *zāwiyah*. There are a significant number of chronicles written by Muslim travellers contemporary with them that use these terms when describing Sufi institutions. However, when these accounts are looked at a little closer, it becomes apparent that

---

[78] Ibid., p. 87.

these three terms are used to refer to the same institution. Ibn Jubayr (d. 1217) explained that by his time the *ribāṭ* had become known as the *khanqah,* and Ibn Baṭūṭah (d. 1369), nearly two centuries later, pointed out that in Egypt the *zāwiyah* had begun to be called *khanqah* as well.[79]

The *ribāṭ* was originally a foundation associated with *jihād* (military activities), and was situated at the frontier during the early period of Islam. By the eighth century, the term's meaning had altered to identify foundations which housed Sufis, who devoted their lives to strive (*mujāhdah*) against their own desires so as to be able to purify themselves and become closer to Allah. According to both the scholar Ibn al-Ḥājj (d. 1336) and the historian al-Maqrīzī (d. 1442), the *ribāṭ* was a positive introduction in Egypt during the Ayyūbid period. On the other hand, the jurist Ibn al-Jawzī (d. 1200) attacked the *ribāṭ* for becoming a place that secluded people from the reality of life. It seems that he believed these people were simply taking refuge there to enjoy idleness.[80] Some sources point towards the *ribāṭ* as not only being used by the Sufis, but also for housing unprotected women, former military personnel and freed slaves. The *Ribāṭ al-Baghdādiyyah* founded by Tidhkar Khātūn, daughter of Sultan aẓ-Ẓāhir Rukn ad-Dīn Baibars al-Bunduqdārī (r. 1260-1277), and the *Ribāṭ as-Sitt Kalīlah,* founded by an amir during the same Mamlūk period have been noted to house women. Most of these *ribāṭs* were supported by *waqf.* It is interesting to note that a number of the *waqfiyyah* documents of certain *ribāṭs* mention that the people staying in the *ribāṭ* needed to have qualities particular to people of the *zāwiyah*, but at the same time they were not to favour innovation opposed to the *sharī'ah.*[81] It can be assumed that the reason behind this condition was that those who

---

79 Fernandes, op. cit., p. 10.

80 Ibid.

81 Fernandes, op. cit., p. 12.

were housed in the *ribāṭ* were to busy themselves in prayers, *dhikr*, recitation of the Qur'ān, and with the 'inner dimension' of Islam, but a warning was given by the authorities that heretical behaviour would not be accepted. The clause in the deed in itself indicates that certain elements of society that were closely associated with Sufis (the people of the *zāwiyah*) were allegedly behaving in contradiction to the *sharī'ah.* By the middle of the fourteenth century the *ribāṭ* seems to have been assimilated by the *khanqah* and the *zāwiyah*; initially the term *ribāṭ* became associated with living units inside the *zāwiyah* or the *khanqah,* and by the end of the fifteenth century the term simply disappeared.[82]

Originally, the term *zāwiyah* appears to have meant a part or a corner of a religious building, such as a mosque. Al-Maqrīzī and Ibn Duqmaq (d. 1406) mentioned eight *zāwiyahs* that were known to be a part of the *Jāmi' al-'Atīq*, the first congregational mosque built by 'Amr ibn al-'Āṣ in Fusṭāṭ. The *ḥalaqah* took place in these *zāwiyahs.* These *zāwiyahs* were not only dedicated to the science of *taṣawwuf* but to all the sciences taught at the mosque. However, similarly to the term *ribāṭ*, the term *zāwiyah* also evolved in the later classical age and began to be referred to a Sufi institution linked to a specific Sufi *ṭarīqah*, built in the name of a particular shaykh for whose family it served as a home as well as a place for the students to learn the way of the 'order'. Often at the death of the shaykh, who was buried at the *zāwiyah,* the grave becoming a shrine for the *ṭarīqah.* In many sources, scholars and jurists are found to criticise some of the annual festivals of these shrines as heretical. By the Mamlūk period, the position of the shaykh had become hereditary. The entry requirements for a *zāwiyah* were very relaxed; in most cases, individual spiritual attraction alone was enough to join and the individual could leave at will. The *zāwiyah*

82 Ibid.

was not only supported by the masses during the Mamlūk period but also by the élite, even the Sultan. A significant number of sultans, amirs and other aristocrats officially supported a particular *ṭarīqah* and shaykh; the architecture of later *zāwiyahs* became grander when built by the sultans as gifts for their chosen shaykhs. By the end of the fifteenth century, the twenty-six *zāwiyahs* mentioned by al-Maqrīzī had multiplied into two hundred and twenty-five. Later on in the sixteenth century, the terms *khanqah* and *zāwiyah* became intermixed, with most of the times, the *zāwiyah* absorbing the *khanqah*.[83] In many ways the rise of the *zāwiyah* vis-a-vis other Sufi institutions was an indication of the rise of 'popular religion'.

According to Mamlūk chronicles it seems that the *khanqah* was a place where Sufis met. The building may have included quarters for living, a kitchen, a bath house and an apartment that belonged to the shaykh. The chronicles are in agreement that this institution first appeared in the Muslim world in the tenth century; it came to Egypt during the next century and flourished during the Mamlūk period. Ibn Khaldūn (d. 1406) mentioned that *khanqahs* increased in number in Cairo during his period and that they were a source of income for the Sufis. Ibn Taymiyyah, as mentioned earlier, made an interesting distinction between the *Ṣūfiyyat al-Arzāq* (salaried Sufis) and the *Ṣūfiyyat ar-Rasm* (cultural Sufis), whom he opposed. He mentioned that the *Ṣūfiyyat al-Arzāq,* who observed the *sharī'ah,* were the people who used the *khanqah*. The *khanqahs* were not named after the shaykhs but rather after their founders; they were also maintained by *waqfs* whose foundational documents stipulated that the shaykhs and the Sufis were required to fulfil their religious duties. The *khanqahs* and the Sufis were independent of the shaykhs, since their funding came from *waqfs*. On the other hand, the *zāwiyah* had an open policy and

83 Fernandes, op. cit., pp. 13-15.

no *waqf*.[84] This meant that, whereas the activities at the *khanqah* were well controlled, at the *zāwiyah* there was no such management.[85]

The *khanqah* was the Sufi institution that gained the most support from the Mamlūk élite. The first *khanqah* to be established by a sultan for the Sufis, was the Sa'īd as-Su'adā' *Khanqah,* built by Sultan Ṣalāḥ ad-Dīn Yūsuf ibn Ayyūb in 1173 CE. The historian al-Maqrīzī reported that the stipulation of the *waqfiyyah* was that the *khanqah* would house Sufis who were poor or destitute. The Sufis were assigned living units, meals and clothes. There is no statement of al-Maqrīzī which links this *khanqah* to any teaching. The first *khanqah* to be associated with teaching was founded by Sultan aẓ-Ẓāhir Rukn ad-Dīn Baibars al-Bunduqdārī (r. 1260-1277) in the thirteenth century where there was an allocated time for teaching religious sciences.[86] The second such *khanqah* was built by Sultan Nāṣir Muḥammad in 1324 CE; it was during this century that permanent teaching of religious sciences at *khanqahs* commenced. The madrasah and the *jāmi'* mosque acknowledged and incorporated *taṣawwuf,* such as *mashyakhah taṣawwuf*, a daily meeting of *ḥuḍūr* meditation and recitation with a shaykh.[87] It is interesting to note that whereas during the classical age the focus was on teaching the theory of *taṣawwuf,* at the madrasah and the *jāmi'* mosque during the Mamlūk era, the emphasis was on the practice of *dhikr*. At the same time the *khanqah* began to incorporate teaching of the major religious sciences due to the increased desire of the *khanqah* students to study such knowledge. The subject most taught at the *khanqah* was the jurisprudence of the four legal schools. Berkey describes this evolution of the *khanqah*:

---

84 Ibid., pp. 17-18.

85 Conversely, the *zāwiyah* as well as being potentially the locus for a more popular and less disciplined form of *taṣawwuf* was also able to be the domain of a more authentic teaching since it was not controlled by outside interests - Ed.

86 Fernandes, op. cit., p. 27.

87 Ibid.

> ....the coming together of Sufism and the law can be traced on an institutional level...madrasah devoted to jurisprudence came to house Sufis and support their worship, while *khanqah* established for the benefit of mystics began to offer lessons in *fiqh* and related subjects.[88]

Due to the rise of Sufism and its acceptance as a part of 'formal Islam', the madrasah and the *khanqah* began slowly to blend into one institution. It can also be argued that the blending of educational and Sufi institutions mirrored the transformation of Sufism from just a mystical trend to the mainstream of intellectual life in Muslim society.[89] The Sufis who wished to learn from the *'ulamā'* normally resided at the *khanqah*, whereas the *zāwiyah* became the residence of more informal groups who tended to lean towards a more 'popular religion'. Hence, the *zāwiyah* became a place where sometimes reprehensible activities were reported to have taken place. For example, in 1359 CE, Sultan Ḥasan went to the *Zāwiyah Qalandariyyah*[90] and admonished the shaykh for not acting according to the Sunnah of the Prophet ﷺ.[91] By the fifteenth century, the most prominent *'ulamā'* and *fuqahā'* were also Sufi scholars.[92] The unification of 'formal Islam' and *taṣawwuf* that commenced during al-Ghazālī's time led, less than two centuries later, to the merger of the larger community of *'ulamā'* with Sufi scholarship.

The question arises as to whether this merger had a negative impact on the study of the sciences? Surprisingly, the most prestigious and advanced academic institutions in the late Mamlūk period

---

88 Berkey, op. cit., 2001, p. 4.

89 Ibid., p. 59.

90 *Qalandar* is almost synonymous with *dervish*, and thus denotes a loose affiliation of individuals often without connection to the teachings of the *sharī'ah* or *taṣawwuf*, and thus often associated with more heterodox expressions of the *dīn* - Ed.

91 Fernandes, op. cit., p. 102.

92 Berkey, op. cit., 2001, p. 102.

were *khanqahs* and madrasahs that combined Sufic and educational functions.[93] A problem appears to have occurred when the distinctions between the madrasah, *khanqah* and *zāwiyah* became blurred. During this period, some madrasahs became institutions with little or no teaching, for example, the Jawhar Lala Madrasah in Cairo was specifically a place where Sufis recited Qur'an, meditated and made *dhikr*. The only teaching was a class on Ḥanafī *fiqh* every three weeks, not the intellectual demand that most madrasahs had usually made of their students in the past.[94] As mentioned earlier, various popular elements such as magic, miracles attributed to false shaykhs and saint veneration created a populace who lacked aspects of independent reasoning and reliance on textual evidence. Saint veneration became an everyday occurrence during the Middle Period even for the upper classes. For example, the grave of Shaykh Ḥusayn ibn Ibrāhīm ibn 'Alī ibn al-Jākī (d. 1337), was visited for seventy years after his death; people made vows and offerings and continuously claimed that requests at the grave were answered. Days were put aside for visiting certain shaykhs' graves; for example, the tomb of Shaykh 'Abdullāh ibn Muḥammad ibn Sulaymān al-Manūfī al-Maghribī (d. 1348) was visited[95] every Saturday.[96] Mamlūk Sultans and dignitaries were also known to visit Sufi figures throughout the Middle Period; for example, an-Nāṣir Nāṣir-ad-Dīn Muḥammad ibn Qalāwūn (r. 1294-1295, 1299-1309 and 1310-1340) visited Shaykh al-Murshidī (d. 1337), since he was such a well known saint (*walī* of Allah).[97] Both authentic *taṣawwuf* and 'popular religion' became highly popular in both 'low' and the 'high' culture; in fact it is safe to assume that 'popular religion' had

---

93 Ibid., p. 84.

94 Berkey, op. cit., 2001, p. 84.

95 Visiting a tomb is not necessarily haram *per se*. Rather, it is visiting the tomb without the requisite *adab* that is reprehensible - Ed.

96 Shoshan, op. cit., p. 22.

97 Ibid., p. 76.

become a common ground between the élite and the common people by the late Mamlūk period. In the later period of the Mamlūk Sultanate, education seems to have suffered due to the Black Death, political instability, harsher taxes and the rise of popular religious sentiments amongst the masses, which contributed to the appearance of a rigid dichotomy between legalised 'formal Islam' and a 'popular religion' that was pseudo mystical and ambiguous.

Reflections

Was there a decline in education during this period? Yes. Decline occurred at the end of the Mamlūk period, but that is historically the case for all events such as the Mongol invasion in the case of the 'Abbasid Caliphate, or internal political instability and Black Death in the case of the Mamlūk Sultanate. They would naturally lead to decline in the intellectual fervour in society.

Perhaps the real question should instead be: how is one to measure phenomena such as success and decline? In previous chapters, the rise and success of education were seen to differ due to the historical conditions of the eras in question. Primarily, the success of education during the foundational period was based upon the formation of a believer, who would be able to attain *ta'līm, ta'dīb* and *tarbiyah,* i.e. he or she learnt the knowledge available to them and their actions conformed to spiritual, ethical and moral directives laid down in the Qur'an and Sunnah. During the next period of education, i.e. the formative period, the success of Islamic education depended not only on acquiring *ta'līm, ta'dīb* and *tarbiyah* (from the previous era) but the advance of various religious sciences and the rediscovery of ancient sciences. According to this study, the reason that the title *'The Golden Age'* was applied to the classical age was not merely on the basis of the success of the religious sciences (even given the prestige of religion in society), but on how successfully all the sciences were blended to create a society that was cultured, richly textured and religious at the same time. During this period, the definition of the attainment of *ta'līm* was very wide and this gave rise to scholars (*'ulamā'*) who had immense knowledge and specialisation regarding Qur'an, *ḥadīth*, mathematics, linguistics, geography, history, medicine, astronomy, etc. All sciences were seen as a part of the wider knowledge necessary to affirm belief in Allah ﷻ. This notion of the unity of science was so widespread that Ibn Rushd argued that anyone studying medicine, specifically anatomy could not but see the unity of Allah in it, "Anyone who studies anatomy will increase his faith in the Omnipotence and Oneness of God the Almighty."[98] Islamic education continued to stress the need for the attainment of *ta'dīb* and *tarbiyah* for the believer. In this way Ibn Sīnā, Ibn Rushd and al-Fārābī were as much a part of the success of Islamic education as al-Ghazālī, aṭ-Ṭabarī and ash-Shāfi'ī. From this point of view, the success of Islamic education was based on how the learned people of the classical Islamic world were living in the light of the inheritance of the Prophet Muḥammad ﷺ, by combining the religious and the secular as one in the *dīn* (although sometimes scholars and groups had conflicting theories).

According to Ibn Khaldūn's theory, it can also be argued that no civilisation can last forever. However, it is also true that no other civilisation on Earth has survived as long as the diverse Islamic civilisation that flourished along with its educational system for over a thousand years. Nevertheless, no matter how successful any education system might be, it will inevitably have weaknesses. This, of course, is also true for the 'Golden Age' and the Mamlūk period. There were certain aspects of the classical society that still evaded the touch of Islamic education or, stated in another way, there were certain issues that Islamic education had not been so successful with. Even though Islamic education had been slowly developing for the

98 Overbye, op. cit., p. 3

previous eight hundred years, there were certain issues of education that had not been resolved by the Muslims. In the political arena connected to the Sultan and the Caliphal court, no progress was made in curbing the fall of sultanates after their initial rise and period of glory, as described so vividly by Ibn Khaldūn. The caliphs of the Umayyad and the ʻAbbasid periods and the sultans of later periods continued at most to be outside the influence of political theory; Islamic education did not produce any political thinking that would provide an alternative to the various clashing sultanates during the period under discussion.[99] However, the second charge of so many historians, that Islamic intellectual sciences disappeared during this time, is baseless according to most evidence.

"No science is created in a vacuum" is a well known statement of Nasr and it is true of both Islamic and Western sciences. Islamic sciences grew out of the cosmological thought of Islamic civilisation and continued to be a major part of the Muslim world until the beginning of the eighteenth century, when the Muslim world was colonised and thus felt that the only way to compete with the West was to adopt Western science. Can science be divided according to religious worldviews when there is essentially only one universe? According to Nasr, science arises from particular circumstances with certain philosophical opinions about the nature of reality.[100] In the Islamic world these views were and are based upon the revelation, whereas in the West, scientific thinking is based upon the eighteenth century Enlightenment. This way of thinking influenced the Muslims during the nineteenth and early twentieth centuries, when they were colonised nations and brought forth modernist 'reformers'. Ibn Khaldūn (d. 1406) described such a process as early as the fifteenth century:

---

[99] M. G. S. Hodgson, *The Venture of Islam Vol. III*, (London: University of Chicago Press), 1974, p. 350.

[100] Overbye, op. cit., p. 5.

> The vanquished always wants to imitate the victor in his distinctive characteristics, his dress, his occupation and all his other conditions and customs....at this time, this is the case in Spain. The [Muslim] Spaniards are found to assimilate themselves to the Galician nations in their dress, their emblems, and most of their customs and conditions.... the intelligent observer will draw from this the conclusion that it is a sign of being dominated by others.[101]

Both Muslim and non-Muslim scholars have given many reasons for what they see as the steady decline of the Islamic world from the thirteenth century onwards. The major crisis of the Islamic world during this time was the Mongol destruction of Baghdad in 1258 CE, which was reported by contemporary Muslims as a turning point in Islamic history. It was to be the first time that the Muslim heartland was so thoroughly defeated and subjugated to non-Muslim domination.[102] There can be no doubt that one of the main effects of this crisis was the deterioration of Islamic education. All agree that when the Mongols launched their attack, the Islamic heartland suffered the death of many scholars and the destruction of numerous libraries, madrasahs, *bimaristans* and other educational institutions. It is also argued that even earlier than the Mongolian invasion, the 'Abbasid power had begun to devolve politically, and various sultans obtained control of local centres. Despite this, Islamic education was maintained along with the international network that the scholars had used throughout the Umayyad and 'Abbasid periods. In addition, the competitiveness of the various sultans and dynasties and their attempts to outdo each other also assisted the educational system. Others have argued that the decline began from the tenth century

---

101 Ibn Khaldun, op. cit., p. 116.
102 Lewis, op. cit., p. 15.

with the rise of the Fatimid Shiite power in the tenth and eleventh centuries, when they seized control of a large number of Sunni Muslim lands, such as Egypt and Iraq. In addition to this there was the invasion of the Crusaders from the West, challenging the Muslims in Syria and Palestine.[103] Many have further cited the growing distrust of the rational sciences during the Mamlūk period as the reason for the decline of the Islamic civilisation.

> During the Mamlūk regime it became a regular practice for the sultans to build both schools and Sufi monasteries, as part of a policy to combat Shiite heresy and pro-Fatimid tendencies by means of education. All these schools concentrated on the religious subjects within the Sunni context of the four orthodox schools. Philosophy and logic were forbidden. Mathematics and natural sciences were demeaned by the scholars as they were combined with philosophy and logic.[104]

Although there is evidence of the existence of suspicion towards the intellectual tradition, these reports are of isolated incidents caused by political and social instability that have unfortunately been highlighted as if they were the norm. In fact the majority of the *'ulamā'* of that time saw nothing inherently anti-rational about Islam and many important Islamic communities continued to be nourished by a continuous and vigorous philosophical discourse, as shown earlier in this chapter. The track record of Islamic education shows that it was able to integrate the majority of the sciences and their institutions in service of a distinct Islamic society for more than a thousand years

103 Stanton, op. cit., p. 184.
104 'Abdullāh Al-Fahad, *Classical Educational Thought, Curriculum and Methods of Teaching in Islam,* (PhD: Cardiff), 1998, p. 117.

and at the same time have an effective social order based upon the *sharīʿah.*

However, weaknesses arise in any society and this is also true of Islamic civilisation. Popular religion in many parts of the Muslim world during the last part of the Mamlūk period created an aura of superstitious belief that helped to reinforce a certain amount of intellectual stagnation.[105] It can be argued that 'popular religion' and the extreme reaction towards it, are inherited from this period. The rise of the Black Death, which decimated Cairo's population by striking more than fifty times between 1348 and 1517, created a dreary atmosphere. Death during this period became a communal affair where approximately three hundred people died daily, until the plague became so intense that the number rose to a thousand a day. Without doubt, this must have had a strong impact on people's psyches and it is not strange that 'popular religion', with its superstitions, magic and miraculous healing, was welcomed with open arms.[106] However, as Ibn Khaldūn argues:

> As long as a nation retains its solidarity, royal authority that disappears on one branch will, of necessity, pass to some other branch of the same nation.[107]

To the west and east of Egypt, three new Muslim Sultanates flourished, in which Islamic intellectual zeal grew once more for a number of centuries. During the time education in the Mamlūk world was fading away, the Ottomans in Anatolia, the Moghuls in India and the Safavids in Persia were simply beginning their intellectual endeavours, which led to the creation of three of the greatest pre-modern Muslim states.

---

105 Stanton, op. cit., p. 180.
106 Shoshan, op. cit., pp. 4-6.
107 Ibn Khaldun, op. cit., p. 115.

Until quite recently the expansion of Islam in Europe, Asia and Africa was a leading fact of world history. Moreover the consolidation of the Islamic heartlands into three great empires, the Ottoman, the Safavid and the Mughal occurred between 1400 and 1600, and gave Islam a firmer political-military framework than it had enjoyed since the collapse of the early Caliphate. Islam in short, continued to enjoy spectacular success in the late medieval and early modern times. Only since about 1700 has the balance between an expansive, aggressive Western European civilisation and a no less expansive aggressive Islamic civilisation shifted sharply against Muslims.[108]

[108] William H. McNeil and Marilyn Robinson Waldman, *The Islamic World*, (New York: Oxford University Press), 1973, pp. vi-vii.

Chapter Five

An Overview of Ottoman Education

The Seljuk Turks

This edition of the book does not have the scope to cover the social history of Islamic education in Moghul India and Safavid Persia. It will instead focus on the Ottomans, but again it is not pertinent to try to cover all of Ottoman educational history in such a small chapter. The Ottoman *dawlah* lasted for six hundred years and detailed research on its education system would require a separate volume. However, an overview of Islamic education during the Ottoman period is needed in order to demonstrate the evolution of Islamic education before the modern era. Hence, we will have a look at the overall development of the Ottoman education system during this period against the socio-historical background described in the earlier chapters of this book.

In order to understand the history of the Ottomans we have to first look at their relationship to the Seljuks. The Seljuks were nomadic Turks who had accepted Islam and settled down on the plains of Iran. Even before the fall of Baghdad in 1258 CE, the Seljuk Turks had begun to carve out a state for themselves in Iran, with Isfahan as their capital. In 1055 CE, the Seljuk Sultan Toghril Beg (r. 1038-1063) restored Baghdad to Sunni rule. Later on, his son Sultan Alp Arslan (r. 1063-1072) began the conquest of Anatolia (Modern Turkey) from the Byzantine Empire. After the Battle of Manzikert in 1071 CE, the Turkish tribes of Central Asia began to migrate in large numbers west into Anatolia. The Seljuks began to rule this land independently long before the fall of Baghdad, and by the thirteenth century had settled firmly in Anatolia, with Konya as their capital. This became known as the Sultanate of Rum, so-named because the land they now ruled had formally been known as Roman land for much of history. The period of the Sultanate of Rum in the twelfth and the thirteenth centuries is well recognised for its architecture, madrasahs, medical institutions and arts. By the end of the fourteenth century most of the Sultanate of Rum, like all other eastern parts of Islamdom, came under Mongol rule; by the fifteenth century this rule disintegrated into smaller emirates. With the Mongol invasion of Central Asia, other Turkish Muslim nomadic groups were also forced to expand towards Anatolia. By the time Mongol rule disintegrated, new Turkish principalities (emirates) had been founded, one of which was the state of Sultan Karaman Beylik, who made Konya his capital and inherited most of Seljuk authority. For a while all of the smaller Turkish Emirates continued to recognise the supremacy of the Sultan in Konya, but by the middle of the fourteenth century the Ottomans had become a force of their own.[1]

The Ottomans

Ertugul (d. ca. 1280) was the leader of one of these new frontier principalities and he had brought four hundred fighters for the service of the Seljuks. According to the chronicles of Karamani Mehmet Pasha,

1 Ira M. Lapidus, *A History of Islamic Societies,* (Cambridge: Cambridge University Press), 2002, pp. 248-250.

Ertugul's son Osman ('Uthmān in Arabic) succeeded his father in 1300 CE and was approved by his tribe.[2] Osman Bey (r. 1259-1326) expanded his principality westwards and made the Byzantine city Bursa his capital. Osman Ghazi, as he became known because of his vocation as a warrior, led a siege in 1301 CE against the former Byzantine capital Nicaea.[3] It was here that he gained fame for his victory over the Byzantine mercenary army. The Turcoman tribes flocked to his standard after this victory, and as in the other principalities, they took the name of their leader and became known as the *Osmanlis.*[4] Osman later crossed the straits to Gallipoli (1345), thus establishing a foothold in Europe, and invaded northern Greece, Macedonia, Bulgaria and the western Balkans. However, during a large part of the fourteenth century, the Ottoman *dawlah*[5] was simply a frontier principality that was advancing at the expense of the Byzantine Empire and on the ruins of the Seljuk Sultanate.[6]

Even though the Ottoman *dawlah* was constantly in a state of *jihād* during this time, it united Muslim Anatolia with the Christian Balkans. Thus, at the same time as being a Muslim *dawlah,* it became the protector of the Orthodox Church and millions of Christians. The Ottomans soon became a cosmopolitan polity, treating all creeds and races as its citizens. At first the main language was Persian and then Turkish

---

2 Rudi Paul Lindner, *Nomads and Ottomans in Medieval Anatolia,* (Bloomington: Indiana University), 1983, p. 19.

3 Later re-named Iznik.

4 Ottoman Turks in Turkish.

5 We follow the usage of Professor Maksudoglu who, in his *Osmanli History,* insisted to use the term *dawlah* rather than the more common 'empire', since the Ottomans never used that word about themselves, or 'state', since the state refers to an entity that came into existence in Europe at the Treaty of Westphalia and denotes a body that legislates, whereas the *dawlah* brings the legislation that Allah has revealed into being. Mehmet Maksudoglu, *Osmanli History (1289-1922) Based on Osmanli Sources),* (Research Centre IIUM: Kuala Lumpur), 1999.

6 Lapidus, op. cit., p. 250.

slowly became the language of the literary arts and administration. From the early 1300s, the Ottomans began their transformation from a frontier principality into a sultanate by annexing most of their neighbouring states, including most of the Seljuk land. According to Inalcik, the event that defined the establishment of the Ottoman Sultanate was the Opening (*fatḥ*)[7] of Constantinople to Islam in 1453 CE by Mehmet al-Fātiḥ (Muḥammad II).[8]

By 1453 CE, the Ottoman Sultanate was not simply a stronger *dawlah*, but also the one which had opened the city of Constantinople to Islam, by which act Sultan Mehmet II (r. 1432-1481) ushered in the era of the Ottoman Sultanate, the city becoming known henceforth as Istanbul. The opening of previously Byzantine land in Anatolia to Islam led to the eventual conversion of the population. Before the Ottoman *jihād*, the vast majority of Armenians, Syrians, Georgians and Greeks living in Anatolia had been Christian. By the time of Sultan Mehmet II, more than ninety percent of the Anatolian population were Muslims. Some of this was certainly due to the migration of Muslim Turks to Anatolia, but the greater part of the change was due to the Christian population converting to Islam. However, the Balkans were still majority Christian according to the Ottoman census taken in 1520-1530 CE, which shows nineteen percent of the Balkans being Muslim and the rest being Christian, with a small Jewish community. The rise of Muslim numbers in the Balkans occurred mostly in Thrace, Macedonia, Thessaly, Bosnia, Herzegovina, and Silistria.[9]

The Ottoman Sultanate did not surpass the Mamlūks politically until the sixteenth century, when Sultan Selim (r. 1512-20), the grandson of

---

7 Here we also follow Professor Maksudoglu who insisted on translating the Arabic term *fatḥ* not as 'conquest' but in a literal sense as 'Opening', i.e. the opening to Islam of the city of Constantinople.

8 Halil Inalcik, *The Ottoman Empire the Classical Age 1300-1600,* (London: Weidenfeld and Nicholson), 1973, p. 23.

9 Lapidus, op. cit., pp. 251-253.

Mehmet II, crushed the Mamlūk forces and annexed not only Egypt, but also the whole of Eastern Islamdom, including the three Holy Cities. In 1517 CE, at the conquest of Mamlūk Egypt and Syria, Sultan Selim initiated the transfer of the last 'Abbasid Caliph, al-Mutawakkil III, from Cairo (d. 1543) to Istanbul. The Syrian chronicler, Ibn Ṭūlūn (d. 1546), well known for his annals *Mufākahat al-Khillān,* began his annals with the name of the reigning 'Abbasid Caliph of Cairo. During the conquest of Cairo by the Ottomans, Ibn Ṭūlūn mentions that, that year the Caliph and the Commander of the Faithful, al-Mutawakkil III, had been sent under escort from Egypt to Istanbul by sea; later on in his annals Ibn Ṭūlūn added that the Caliph was now living in Istanbul.[10] Following this event, a popular story has been told about Sultan Selim marrying the daughter of al-Mutawakkil III and appropriating the title of Caliph after him. Historically it has been documented that Sultan Selim was the first Ottoman Sultan to have used the title '*Khādim al-Ḥaramayn* - Servant of the two Holy Sanctuaries'.[11] By the reign of his son Sulaymān (r. 1520-66), Ottoman Sultans became widely known as Caliphs. The Ottoman leader became recognised by his subjects as Ghazi, Caliph and Conquering Emperor.[12] This is also true for those from outside the Ottoman *dawlah*, as is evident from the incident in 1565 CE when the Acehnese Sultan 'Alā ad-Dīn Ri'āyah Shah al-Qahhār sent his ambassador to Istanbul from Indonesia to plead for military support against the Dutch; the ambassador addressed Sulaymān by the title of Caliph.[13]

Soon the Ottoman Caliphate stretched from North Africa to Madīnah and from Baghdad to Hungary. Even though the rulers of the

10 Holt, op. cit., pp. 501-507.

11 Virginia H. Aksan and Daniel Goffman (eds.), *The Early Modern Ottomans: Remapping the Empire,* (Cambridge: University of Cambridge Press), 2007, p. 94.

12 Lapidus, op. cit., p. 263.

13 Azyumardi Azra, *Islam in the Indonesian World: An Account of Institutional Formation,* (Indonesia: Mizan), 2006, p. 171.

Ottoman Caliphate claimed the title of Caliph, it is vital to point out that they were not the sole rulers of the Islamic world, primarily due to there being at least four major sultanates that were independent of the Ottoman *dawlah* during this period: the Moghul Sultanate in India, the Borneo Sultanate, the Golden Horde in the Russian steppes and the Safavid in Persia. It may still be argued that the Sunni sultanates did accept the Ottoman ruler as the symbolic Caliph and therefore the rightful protector of Makkah and Madīnah. A good example of this is the above request of the Aceh Sultanate for aid against the Dutch from the Ottoman Caliphate which was seen as the protector of the pilgrimage route.

The Caliph of Istanbul became the inheritor not only of the Byzantine Emperors, but also of the Baghdad Caliphs. The Ottoman Caliphate reached its zenith under Caliph Sulaymān (r. 1520-66), the son of Sultan Selim.[14] Historians claim that the Ottomans may have created the greatest Muslim polity in modern history and although this claim may be contested, the fact remains that it was the longest lived Muslim *dawlah* because it endured for six hundred and twenty-two years. There were thirty-six sultans/caliphs who reigned from 1300 to 1922; all direct descendants of Osman Ghazi.[15]

However, the purpose of this chapter is not to explore and analyse the political history of the Ottoman sultans and caliphs; it will try to establish the role of education within Ottoman society and the heritage of the Caliphate. The history of Ottoman education can be divided into two stages: early and late Ottoman education. The two periods can be further sub-divided into stages: within early Ottoman education there was the formative period, the classical period and the years of change or decline. There is no exact way of dividing these

---

14 V. J. Parry, *A History of the Ottoman Empire to 1730,* (Cambridge: Cambridge University Press), 1976, p. 79.

15 Ibid.

stages into historical years, since the likelihood is that they all overlap each other at certain junctures. However, for the purpose of research it is necessary to loosely fit them into a timeline. Accordingly, in the Ottoman *dawlah* the earliest work on education, i.e. the formative period, began during the early fourteenth century. The classical period of Ottoman education seems to have sprung from the political idea of the Ottoman *dawlah* as a sultanate, during and after the opening of Constantinople to Islam in 1453 CE. The early period of decline of Ottoman education seems to have commenced in the seventeenth century and by the eighteenth century, the Ottomans realised they had to take drastic measures regarding all aspects of their society, beginning with education.[16] The late stage of Ottoman education commences from this point of decline during the period known as the Enlightenment in Europe. To change the decaying structure of their education system, the Ottomans initiated the *Tanzimat* reforms.

Early Ottoman Education

> The parallels between the course of Turkish political history and the changes in the educational system are striking.[17]

The formative period, as stated earlier, commenced during the infancy of the Ottoman *dawlah*. Early on in its formative stage, the Ottoman *dawlah* adopted the traditions and the institutions of the previous Seljuk Sultanate including the education system. Scholars such as Karpat argue that the early Ottoman *dawlah* was not even labelled 'Ottoman' or 'Turkish' until the reign of Sultan Muḥammad I (d. 1421) because everything in the *dawlah* was in constant flux during the era of the frontier marches. It was only by the fifteenth century

---

16 Ihsanoglu and Gunergun, op. cit., pp. 40-45.

17 Kemal H. Karpat, *Ottoman Past and Today's Turkey*, (Leiden: Brill), 2000, p. 50.

that the state began to be labelled 'the sublime state of the *Osmanlis*' (*Devlet-i-ali-i-Osmani*).[18] Due to the slow centralisation of the frontier state, education began as a local enterprise.

The Ottomans inherited the madrasah from the Seljuk Turks. According to the chronicler Ashikpashazade (d. 1362), it was Sultan Orhan, the son of Osman Bey who had established his capital in Bursa, who established the first *medrese* (madrasah as pronounced in Turkish) in the city of Iznik (Nicaea) in 1331 CE, after its capture from the Byzantines.[19] Ibn Baṭūṭah, the adventurer, described his travels to the capital Bursa during the reign of Orhan; his narrative is one of the few first-hand accounts historians possess of the early Ottomans.

> We journeyed next to Bursa, a great city with fine bazaars and broad streets, surrounded by orchards and running springs. Outside it are two thermal establishments, one for men and the other for women, to which patients come from the most distant parts....The sultan of Bursa is Orhan Bek, son of Othman Chuk. He is the greatest of the Turkmen kings and the richest in wealth, lands and military forces and possess nearly a hundred fortresses which he is continually visiting for inspection and putting to rights....Orhan besieged it [Iznik] twelve years before capturing it and it was there that I saw him.[20]

Orhan Ghazi was the founder of the basic education system in his state; he established a *waqf* for the madrasah in Iznik and personally appointed the trustee of the institution. Like most scholars of that

---

18 Ibid., p. 5.

19 Inalcik, op. cit., 1973, pp. 3-8.

20 Ibn Batutah, *Ibn Batutah: Travels in Asia and Africa,* (London: Routledge and Kegan Paul), 1984, p. 136.

time, the trustee and lecturer of this *medrese,* Mevlana Davud al-Kayseri (1324-1351), was educated abroad in Egypt.[21] The sixteenth century scholar Tashkopruluzade (1495-1561), wrote extensively about Mevlana Davud al-Kayseri's appointment at the first Ottoman *medrese*:

> He [Davud] studied in his own land, and then journeyed to Cairo, to study Qur'anic exegesis, Traditions and the principles of Jurisprudence under its scholars. He distinguished himself in the rational sciences and acquired the science of *taṣawwuf*....Sultan Orhan built a madrasah in the city of Iznik. From what I have heard from reliable sources, this was the first *medrese* to be built in the Ottoman realms and he appointed Davud of Kayseri to its Professorship.[22]

The scholars of the early Ottoman period were all educated abroad; the majority of them carried out their higher studies in Mamlūk Syria and Egypt or in Seljuk Iran and Iraq. According to one statistic, of the majority of the one hundred and fifteen known scholars during this period in Anatolia, approximately forty-three percent were educated in Iran, which was not then the solidly *shīʿah* entity it has since become, with 23.4% receiving their education in Egypt, followed by Seljuk Anatolia where 14.7% scholars obtained their education in Transoxania; Syria and Iraq were listed as the places where the fewest number of scholars were educated. According to these statistics, and from studies of the residences of the authors who wrote the main textbooks that were used in early Ottoman madrasahs, it becomes

---

21 Ekmeleddin Ihsanoglu, *Medrese Education during Early Ottoman Period,* http://www.muslimheritage.com/uploads/madrasahs.pdf, (accessed 21/08/10).

22 Colin Imber, *The Ottoman Empire 1300-1650,* (London: Palgrave Macmillan), 2002, p. 226.

clear that certain Islamic centres, especially in Iran and Egypt, were the principal influences on the development of Ottoman education.[23]

The Ottoman *dawlah* differed intellectually a great deal from their counterparts in the Mamlūk domain. Whereas, in the Mamlūk domain during the fourteenth to sixteenth centuries, the notion of 'popular religion' was becoming 'rife', the Ottoman *dawlah* instead carried on the legacy of the two most famous intellectuals of Islam: al-Ghazālī (d. 1111) and ar-Rāzī (d. 1209). The majority of Ottoman scholars throughout the fourteenth to sixteenth centuries, developed under the ar-Rāzī and al-Ghazālī schools of thought. Thus, due to the characteristics of these schools, the educational system was influenced by a rational and practical outlook on religion. Inalcik explains that, "The Ottoman madrasahs followed the most broad–minded tradition of Sunni Islam."[24] The school of ar-Rāzī, for example, was established at the Ottoman *medrese* by Molla Shemseddin Mehmed Fenari (1350-1431), who was a professor at a Bursa madrasah, as early as the fourteenth century. This tradition continued all the way into the sixteenth century with Ebu's-Su'ud (Abu's-Su'ūd) Effendi (1490-1574) as its last prominent scholar during the reign of Sulaymān (r. 1520-66).[25] From the second half of the fifteenth century and then in later centuries, all scholars were educated within the Ottoman realms, which had incorporated much of the Middle East. Scholars such as Molla Husrev (d. 1480), Ibrāhīm of Aleppo (d. 1549), Ibn Nujaym (d. 1563) and Timitashi (d. 1595), who rose to prominence during the Ottoman Caliphate, were all educated at madrasahs in Ottoman lands.[26]

---

23 Ekmeleddin Ihsanoglu, *Medrese Education during Early Ottoman Period,* http://www.muslimheritage.com/uploads/madrasahs.pdf, (The Foundation for Science, Technology and Civilisation), (accessed: 21/08/10).

24 Inalcik, op. cit., 1973, p. 176.

25 Ihsanoglu and Gunergun, op. cit., p. 42.

26 Imber, op. cit., p. 227.

During the early days of the Ottoman *dawlah*, among the eighty-two madrasahs that were founded between 1331 and 1451, the *waqf* document of the individual *medrese* was normally based upon the teaching of religious and literary sciences. For example, the *waqf* document of the first *medrese* of Sultan Orhan only states that instruction is to be given to the students daily. In the endowment deed of the *medrese* in Bursa by Lala Sahin Pasha, it specified that every individual teacher should be eloquent and acquainted with knowledge, and that he would teach every day with the exception of established holidays. One endowment criterion of an Edirne *medrese* went as far as to stipulate that philosophical issues should be avoided at all costs. Nevertheless, there is evidence of medicine being studied at hospitals and observatories being built adjunct to madrasahs throughout this period. In this time, the building of madrasahs began to increase rapidly throughout the Ottoman Sultanate such that by the time of Mehmet II, a new way of ranking the different madrasahs was developed.[27] Numerous scholars were invited to work in the Ottoman Sultanate when new madrasahs were established. For example, during the reign of Murād II (r. 1421-1451), renowned scholars such as 'Alā ad-Dīn of Tus (d. 1482) and Fakhr ad-Dīn 'Ajamī from Persia, enhanced the reputation of many of the new madrasahs in Anatolia by accepting their professorships.

By the reign of Mehmet II (r. 1451-1481), the school of ar-Rāzī became the strongest influence within academia and Mehmed al-Fenari, an early Ottoman scholar of the above mentioned school, specialised in the science of logic, which became an essential part of the madrasah curriculum. Other scholars such as Molla Lutfi (d. 1494) and Mirim Celebi (d. 1525) were great contributors to the sciences

---

[27] M. Bilge, *Ilk Osmanli Medreseleri*, (Istanbul: Istanbul Universitesi Edebiyat Fakultesi), 1984, pp. 20-21.

of mathematics and scholastic theology. Ibn Kemal (1468-1534) was another scholar who influenced Ottoman thought by his writings on history, theology and jurisprudence. Consequently, this style of madrasah in the formative period continued to be established at Iznik, Bursa and Edirne until Constantinople was opened to Islam by Mehmet II. In total, twenty-five madrasahs were built in Bursa, thirteen in Edirne and four in Iznik.[28] As stated earlier, the greatest influence on early Ottoman education was from Iranian educational centres. In fact, the main language that was used for a long time in the Ottoman Sultanate was neither Turkish nor Arabic, but Persian. However, it has to be remembered that it was common for Ottoman scholars to know all three languages, i.e. Arabic, Persian and Turkish.[29]

It was during the reign of Mehmet II, that the Ottoman *dawlah* acquired a centralised structure, which had far-reaching consequences for pedagogy in the Ottoman *dawlah*. After the opening of Constantinople to Islam in 1453 CE, Mehmet II immediately converted eight churches and monasteries into madrasahs. The most significant change in Ottoman education was when he established the *külliye,* a mosque complex, which had within it numbers of madrasahs. The Fātiḥ *Külliye* had within it eight higher madrasahs, which surrounded the Fātiḥ Mosque, each entitled the *Sahn Semâniye medrese*. Behind the *Semâniye* madrasahs were eight further smaller madrasahs known as *Tetimme.* In addition, a *kuttāb* (known as *Dār at-Ta'līm*) was constructed beside the western door of the Fātiḥ Mosque for primary education. According to the legal document drawn up for the Fātiḥ *Külliye,* the complex also housed a hospital, a library and a kitchen for the use of students and staff.[30] This *külliye* needs to be recognised as another

[28] Ihsanoglu and Gunergun, op. cit., p. 38.

[29] Carl Brockelman, *History of Islamic Peoples,* (London: Routledge and Kegan Paul), 1949.

[30] Ihsanoglu and Gunergun, op. cit., p. 38.

development of the madrasah whose long history began during the eleventh century.

A distinct curriculum, differing from the previous one, and a new hierarchical structure was introduced into the madrasahs. In the charter of the Fātiḥ *Külliye* there is a clause that specifies that teachers who want to be employed in its madrasahs have to cover teaching in both religious studies and rational sciences. Sciences other than those of the *dīn* that were mentioned in the new curriculum were: grammar, syntax, logic, rhetoric, geometry, astronomy, philosophy and mathematics. This is clearly a move away from previous madrasahs that had rather ambiguous clauses in their endowment deeds with regards to the teaching of non-*sharīʿah* sciences.[31]

In addition to the inclusion of literary and rational sciences, the charter stipulates a hierarchy of the madrasahs based upon the salaries of the teachers. The lecturers at the *Tetimme* madrasahs received lower salaries than the lecturers at the *Sahn medrese,* who were considered the most distinguished of the *ʿulamāʾ*. Furthermore, lecturers at the madrasah were paid salaries according to their expertise. A student who had completed his study at the *Tetimme medrese,* which was referred to as *Musila-i-Sahn* (Preparatory to the *Sahn*), was therefore able to continue his studies, if he wished, at the *Sahn medrese.* Across the Sultanate there were other lower levels of madrasahs, such as the *Dahil, Hasiye-i Tecrid, Miftah* and *Telvih.* The *Dahil* madrasahs were normally constructed by the Sultan or the mothers and daughters of sultans. These *medrese* ranked on the same level as the *Tetimme* madrasahs.[32]

This hierarchical formation of the madrasahs during Muḥammad al-Fātiḥ's time continued, with the *Aya Sofia medrese* being at the highest

---

31 Franz Babinger, *Mehmet the Conqueror*, (Princeton: Princeton University Press), 1978, p. 296.

32 Ihsanoglu and Gunergun, op. cit., p. 40.

level, until the establishment of the Suleimaniye *Külliye* in 1557 CE. After students had completed their studies at the *Sahn medrese, Aya Sofia medrese* or in later centuries, at the Suleimaniye *Külliye* with the status of *danismend*, they were eligible to commence their teaching careers at a higher education institution. The madrasahs seem to have been classified according to the level of instruction provided in them; the text books that were used at the madrasahs became the labels that identified the various madrasahs. According to Ugur, although the curriculum of the various levels of madrasahs was uniform throughout the Ottoman *dawlah*, the higher madrasahs were not spread throughout the land. For the highest level of the madrasah, students needed to come to the heart of the Ottoman *dawlah*, Istanbul.[33]

Why did Mehmet II include the rational and literary sciences in the madrasah curriculum and establish a hierarchical system for the madrasahs throughout the Ottoman *dawlah*? The Ottoman historian Inalcik reasons that Sultan Muḥammad's ambition was to make Istanbul the leading metropolis of the world and this becomes more evident with the various reforms that Mehmet II established in Istanbul. First of all, he re-populated the city with Jews, Christians and Muslims from various parts of the Ottoman *dawlah*. He extended his recognition to the Greek Patriarchate of Istanbul, built commercial centres and boosted trade in the city. Before the opening to Islam, Constantinople's population was approximately thirty thousand and after the conquest, the population rose to around seventy thousand.[34] In addition, according to Lekesiz, Mehmet II sought to establish the city as the religious and scientific centre of the Muslim world.[35] Mehmet II

---

33 Ali Ugur, *The Ottoman 'Ulema in the Mid-17th Century,* (Berlin: Klaus Swarz Verlag), 1986, p. xxxix.

34 Halil Inalcik and Donald Quataert (eds.), *An Economic and Social History of the Ottoman Empire*, (Cambridge: Cambridge University Press), 1997, p. 18.

35 Ihsanoglu and Gunergun, op. cit., p. 40.

saw the rational and literary sciences as important tools to raise the profile of the Ottomans as a leading state in the world. The history of Baghdad and its intellectual heritage must also have been very fresh in the minds of the Muslims during this period. With regards to the hierarchical system of the madrasahs, it seems that Mehmet II intended to centralise the *dawlah*, thus making the education system into a hierarchy to fit the wider picture of governance. The main motive behind the training at this point was to have qualified functionaries who would work at religious and judicial administrative institutions.

There is historical evidence that points towards Sultan Muḥammad's personal interest in scholarship. He is known to have favoured the company of scholars and poets and also seems to have made appointments of lecturers based on the merits that he himself noted down. He was therefore, during his own time, known as a patron of all the sciences.[36] His personal interest in scholarship and its standards supports a wider picture of a ruler, who not only patronised education for political purposes but was also something of an educationalist himself.

It was during the early sixteenth century in the reign of the Caliph Selim I (r. 1517-1520), the grandson of Mehmet II, that the political status of the Ottoman Sultanate changed from a simple sultanate to the Caliphate which filled the vacuum left by the Mamlūks. At the beginning of Sultan Selim's reign, Anatolia to the west of the Euphrates was predominantly a Muslim country settled by immigrant Turks or converted native populations. Previous centuries had seen a widespread Islamisation of Anatolia and certain parts of the Balkans.[37]

[36] Babinger, op. cit., p. 296.

[37] Inalcik, op. cit., 1997, p. 27.

The scholar Tashkopruluzade Aḥmad (1495-1561) took upon himself the task of defining knowledge and classifying the various sciences, which provided the starting point for madrasah learning in the Ottoman realm. Following in al-Ghazālī's (d. 1111) footsteps, Tashkopruluzade divided knowledge into four stages: written, oral, intellectual and spiritual. The spiritual sciences were further subdivided into branches of theoretical, practical, religious and rational sciences. Here is the full outline:

1. The calligraphic sciences: writing implements, styles of writing etc.
2. The oral sciences: the Arabic language and phonetics, lexicography, etymology, grammar and syntax, rhetoric, prosody, poetry, composition, history and the other literary sciences.
3. The intellectual sciences: logic and dialectics.
4. The spiritual sciences:

    i. The theoretical rational sciences: general theology, natural sciences, mathematics.
    ii. The practical rational sciences: ethics, political science.

        (a) The theoretical religious sciences: the Qur'an and the *ḥadīth*, and the sciences devoted to their interpretation, i.e. Qur'anic exegesis, the study of *ḥadīth*, Islamic theology and the principles of Islamic law and jurisprudence.
        (b) The practical religious sciences: practical ethics, etiquette, *iḥtisāb*[38] and all the subjects relating to Muslim life and worship.[39]

---

38 *Iḥtisāb* is sometimes known as the office of the *ḥisbah*, which was responsible for the oversight of markets to ensure that standards such as weights and measures were observed and that fraudulent practices such as usury were not practised.

39 Adapted from Inalcik, op. cit., 1973, p. 165.

A madrasah student of this period was expected to study all the above sciences, but before studying any other subject, every student was expected to master the religious sciences and the Arabic language which would lead the student to study with a *muderris,* a scholar of recognised authority in the religious and spiritual sciences.[40]

Classical Ottoman Education

The whole process of centralisation started by Sultan Mehmet II reached its peak during the Caliph Sulaymān's reign (r. 1520-1560). This period saw, without doubt, the most well organised, hierarchical, bureaucratic system of education of any Islamic *dawlah.* As Yasar points out:

> The extraordinary bureaucratic hierarchy extended from the level of professorship of a small provincial *medrese* to that of the *Sahn* professorship in the Caliphal capital, and from the *Sahn* professorship to the Caliphate's highest *'ulamā'* position, that of the '*Shaykh ul-Islam.*'[41]

The tables[42] below show the increasing number of madrasahs being built throughout the Ottoman lands during the first three centuries of the Ottoman *dawlah*; this process accelerated during the reign of the Caliph Sulaymān.

40 Inalcik, op. cit., 1973, p. 166.

41 Ahmet Yasar Ocak, (Hacettepe University, Ankara), *The Ottoman Empire and Islam Framework for a New Interpretation*, http://humanities.uchicago.edu/orgs/institute/sawyer/archive/islam/ocak.html, (accessed: 07/01/12).

42 Adapted from Ekmeleddin Ihsanoglu, Medrese *Education during Early Ottoman Period,* http://www.muslimheritage.com/uploads/madrasahs.pdf, (The Foundation for Science, Technology and civilisation), (accessed: 21/08/10).

City/ Region	14th century	15th century	16th century
Iznik	4	0	0
Bursa	19	11	6
Edirne	1	20	10
Istanbul	0	23	113
Anatolia	12	31	32
Balkans	4	12	18
Syria	0	0	3
Hijaz	0	0	6
Yemen	0	0	1
Total Madrasah	**40**	**97**	**189**

Reigning Sultans/Caliphs	Madrasahs Founded
Orhan Ghazi (r. 1326-1359)	10
Murād I (r. 1359-1389)	7
Bayezid I (r. 1389-1402)	23
Chelibi Mehmed (r. 1402-1421)	7
Murād II (r. 1421-1451)	38
Mehmed II (r. 1451-1481)	30
Bayezid II (r. 1481-1512)	33
Selim I (r. 1512-1520)	8
Suleyman I (r. 1520-1566)	106
Selim II (r. 1566-1574)	17
Murād III (r. 1574-1595)	42
Mehmed III (r. 1595-1603)	5
Uncertain	24
Total	**350**

Distribution of Madrasahs across the European part of the Ottoman Caliphate	**Madrasahs**
Greece	189
Bulgaria	144
Albania	28
Bosnia-Herzegovina, Croatia and Montenegro	105
Kosovo, Macedonia, Serbia, Slovenia and Voyvodina	134
Romania	9
Hungary	56
Total	**665**

By the time of the Caliph Sulaymān, the Ottoman capital Istanbul and other major cities such as Edirne and Bursa had become great cities not only with regards to trade and education, but also other public works and developments such as bridges, roads, canals, hospitals and madrasahs. According to an official Ottoman survey in 1546 CE, Istanbul had two thousand five hundred and seventeen *awqāf* (*waqfs*) devoted to Istanbul alone and it had also become a multicultural, multi-faith metropolis; as early as 1477 CE, the Jews formed the third largest section of the population after the Muslims and the Orthodox Greek Christians. By the mid-seventeenth century the city's ovens consumed two hundred and fifty tons of wheat daily, and two thousand ships carrying food docked in Istanbul every year.

> Wheat, rice, sugar and spices from Egypt; livestock, cereals, edible fats, honey, fish and hides from the regions north of the Black Sea; cereals and hides from Thessaly and Macedonia; ....and other Mediterranean products from Morea and the Aegean islands continually poured into Istanbul.[43]

[43] Inalcik, op. cit., 1973, p. 145.

The road systems were as sophisticated as the sea transport during this era of the Ottoman Caliphate. Not since the Roman period had Europe had such an organised road system by which, for example, one could cover the distance from Istanbul to Belgrade in fifteen days as the Caliph Selim II (r. 1566-1574) did in 1566 CE. In most of Anatolia, wagons with people, food and goods could be seen travelling up and down the nation and even further afield. There were caravans to and from Istanbul and far off places such as Poland, Iran, Basra, Aleppo, Ragusa, Belgrade, and of course, Arabia. On these routes caravanserai, inns and hostels, which were maintained by *waqf*, were established for travellers. As early as 1443 CE, Sultan Murād II (r. 1421-1451) had constructed a bridge near Edirne over the River Ergene towards Bulgaria; on the other side he built an inn, bazaar, mosque and madrasah, and revenue from the inn and bazaar maintained the bridge, the mosque and the madrasah. For safety on the roads, many sultans and caliphs established *yayas* or farmer-soldiers as a means of protection for travellers. Later on, many of these small stations grew to become towns and their madrasahs became well known as educational centres.[44] In this environment, the *Ahi* order grew, which was a social organisation in the towns, and they developed their own hospice for travellers. In the fourteenth century Ibn Baṭūṭah described them vividly:

> An *ahi* in their idiom is a man whom the assembled members of his trade, together with other of the young unmarried men and those who have adopted the celibate life, choose to be their leader. The *ahi* builds a hospice and furnishes it with rugs, lamps and what other equipment it requires. His associates work during the day and bring him their collective earnings and with this they buy fruit, food and

[44] Ibid., pp. 140-150.

> other things needed for consumption in the hospice. If during the day a traveller alights at the town, they give him lodgings with them.[45]

In this metropolitan society the madrasahs were the universities of the Ottoman Caliphate, producing scholars of religion and science.

The Caliph Sulaymān was the last person to develop the *medrese* system nearly five hundred years after its establishment by Nizam al-Mulk in the eleventh century. He made an important change to the hierarchy of the Ottoman madrasahs that Sultan Mehmet Fātiḥ (Muḥammad II) had instituted during the fifteenth century. From the late sixteenth century, the Suleimaniye *Külliye* ranked as the highest *medrese* complex of the Ottoman Caliphate. Surrounding the famous Suleimaniye mosque, the Caliph Sulaymān established four general madrasahs and two specialised madrasahs, one for *ḥadīth* and one for medicine. A hospital, kitchen and a pharmacy were added to this complex. These madrasahs were given the highest ranking in the Ottoman Caliphate and the most successful scholar would rise through the ranks by teaching first at the provincial colleges, eventually leading to a post in one of the madrasahs of the Suleimaniye *Külliye*.[46]

During his reign, the Caliph Sulaymān introduced the first legal educational code (*kanûnnâme*) which highlighted the need for an education that explained the creation of Allah ﷻ, informed the subjects of an orderly state and taught people to comprehend the universe created by Allah, furthermore, that it would include the teachings of the prophets in order to benefit humanity. Ottoman administrators highlighted the importance of the pursuit of sciences and their wisdom, and a necessary explication of this through religious virtue and the *sharīʿah*. The success of the balance and the rigour with which

45 Ibn Batutah, op. cit., p. 419.
46 Imber, op. cit., p. 230.

the religious sciences and the rational sciences were taught during this era is easily seen through the description of the curriculum of the Ottoman madrasah of that period by the contemporary scholar Ihsanoglu:

> During the course of their education, the books a student would read were ordered as follows. The first three were morphology (*sarf*), syntax (*nahiv*) and logic (*mantik*). The last two were *ḥadīth* and commentary on the Qur'an (*tefsîr*). In between the first three studies and the last two, subjects such as elocution (*âdâb-i bahs*), preaching (*vaaz*), rhetoric (*belâgat*), study of philosophical theology (*kelâm*), philosophy (*hikmet*), jurisprudence (*fikih*), inheritance (*ferâiz*), tenets of faith (*akaid*) and legal theory and methodology (*usûl-i fikih*) were pursued.[47]

In addition to the above sciences, sciences such as arithmetic, geometry, algebra and astronomy and classical physics were also taught in Ottoman madrasahs. According to studies of autobiographies of this period by Ihsanoglu, these subjects were studied by students after philosophy and before the advanced study of Qur'anic exegesis. Below is another description of the madrasah curriculum of this period, this time focusing upon the rational sciences:

> There is a book titled *Eskâl-i Te'sis* in geometry at the *iktisar* level that they would read. Following that, they would read Euclid with its proofs at the *istiksa* level. For arithmetic at the *iktisar* level there is *Bahâiyye*, which they would read. Subsequently, they would report on *Ramazan Efendi* and *Culli*,

[47] Ekmeleddin Ihsanoglu, *Madrasahs of the Ottoman Empire,* FSTC Limited, April 2004, p. 14, http://www.muslimheritage.com/uploads/madrasas.pdf, (accessed: 18/03/2011).

which were close to the *iktisad* level. Because astronomy involves the use of the imaginative powers and supposition and is therefore more difficult than geometry, they would study that later as a separate subject. It is offered at the appropriate level. It is common knowledge that scholars do not weary of the temperament of students and always give Tuesdays and Fridays off from classes in order to encourage them in their studies. Students use those two days for the preparation of materials they need and during the summertime they go off on trips and picnics. Even there they do not remain idle, but undertake discussions of arithmetic, geometry, astrolabes, land surveying, Indian, Coptic and Ethiopian arithmetic, *parmak hisâbi* (abacus), mechanics and other such sciences which do not require independent lessons. During the winter, they engage in conversation, devote themselves to solving puzzles (*muammâ*) and riddles, to *mukadarat* (measuring and comparing), to history, poetry, prosody and to classical *dîvân* poetry. Some of them are occupied with the occult sciences, but the teachers do not allow them to follow such pursuits because such subjects occupy too much of their time.[48]

The Period of Crisis

From the fourteenth century to the seventeenth century, the Ottoman Caliphate had kept a balance between the rational and the religious sciences; it had done exceptionally well in comparison to any other contemporary state to create a successful centralised education system. During this period, the Ottoman education was recognised for

48 Ekmeleddin Ihsanoglu, *Madrasahs of the Ottoman Empire,* FSTC Limited, April 2004, p. 14, http://www.muslimheritage.com/uploads/madrasas.pdf, (accessed: 18/03/2011).

its *ta'līm* (imparting knowledge). Numerous scholars had distinguished themselves in subjects such as mathematics, medicine, astronomy and scholastic theology. There were also numerous books on *tarbiyah* and *ta'dīb*, exemplifying the good behaviour and the manners of the believers. This period was recognised as well for the Sufi orders' quest for spiritual enlightenment; Jalāl ad-Dīn Rumi (d. 1273) and his legacy of teachings on Islamic spiritualism stand out during this era. At the same time the Ottoman *dawlah* was politically stable and militarily successful, dominating trade in the Middle East and the Mediterranean; economically it was relatively self sufficient. During these three centuries all this stability and success led to large public works by the centralised *dawlah*, in addition to private wealthy endowments of hospitals, schools, roads, bridges and madrasahs. However, by the seventeenth century a number of social, political and economical factors began to lead much of the Ottoman *dawlah* apparatus and its institutions, including education, into a lengthy decline.

By the eighteenth century, the central Ottoman *dawlah* began to increasingly lose previously conquered territories; at the same time economically the Ottoman *dawlah* was losing trade since European powers had been able to create direct links with India and Iran, which had once been only accessible through Ottoman lands. The discovery of the Americas also opened up new sea routes for the European powers which gradually bypassed Ottoman trade routes that had been controlled and managed successfully by the Ottoman Caliphate for three centuries. At the same time, silver from the Americas flooded the Ottoman market which led to inflation in Ottoman society.[49] The final blow to the Ottoman economy was the rise of industrialisation in England during the early seventeenth century, because of which

[49] See: Suraiya Faroqhi, Bruce McGowan, Donald Quataert and Sevket Pamuk, *An Economic and Social History of the Ottoman Empire 1600-1914: Volume 2*, (Cambridge: Cambridge University Press), 1997.

mass production through machines meant that handmade goods lost their attractiveness in the market since the prices of manufactured goods dropped. During the early nineteenth century, the European powers convinced the Galata bankers within the Ottoman Caliphate to persuade Mahmut II (r. 1808-1839) to permit the entrance of European products into the market.[50] However, even with falling trade and the economic crisis during this period, the Ottoman *dawlah* was the only state of that size which never contracted a foreign debt, until the 1850s that is.

During this period of crisis many Ottoman scholars began to write about the decline of education in the Ottoman Caliphate. In fact the Ottoman scholar Tashkopruluzade was criticising the declining popularity of mathematics and the falling standards of scholastic theology as early as the middle of the sixteenth century.[51] His criticism was that most of the scholars considered themselves learned after reading a few 'handbooks'; they did not attach importance to theology, Qur'anic exegesis or non-religious sciences. On the other hand, they had become obsessed with poetry, composition and anecdotes that were used to acquire worldly possessions.[52] It is evident from the writings of the seventeenth century Ottoman scholars Katib Chelebi (d. 1658) and Koci Bey (d. 1650) that the rational and the physical sciences were being taught during the seventeenth century; however, these scholars also criticised how these sciences were losing prominence during this period.[53] Katib Chelebi wrote concerning the lack of rational sciences:

---

50 Arikan Tarik Saygii, 'Impacts of Wrong Financial Decisions on the Collapse of an Empire: The Ottoman Case', *African Journal of Business Management,* Vol. 3, April 2009, pp. 151-159.

51 Francis Robinson, 'Ottoman-Safavids-Mughals', *Journal of Islamic Studies,* Vol. 8, No. 1, January 1997, p. 156

52 Inalcik, op. cit., 1973, p. 179.

53 Ihsanoglu and Gunergun, op. cit., p. 41.

> But many intelligent people remained as inert as rocks, frozen in blind imitation of the ancients. Without deliberation, they rejected and repudiated the new sciences. They passed for learned men, while all the time they were ignoramuses, fond of disparaging what they called 'the philosophical sciences' and knowing nothing of earth or sky. The admonition '*Have they not contemplated the kingdom of heaven and Earth?*' made no impression on them; they thought 'contemplating the world and firmament' meant staring at them like cows.[54]

Gelibolulu Mustafa 'Alī Efendi (d. 1599) argued that the decline of the madrasahs was because of a lack of interest in scholarly studies, decline in the writing of scholarly works, nepotism amongst senior scholars, bribes in the educational profession and no real differentiation between scholars and opportunist charlatans masquerading as scholars.[55] The educational standard had fallen so much that when the scholar Takiyyuddin Mehmed (d. 1578) built an observatory and an astronomical clock which matched the most advanced observatory (Tycho Brahe's) in Europe, the scholars saw it as blasphemy and used an outbreak of plague as a pretext to raze it to the ground in 1580 CE. In 1716 CE, 'Alī Pasha's books were confiscated, and the Shaykh al-Islam of that period issued a *fatwa* against libraries having books on astronomy, history and philosophy.[56] This fanatical way of understanding religion also blocked contemporary technology coming from Europe.

54 Robinson, op. cit., pp. 151-184.

55 Ekmeleddin Ihsanoglu, *Madrasahs of the Ottoman Empire,* FSTC Limited, April 2004, p. 15, http://www.muslimheritage.com/uploads/madrasas.pdf, (accessed: 18/03/2011).

56 Inalcik, op. cit., 1973, pp. 179-181.

It is well known that the first Arabic script printing press in the Ottoman Empire was not used until 1726 CE, when it was specifically allowed by a *fatwa* from the Mufti. However, this technology had been available since 1493 CE in Istanbul. The question arises as to why it was not used earlier? It may be interesting to compare this scenario to the introduction of paper to the Islamic world during the eighth century. The Muslims came across the idea of paper-making at the Chinese border and they applied it in their society with zeal. This enterprise[57] was not only successful in its own right but was a contributing factor to the rise of the translation movement and of advanced scholarship in the Islamic world. Unfortunately, this same zeal was not applied to the printing press, and it took the Islamic world two hundred years to reach the conclusion that they needed it.

On the other hand, the success of the Reformation and the rise of scholarship in Christian Europe were inseparably linked to the success of the printing press. What is even more amazing with regards to the Ottoman Empire is that the *fatwa* of the eighteenth century permitting the printing press was specific about which books were permissible to publish, such as dictionaries, and books on logic and natural sciences. These subjects were listed under the *'ulūm-i-'aliyye* (auxiliary sciences) in a publication programme that preceded the above *fatwa*. Thus, *ḥadīth*, *fiqh* and religious books were excluded. It seems that the *fatwa* may have been strongly influenced by a group of calligraphers, scholars and scribes who wanted to resist the printing press even as late as the eighteenth century; thus, the press only existed for nineteen years until it was shut down, and it was only fifty years later that it would recommence operations, but by then the Ottoman *dawlah* had fallen into a long stagnation.[58] As a result of

---

57 See chapter 3.
58 Ihsanoglu and Gunergun, op. cit., p. 27.

the strong opposition to any change, slowly but steadily, the Ottoman *dawlah* closed in on itself.

What was the reason for such a decline when only a century earlier education had reached its peak? According to Ugur, even though the organisation of education had become structured and hierarchical, corruption and nepotism had become so widespread that virtually any post was open to anyone as long as they had the proper connections and enough money.[59] Another argument put forward by Tashkopruluzade for the decline of Ottoman education was conservatism in religion that was against *taṣawwuf*, poetry, intellectual sciences and music and considered them as impious; he believed that these so-called scholars exploited people's ignorance to lead them astray. It is argued that one of the strongest proponents of this thought was Mehmed of Birgi (1522-1573), and this way of thinking was continued by his student Kadizade (d. 1635) and his followers known as *fakis*.[60] This seems to be reminiscent of the conflict between orthopraxy and popular folk religion that arose during the Mamlūk period. There is no doubt that the strict conservatism of Mehmed of Birgi originated as a reaction to the rise of popular religion and the changing times in the Ottoman *dawlah*. The historian Idris of Bitlis (d. 1520) wrote about contemporary popular religion in the Ottoman *dawlah* during his period; he warned against such people as Shaykh Bedreddin and his followers specifically thus: "He thought of himself as the *Mehdi*...his own latitudinarian sect would make many forbidden things lawful."[61] According to Idris, Bedruddin gathered thousands of ignorant and simple people who followed him just as many had followed such leaders during the Mamlūk period.[62]

59 Ugur, op. cit., pp. lxx-lxxi.
60 Inalcik, op. cit., 1973, p. 185.
61 Ibid., p. 189.
62 Inalcik, op. cit., 1973, p. 190.

Thus, popular religion transcended the different classes of the Ottoman Empire. Again, as in the Mamlūk era, the two opposite poles of 'fanatical Islam' and 'popular religion' created a rigid dichotomy between 'state Islam', which began to be represented as a religion that was official and legalistic, and mystical and superstitious 'popular religion'. However, this was not the only reason for the decline of Ottoman education; there were numerous other factors, as Inalcik argues:

> As factors paving the way for the crisis of the late sixteenth and early seventeenth centuries, we can cite the influence of increased population, Europe's new military technology and the monetary and financial crisis.[63]

It is obvious that numerous events occurred to influence the educational establishment in the Ottoman *dawlah*. Further causes for the crisis cited by numerous Ottoman historians are: civil war between rival princes, such as the event in the middle of the sixteenth century involving Prince Mustafa and Prince Bayezid, the interference of different scholars at this time in the administration of the nation, and again the war with Iran, the crisis spiralling even further out of control due to pressure on the already burdened financial state of the Ottoman *dawlah*. Disunity amongst the *'ulamā'*, which grew from a very competitive society, nepotism, growing corruption and the intrigue that competition bred, continued to lead to the lowering of the standards of education.[64] All of this seems to have reinforced, on one hand, a conservative and rigid 'religion' and on the other hand, a superstitious and ambiguous 'popular religion'.

---

63 Inalcik, op. cit., 1997, p. 22.

64 Ibid., pp. 22-25.

Education in the *Tanzimat* and the Hamidian Periods

By Mahmut II's reign (r. 1808-1839), there was a feeling in the Ottoman lands that the traditional ways had to be abandoned to make way for 'advanced' European ways. Mahmut II led the way to modernisation by beginning to dress like a European monarch, and his son and successor Abdul Majid I (r. 1839-1861) transferred his residence from the Topkapi Palace, which had been built by Mehmet II in 1465 CE, to the new European styled Dolmabahçe Palace. Western sofas and tables replaced the old divans and it seems that the turban was for the first time banned in court and the fez endorsed instead.[65] Even then, the Ottoman Caliphate was the only contemporary empire not yet to have contracted foreign debt.

By 1838 CE, there was agreement amongst the Ottoman leadership that reform was necessary throughout the Caliphate. A reform edict was introduced with the name *Tanzimat Fermani.* The same year, major trade agreements were made between the Ottomans and Great Britain and France. In both agreements, the Ottoman Caliphate dropped its traditional customs tax on French and British goods coming into the nation to three percent. Since Ottoman subjects were not producing anything on a mass scale, the market was flooded with imported French and British goods; it led to cheaper products from the West causing the disappearance of traditional craftsmen and producers, who could not afford to compete with the new foreign goods.[66]

In the final year of Sultan Mahmut's reign, an imperial edict (*Hatt-i Sherif of Gulhane*) was drafted to proclaim his commitment to modernisation.[67] With the death of Mahmut II in 1839 CE, the era of

---

65 S. J. Shaw and E. K. Shaw, *History of the Ottoman Empire and Modern Turkey,* (Cambridge: Cambridge University Press), 1995, p. 49.

66 Arikan Tarik Saygii, 'Impacts of Wrong Financial Decisions on the Collapse of an Empire: The Ottoman Case', *African Journal of Business Management,* Vol. 3, April 2009, p. 151-159.

67 Ibrahim Vehbi Baysan, *State Education Policy in the Ottoman Empire during the Tanzimat Period,* (PhD: University of Manchester), 2004, p. 226.

the *Tanzimat* commenced. Thus, *Tanzimat,* which in Turkish means the era of reorganisation or reform, targeted not only education but all spheres of the state. These reforms were instituted from 1839 until 1876 CE under two of the Ottoman Caliphs: Abdul Majid I (r. 1839-1861) and Abdul Aziz (r. 1861-1876).[68] The reorganisation of education was not the priority of the *Tanzimat*; in fact the first reforms occurred in the political and financial establishments.[69]

Due to major changes to the financial system in the Ottoman *dawlah* in 1839 CE, with the introduction of paper money and the inability to deal with its governance, the Ottoman *dawlah* fell more and more into financial crisis. By 1854 CE, the Ottoman Caliphate became involved, along with France and Great Britain, in the Crimean War against Russia, which forced their hand to begin a foreign loan. This foreign loan came from France and England through the international market controlled by Western powers. The whole of the *Tanzimat* period (1839-1876) was funded by foreign entities with continuous attempts by Britain and France to impose some kind of control on the spending of this money. By the late nineteenth century it became obvious that the Ottoman *dawlah* had accumulated a vast amount of debt which was not payable by the bankrupt empire. The Ottoman *dawlah* had been granted fifteen foreign loans between the years 1854 and 1874 with high interest rates. The exact amount borrowed was 127,000,000 Ottoman Liras and the debt by the end of it stood at 239,000,000 Ottoman Liras.[70] By 1882 CE, the Ottoman *dawlah* was paying off its debt through a general debt administration in conjunction with European powers, by raising funds through more foreign debt.[71]

---

68 Shaw and Shaw, op. cit., p. 172.

69 Baysan, op. cit., p. 225.

70 By 1925 the new Turkish Republic accepted 62% of the foreign debt borrowed before 1912 and 77% afterwards and was able to pay it back in 1954.

71 Olive Anderson, 'Great Britain and the Beginning of the Ottoman Public Debt: 1854-1855', *The Historical Journal,* Vol. 7, No. 1, 1964, pp. 47-63.

Even though the financial crisis deepened during these years, the need for change was widely contested between modernists and conservatives across the Ottoman *dawlah*. The modernists saw it as the only way to cure the 'the sick man of Europe' whereas the conservatives saw modernisation as the Westernisation of their Caliphate. Due to the increasing decline of the Ottoman *dawlah* in the economic and political arenas of Europe during the eighteenth and nineteenth centuries, the pressure from the government to change Ottoman society increased further. During the eighteenth century, Europe had begun to develop an advanced weapons industry which left the Ottomans, once superior in this field, behind. During this century the Ottomans became used to importing military experts, gunpowder, weapons and warships directly from European nations. At the same time, new military institutions in the Ottoman Caliphate were established based upon European designs. Hence, in the military field, Ottoman modernisation began on the basis of its necessity simply for survival; this was further followed by economic and political reforms that were based on Russian and French state systems. The establishment of educational reforms began much later in the late eighteenth and early nineteenth centuries.[72]

During the late eighteenth century, the *medrese* system in the Ottoman Caliphate, which had been an evolving higher education system since the classical Islamic period in the eleventh century, was bypassed by major educational reforms based on contemporary European structures.[73] By the eighteenth century and before the reform period, Ottoman education had begun to trifurcate into three streams. The major stream of education within the *medrese* system was in Islamic

[72] Karpat, op. cit., p. 47.

[73] R. Hefner, 'Introduction: the Culture, Politics and Future of Muslim Education', in *Schooling Islam: the Culture and Politics of Modern Islam*, Hefner and M. Q. Zaman (eds.), (Princeton: Princeton University Press), 2007, pp. 13-14.

law, from primary to higher education. The second stream was apprenticeships within the *dawlah*, such as clerical work in the Palace and government. This was the first stream to be reformed since it was linked with the military and finance. The last stream was part of the apprenticeship in the bazaar and the craft organisations which began to suffer financially with the flood of European goods.[74]

The first reform influencing mainstream education was the establishment in 1857 CE of the Ministry of Education, which had the policy-shaping powers to create numerous Western-style educational institutions in a short time.[75] Due to these reforms the Ottoman *dawlah* acquired a dual higher education system that consisted of the traditional structure (*medrese*) and the Western type (*mekteb*).[76] The primary-secondary school was reformed and given a new name, the *Rushdiye*, and it offered training in subjects such as composition, Arabic and Persian, bookkeeping, geography, mathematics and history. The new reforms across the state led to a reformed bureaucracy, which relied on Ottoman subjects being educated accordingly. This inevitably led to a gradual minimisation of the influence of the *medrese* and the *'ulamā'* on Ottoman society, and by the time the Turkish republic was established in 1923 CE, their traditional hegemony had disappeared.

As stated above, the earliest reforms were of military institutions since the Ottoman Empire was on the defensive against Europe. The Ottoman *dawlah* felt it was essential to reform its navy and army, thus the need to learn the fundamentals of Western scientific knowledge. In 1735 CE, the Corps of Bombardiers was established by the French

74 Şerif Mardin, *Religion, Society, and Modernity in Turkey,* (Syracuse, NY: Syracuse University Press), 2006, p. 165.

75 Selçuk Akşin Somel, *The Modernization of Public Education in the Ottoman Empire 1839-1908*, (Brill: Leiden, 2001), pp. 20-22.

76 Yasin Aktay, *Political and Intellectual Disputes on the Academisation of Religious Knowledge,* (MPhil: Ankara University), 1993. Available at *http://www.angelfire.com/art/yasinaktay/tezler/MSThesis*, (accessed 18/02/08).

convert Aḥmad Compte de Bonneval. This corps was educated in subjects such as geometry, trigonometry, ballistics and technical drawing as well as receiving practical training.[77] In 1734 CE, the School of Engineering (*Hendesehane*) for military purposes was opened, followed by the Imperial Naval Engineering School (*Muhendishane-i Bahri-i Humayun*) in 1773 CE, the Imperial Army Engineering School (*Muhendishane-i Berry-i Humayun)* in 1793 CE and the Imperial Military College (*Mekteb-i Harbiye-i Sahane)* in 1835 CE.[78] French experts were imported to train Ottoman students and students were also sent abroad for higher education. However, very soon afterwards the French became allies with Russia during the fourth Russo-Turkish War of 1877-78 CE between Russia and the Ottoman *dawlah*, during which French experts left the Ottoman lands and the teaching was taken over by Ottoman instructors.[79]

The *raison d'être* of the *Tanzimat* was to bolster the Ottoman military so as to counter recent defeats of the Ottoman forces by nations such as Russia and Egypt. However, very soon reform was initiated within civilian fields. Medical education was introduced in 1806 CE with the establishment of the Imperial Shipyard Medical School (*Tersane Tibbiyesi*) and modern medical education began to be conducted in Italian and French. It was during this time that the European manner of graduation was adopted so that the graduating student received a diploma from his educational institution instead of the *Icazet* (certificate) from the teacher which included the chain of teachers. By 1870 CE, it was decided that medical education should be taught through the Turkish language. Sixty-five years after the

77 Ekmeleddin Ihsanoglu, *Ottoman Educational Institutions during the Reform Period,* (FSTC), 2004, pp. 1-18, http://www.muslimheritage.com/uploads/reformottomans.pdf, (accessed: 18/03/2011).

78 Baysan, op. cit., p. 227.

79 Ihsanoglu, op. cit., 2004, pp. 1-18.

foundation of the School of Naval Engineering, the first civil government schools were established; the Translation Bureau was formed in 1833 CE and the Civil Service School was founded in 1859 CE for diplomats and administrators. Civil engineering education began as early as 1874 CE.

This evolution of the education system was closely related to the ineffectiveness of the Ottoman army against its Habsburg and Russian counterparts, especially in the Russo-Ottoman War of 1768-1774 CE.[80] This forced the Ottoman *dawlah* to introduce military innovations, which were imported from the West. As stated earlier, the first modern education institution, which introduced practical and natural sciences, was the Naval Engineering College *(Muhendishane-i bahri-i Humayun),* which was supported by the French military expert Baron De Tott. Before the 1830s, numerous institutions were formed in the Ottoman *dawlah* for the purpose of defending the Ottoman *dawlah* against the growing powers of the West. What distinguished the *Tanzimat* era from earlier periods was the government's attempt to take education away from the monopoly of the religious authorities and put it under state administration.[81]

Due to these changes, the *'ulamā'* and Janissary corps stood against any kind of attempt at institutional modernisation. The *'ulamā'* were legitimately worried that the new civil educational institutes would destroy their traditional monopoly over education. The Janissary corps regarded military modernisation as a threat to their own existence, since they were the traditional military organisation. Nevertheless, after so many successive defeats the Ottoman *dawlah* saw modern European military education as the most effective means to reach the goal of modernisation. The traditional Janissary corps was disbanded

---

80 Somel, op. cit., pp. 20-22.
81 Karpat, op. cit., 2000, p. 50.

by Mahmut II in 1826 CE and replaced by the new War School in 1831 CE, which provided officers for the new military organisation called *Asakir-i Mansure-i Muhammediye.* The Ottoman *dawlah* was trying to take as its example Egypt's modernisation of education; by 1813 CE, the separatist governor of Egypt, Mehmed 'Alī Pasha had sent many students abroad for studies. This had brought many developments in the military field with concrete results for the new Egyptian educational system. Thus, Egypt inflicted a humiliating defeat on the Ottoman *dawlah* during the 1831 Egyptian-Ottoman War.[82]

Another problem facing the Ottoman *dawlah* was that many of its subjects were illiterate. Literacy was high at the apex of the Ottoman Caliphate (which would have been around the sixteenth and seventeenth centuries) according to European travellers like Schweigger (late sixteenth century) and Ottoman scholars like Evliya Celebi (middle of the seventeenth century); at least a quarter of the population could read and write in Turkish or Arabic. However, after administrative decentralisation from the seventeenth century, public order and safety was weakened throughout the Ottoman *dawlah*, affecting the efficiency of pre-*Tanzimat* education.[83] Economic and political destabilisation during the late seventeenth century led the founders of religious endowments, in many cases, to appoint family members as teachers without any regard for their actual qualifications. In such cases, these Islamic educational institutions became places for acquisition of material profit. Even the profession of teachers became hereditary and by the end of the first half of the nneteenth century, reports mentioned illiterate persons acting as Qur'an school teachers and of students who only acquired the ability to read and write after seventeen years of instruction.[84]

---

[82] Somel, op. cit., p. 27.

[83] Karpat, op. cit., pp. 19-20.

[84] Ibid., p. 20.

In 1845 Abdul Majid I issued an Imperial Edict with regards to Public Education. The Ottoman government's reaction to these events was to establish the already mentioned *rushdiye* school, which was directly under the control of the Ottoman *dawlah* and which created literate civil servants.[85] The founding of the *rushdiye* schools also boosted the establishment of teacher training schools (*dār ul mu'allimīn*) in 1848 CE, which accepted women as well as men. These teachers began to supplant the *'ulamā'*, who had been the traditional teachers, with a new profession, i.e. government appointed teachers. Some historians, such as Somel, argue that although the *Tanzimat* era under the Ottoman Caliphs Abdul Majid I and Abdul Aziz, seemed to be a change towards secularisation, it still embodied strong Muslim sentiments. He argues that the basic aim of the government's education in the 1840s was reinforcing moral and religious ethics. Although the *'ulamā'* were supplanted in 1846 CE by the *rushdiye* schools which had a more secular educational administration, this administration still stressed the importance of *tarbiyah* based upon an Islamic theosophy. Therefore looking at the curriculum during the *Tanzimat* period, it can be argued that the education system still had an Islamic character and a number of the teachers of the *rushdiye* schools were still *'ulamā'*. However, since the Qur'an schools were still under the *'ulamā'*, they saw these specifically as their domain. Although both the *rushdiye* and the Qur'an schools considered themselves within the Islamic realm, the fear of not being able to adapt to reform and that therefore the *'ulamā'* would lose their jobs, led to anti-reformist reactions that were justified by an 'Islamic' discourse.[86]

The Ottoman government divided education into five stages: *sibyan, rushdiye, idadiye, sultaniye and aliye,* thus covering both private and state, primary and higher education. The effort to educate all

85 Somel, op. cit., p. 44.
86 Ibid., p. 27.

children of a certain age began with Caliph Mahmud II (r. 1808-1839), but since the state did not have enough teachers and resources to cover such a task, people did not send their children to the primary school. During the *Tanzimat* era (1839-1876), the government made it obligatory to send children to *sibyan*, but despite the warnings of fines and irreligiousness, compulsory primary education was only partially successful.

The *Tanzimat* period also became well known for people's political and patriotic feelings towards the declining Ottoman *dawlah*, the idea of a modernised centralised state, cultural and material progress and the promotion of the economy for industrial, artisanal and individual profit. It can be argued that this period was very compatible with early European, absolutist state policies of social discipline. The Ministry of Public Education was founded in 1857 CE due to the need to effectively coordinate government schools, as was true for European Empires and nations. The *rushdiye* schools were divided into classes in the modern sense, with division of age and knowledge. These schools imported their disciplines from Western Europe, especially France and Russia. The *rushdiye* schools offered tidy uniforms, not dissimilar to the military's, separate rooms according to the level and age of the pupil, and an attempt was made at having standard textbooks. The contents of the textbooks were homogeneous throughout the State for each level, and in order to progress to the next level, pupils had to graduate from the previous level. It is important to note that this system was not fully implemented until the Hamidian period. The aim of education was mainly to promote the modernisation of the Ottoman *dawlah* and to keep the multi-ethnic state together.[87]

During the *Tanzimat* period, reforms were introduced to attempt to change the Qur'an schools into primary institutions, providing

87 Somel, op. cit., pp. 27-35.

religious as well as basic practical knowledge, including literacy. The objectives behind the reforms were seen as military and utilitarian in nature. It could be argued that the aim of the *Tanzimat* was not to achieve the values of the eighteenth century European 'Enlightenment' or the ideals of the French revolution, where the individual was perceived as having become mature by means of critical reasoning and to have gained independence from traditional values. Instead, the *Tanzimat* aimed to discipline the individual in morals by means of traditional and social values.[88] However, it may be argued that groups such as the Young Ottomans (founded in 1865) and later the Young Turks may have instead picked up the same ideals as their European counterparts had regarding the nation state and independence from traditional values, which were perceived to be backward and superstitious. These groups were strongly influenced by Western thinkers with regards to constitutional parliamentary government and materialism.[89]

With a more formidable West in the eighteenth century, several defeats suffered from Western armies, and with an aggressively expanding Russia entertaining Balkan ambitions, the Ottoman *dawlah* began to decline drastically. The Ottomans lost Hungary early on in 1718 CE, while their Crimean Khanate (modern-day Ukraine) became a vassal to Russia in 1783 CE, and furthermore, Greece won its independence in 1829 CE. Although the reigning Caliphs of this period sought alliances with Europe against Russian incursions, there was a heavy price to be paid in the form of concessions and capitulations of lands, chiefly to England and France. The Ottoman Caliphate that had once been the cause of apprehension and fascination for Europe had now become known as the 'sick man of Europe'. Even before Abdul Hamid's

88 Ibid., p. 64.

89 See: Kristin Fabbe, *Disciples of the State? Historical Legacies and State Control of Social Discipline in Turkey and Greece*, MIT, Paper originally prepared for presentation at APSA 2010.

ascension in 1876 CE, Bosnia, Bulgaria and Romania were in danger of being lost by the Ottomans to the Russian and Austrian Empires.

In 1876 CE, the Caliph Abdul Hamid II inherited a host of external and internal political and fiscal problems. The Ottoman *dawlah* proclaimed a national Constitution, written very much in the European style, and it was seen as a means to safeguard the Ottoman *dawlah* from foreign powers. In this constitution it was also made clear that Ottoman sovereignty included the Caliphate of Islam and it was vested in the eldest son of the dynasty of Osman.[90] Unfortunately, this constitution did not deter the Russians from attacking the Ottoman Caliphate in 1877-1878, which led to the peace treaty of San Stefano. The Ottomans had to accept the independence of Romania, Serbia and Montenegro, the autonomy of Bulgaria and the loss of southern Bessarabia to Russia. During the following years, Muslim refugees flooded from Bulgaria and Russian occupied lands into Istanbul and other larger cities. Taking the opportunity this situation afforded, Abdul Hamid dissolved parliament; for the rest of his thirty year reign, he ruled as an absolute ruler.

It was during this period that the Young Turks, a generation after the nineteenth century Young Ottomans, who were progressive *Tanzimat* thinkers, began to call for the removal of the Sultan's powers. It is clear from the sources that some of the youngest collaborators in the Young Ottomans' movement, later on played a role in the Young Turk movement. This new élite group consisted of members who were mainly from lower rank bureaucrats and the military; it seems that they emerged in 1889 CE from the military medical school at *Gulhane,* where they had formed the secret organisation called the Committee of Union and Progress.[91] The CUP strongly believed in a centralised government and in nationalism based upon ethnicity and

[90] Shaw and Shaw, op. cit., p. 175.

[91] Mardin, op. cit., p. 165.

secularism. It showed a strong commitment to the ideals of social Darwinism, materialism, positivism and élitism. Many amongst this group had been influenced by the anti-religious feelings and ideas that were circulating in Europe at this time and they exhibited a wide range of ideas regarding how to import secular Western institutions of education and law.[92]

By the Hamidian period, which commenced at the end of the *Tanzimat* period, under the reign of the Caliph Abdul Hamid II (r. 1876-1908), the distinction between religious and state institutions began to be blurred.[93] In 1887 CE, the government established the *ibtidai mekteb* which began to replace the *sibyan* (primary) schools. Graduates began to teach at these schools and *medrese 'ulamā'* were gradually excluded from teaching at these schools. The *idadiye* schools were newly established secondary education institutions that also began to be built in large numbers during the Hamidian period. However, there was a major lack of teachers[94] and most schools were not in any way close to our contemporary idea of 'modern' schools, with spacious classrooms and neatly aligned desks. Nevertheless, the Hamidian period stands out in the history of education as a time when regardless of the subject taught, the majority of the school texts emphasised Islamic values, ethics and conformity to the *sharī'ah.*

During this period the *dawlah* founded the Higher Education Institution for Civil Servants (*Mekteb-i Mülkiye*), the Higher Education Institution for Law (*Mekteb-i Hukuk*), the Higher Education Institution of Fine Arts (*Sanayi-i-Nefise*),[95] and eventually, after two unsuccessful attempts at establishing a modern university, the Great House of the

92 Fabbe, op. cit., p. 5.

93 Ibid., p. 172.

94 Hence, during this time the *'ulamā'* continued to hold key places within education as both teachers and ministers.

95 This formed the basis of today's Mimar Sinān University in Istanbul.

Sciences (*Dār al-Funūn-i Şahane*) in 1900 CE. This latter institution was the blueprint for all the universities throughout the new Republic of Turkey and later became Istanbul University.[96]

It is clear that the Caliph Abdul Hamid II wanted to raise a generation that would be loyal to Islam and the Ottoman Caliphate. He had a pan-Islamic policy; not one of expansion, but one of keeping the different ethnic Muslims together under the Ottoman Caliphate. From 1882 CE, the Caliph strongly approved of moral, religious and Arabic instruction in the *idadiye* schools. The entire curriculum was given overtones of religiosity and loyalty to the Ottoman *dawlah*. The education curriculum was used to honour the Ottoman *dawlah* and its leader Caliph Abdul Hamid II.[97] It seems that the main emphasis of the Hamidian era was to educate the citizens morally. Thus, *tarbiyah* was seen as the defining character of the government. On the other hand, the *Tanzimat* period tried to adopt Western policies in order to achieve reform, especially military reform. Abdul Hamid II's policies appear to have sought to use Western pedagogical techniques in order to face the challenges of the West. The Hamidian period tried to draw on both Islamic and Ottoman identity to reform the state from within; it seems that the aim of Abdul Hamid II was to educate the younger generation to be skilled in modernity and to be politically loyal to the Islamic *dawlah*. However, secularism had begun to appear in all quarters of society and it is no surprise that the *idadiye* schools were clearly labelled 'Muslim schools' so as to differentiate them from *secular* schools.[98]

In 1908 CE, the Committee for Union and Progress proved itself a major force within modern politics. With the Young Turk Revolution

---

96 Ihsanoglu, op. cit., 2004, pp. 1-18.

97 Karpat, op. cit., 2000, pp. 68-74.

98 Selim Deringil, *The Well Protected Domain: Power in the Ottoman Empire 1876-1909*, (London: I.B. Tauris), 1998, pp. 93-111.

they were able to depose Caliph Abdul Hamid II and establish a new constitution for the Ottoman *dawlah*. With the removal of Caliph Abdul Hamid II, the Young Turks legitimised rule by a new group who had been trained at the professional schools formed during the *Tanzimat* period. By the end of the First World War this same group gathered around Mustafa Kemal's movement of resistance against Greek and Allied invaders. This national movement was widely supported by local organisations with Islamic foundations. By 1922 CE, after victory against the invading Allies, the Ottoman Sultanate was abolished and the Republic was proclaimed in 1923 CE. One year later the Caliphate of Islam which had been in Istanbul since the sixteenth century was abolished.[99]

The ideas of Young Turk writers, such as Ahmet Riza Bey in 1894 CE, moved away from the ideas of the Young Ottoman writers such as Namik Kemal, who had based their ideology heavily on explaining natural law within the belief in God and religious law; in contrast Ahmet Riza Bey argued the need to explain natural law as a positive science devoid of God. These thinkers of both the T*anzimat* and the Hamidian period were heavily influenced by Western materialism, agnosticism and atheism. Another Young Turk thinker, 'Abdullāh Cevdet Bey, began to espouse the idea that Islam was the reason for the backwardness of the Ottoman *dawlah*; he argued against the validity of Islam as a revealed religion. Interestingly both of these Young Turk thinkers agreed that revealed religion had no claim to truth, but both saw religion as an instrument of social control that needed to be used to create a cohesive society. During the early years of the Republic, changes within educational thought highlighted Riza's emphasis on positive science as an ideology of the state. Islam was deemed to be a backward faith and positive materialism and anti-imperialism became

---

99 Mardin, op. cit., p. 234.

the major focus of the new Republic.[100] The reforms of the *Tanzimat* and the Hamidian eras had unconsciously brought forth secularism in a world which for six hundred years had been dominated by religion in all spheres of society.

[100] Ibid., pp. 164-182.

Chapter Six

The Future of Islamic Education

Islamic education is the product of a fourteen hundred year old Islamic civilisation that spanned Arabia and Spain, India and Indonesia. It can never be seen as separate from Islamic civilisation. The existence of this civilisation has meant that its teachings have been widely imparted. This book has only been able to cover some substantial parts of it, but so much is still to be researched. For example, this book has not been able to provide any substantial history of education in Muslim Spain, the Fatimid Caliphate nor of the Moghul and Safavid Sultanates. With regards to the Ottoman *dawlah*, only a brief overview has been presented of its continuation of an education that began in seventh century Makkah. There is no doubt that much research still needs to be carried out on the curriculum, thought and structure of education in the different parts of the Islamic world during the various epochs.

Nevertheless, it becomes quite clear to the reader, even from the limited perspective of this book on education in Islamic civilisation, that Islamic education has always been both unified in its worldview and at the same time diverse, due to variations in culture, geography and history. Islamic education is singular in its Qur'anic worldview, yet it still cannot be understood as a single concept but as a phenomenon with many aspects, all influenced by intellectual, social and political forces of its geography and time. Through this book it also becomes quite clear that education and Muslim society were bound together and the affect of education on society and vice versa, has always been strong and deep throughout Muslim history.

This research has tried to give a glimpse of traditional Islamic intellectual life and education. It is important to understand the diversity that existed within the Muslim world before the eighteenth century. The diversity of scholars such as Ibn Khaldūn, Ibn Rushd, al-Bīrūnī and Ibn Taymiyyah, the diversity of schools of law and thought and the diversity of educational institutions demonstrate the richness of the Islamic tradition and the unification of them all through the simple (but not simplistic) principle of *Tawhīd.*

For many different reasons, this traditional Islamic world began to decline and reached a certain degree of decadence, especially around the middle of the eighteenth century. European colonialism across most of the Muslim world added to the problem and by the nineteenth century, decadence in the Islamic world increased to such an extent that the memory of a relatively successful Islamic world before the eighteenth century slowly disappeared from memory and was replaced by a newfound inferiority complex. It is therefore not a surprise that the two main types of Islamic thinking today belong to two particular groups often referred to as modernist/progressive and fundamentalist/traditionalist. Both groups have been highly influenced by the secular humanism of the eighteenth century with the only difference being that modernists have directly tried to secularise all fields within Islamic knowledge through science, art and law, whereas fundamentalists think they are trying to revive Islam in opposition to modernism. However, these revivalists are just another product of the same secular humanism which is often pseudo-traditional; they think it is acceptable to simply refer back to the original sources, and insist on one rigid interpretation without realising the value of the intellectual history of the worldwide *ummah* over the last fifteen centuries.

The main strength of the Islamic world in the past has in fact been its unity, but without that leading to rigid uniformity. Within the intellectual, political and social history of Islam, the existence of numerous schools of thought with a wide range of interpretations, yet each differing interpretation in conformity to the Qur'an, *ḥadīth* and the *sharīʿah*, highlighted the strength of traditional Islam to uphold the ideal of diversity within Unity.

> *Mankind! We created you from a male and female, and made you into peoples and tribes so that you might come to know each other. The noblest among you in Allah's sight is the one with the most taqwa. Allah is All-Knowing, All-Aware.*[1]

In modern times, the Muslim world faces numerous economic problems and political turmoil which is inextricably linked to Islamic education. Education for Muslims has faced and faces numerous challenges from fundamentalists, liberalists, Marxist socialists and capitalists, all a product of the secular sphere. It could be argued that many liberal thinkers do not hide their hope that Islam will eventually find 'enlightenment' as the West did, whereas much of the fundamentalists' hope is to lock up the Islamic faith within a rigid system that in itself is a product of modern times, instead of a traditional system. These groups offer either puritanism or rationalist reform inspired by a colonial heritage. Islamisation from this perspective only deals with issues superficially, at best.

---

1 Bewley and Bewley, op. cit., Sūrat al-Ḥujurāt 49: 13.

Today most Muslim societies' education systems, West or East, have dualistic natures. They divide their education into secular and religious spheres; state schools represent the secular sphere and the weekend or after-school hours madrasahs are devoted to the religious sphere. This is not true only in the West due to the immigration of Muslims to a Christian and later post-modern society during the twentieth century, but it had also become a major part of the Muslim world as early as the 1830s as we have seen in the previous chapter of this book. Today in many circles, the call for Islamisation of science and modern technology is perceived as a part of the Islamic educational programme. In the West and the East, the same argument is frequently advanced for having Muslim schools that combine the secular and the religious. Both agree that all knowledge should be consistent with Islam.

It is interesting to note that within the historical documents there is no mention of 'Islamic education' *per se* except the use of terms found within the sciences of the *dīn* such as *ḥadīth*, *tafsīr* and *fiqh* etc.; this is clearly because within Islamic civilisation there was never a need to highlight something that was so obvious within the society. Islamic theology and cosmology were embedded within the society and without any major challenge to this creed; no one felt the need to highlight the *Islamicness* of it. In the same manner, today no one needs to highlight that our education across the world (including the Muslim world) is secular; i.e. most books and courses in any science, humanities or art subjects are firmly embedded within an atheist or agnostic cosmology and worldview. Thus, even in Muslim nations, many people feel the need to apply the term 'Islamic' to education as an *alternative* to secular education and furthermore they feel the need to speak of *Islamisation.*

For us to understand the dual nature of education amongst Muslims it is important to understand its origin. Secularisation of education in Europe began as early as the seventeenth century with the rise of the European'enlightenment'. This movement in Europe led Western thinkers to assert the primacy of science and absolute rationalism, which led in turn to 'higher' Biblical criticism, radical approaches to Christian and Jewish doctrine and even denial of any supernatural elements in religion. Today, these liberal thinkers' presumption is that Islam is comparable to the other Abrahamic faiths that went through the enlightenment two to three centuries ago and thus that Islam will follow a similar theological trajectory as the other two Abrahamic faiths. Thus, these so-called enlightened thinkers believe that eventually Islam will come to this self-proclaimed 'enlightenment' and follow suit by accepting the primacy of science, leading to modern Qur'anic criticism and a radical reformulation of Muslim doctrine.

An argument of this kind sometimes resembles that made about another minority group in the West, the Jewish Diaspora. It is argued that even though with Europe's long history of Jewish persecution and extreme inhospitality towards Jews, the Enlightenment period did create the atmosphere for the Jewish nation to produce heroes like Freud, Einstein and Marx who are revered by Jews and non-Jews alike, in Europe and all over the world. Hence, Silverstein argues that "given time and favorable circumstances Muslims are also to create crossover heroes".[2] The obvious mistake made here is to assume that these Jewish heroes somehow represent traditional Judaism, whereas Freud labelled religion an illusion and the existence of God a response of the primal human horde to the father complex,[3] and Marx called religion, including Judaism, an opium for the people which trapped them in the 'vale of tears'.[4] Most Jews who went down

2 Adam J. Silverstein, *Islamic History: A Very Short Introduction,* (Oxford: Oxford Press), 2010, p. 135.
3 Michael F. Palmer, *Jung and Freudon Religion,* (London: Routledge), 1996, pp. 34-40.
4 Julius Carlebach, *Karl Marxand the Radical Critique of Judaism,* (London: Routledge and Kegan Paul), 1978, p. 153.

in European history as 'heroes' during this period were transformed beyond recognition from what had historically been considered adherence to traditional Judaism.

Islamic education, in both the West and the East, ideally shapes the human being to become the vice-regent of Allah; this is seen as being the original destiny of the primordial human being in Islamic theology. The philosophy of Islamic education is to bring about inner perfection of a metaphysical nature. However, this does not mean that Islamic education ignores worldly knowledge; rather it stresses worldly knowledge's importance but with the cultivation of a deeper meta-knowledge. Divine revelation guides human beings on the path of life, whereas the human intellect is in constant interaction with the physical universe through observation, meditation, experimentation and application. Thus, Islamic education for Muslims is just an element of the wider Islamic theology in which the self-proclaimed primacy of science and of the autonomous human and secular reality is non-existent.

The future for Islamic education lies only within the practice according to the belief that knowledge not only supports life in this world but is also paramount for the life in the hereafter.[5] Numerous scholars of the past, such as Imam al-Māturīdī (d. 944), describe the sources of knowledge as three: sensory perceptions which include experience and experiment, reports of divine revelations or from the prophets and messengers, and reason. Al-Fārābī (d. 951), the renowned Muslim philosopher, classified knowledge in a two-fold scheme: practical knowledge, which deduces what needs to be done and theoretical knowledge which helps the soul to attain perfection. Ibn Khaldūn (d. 1406), the distinguished Muslim sociologist, argued that knowledge is of three kinds: knowledge by inference, knowledge by perception

---

5 Al-Attas, op. cit., p. 157.

and knowledge by personal experience.[6] In the West, Shaykh ʿAbd al-Wāḥid ibn ʿĀshir (d. 1631) spoke about a threefold division in his poem *al-Murshid al-Muʿīn*.[7] Even if these three different classifications of knowledge create distinct routes to understanding Islamic education, all scholars of Islam acknowledge not only sensory/experiential and intellectual perceptions but also revelation, which is recognised as the highest level.[8] In modern times, the only way that we can do justice to Islamic education is to accept that belief and the sacred must permeate the so-called secular life. Without truly understanding the reality of our modern life we can not begin to challenge it intellectually and without truly understanding our own Islamic heritage we can not apply it to our world.

Abū Hurayrah ﷜ reported Allah's Messenger ﷺ as saying: "The words of wisdom are the lost objects of the believer; he must claim them wherever he finds them."[9]

---

[6]   Nasr, op. cit., 1976, p. 95.

[7]   In his commentary on the poem, contemporary author Shaykh Ali Laraki explains the three types of proposition thus: 1. Rational propositions (*ḥukm ʿaqlī*), such as 2+2=4, are confirmed or rejected by the intellect and do not need verification using the following two categories: 2. Empirical propositions (*ḥukm ʿādī*), such as: it hurts to put your hand into an open flame, which are confirmed or rejected by experience and; 3. Religious propositions (*ḥukm sharʿī*), such as: there is life after death, which are confirmed or rejected by the Qurʾan or Sunnah. See: Ali Laraki, *The Practical Guidebook*, (Norwich: Diwan Press), 2012.

[8]   Michael S. Merry, 'Islamic Philosophy of Education and Western Islamic Schools; Points of Tension', in Salili, Farideh and Hoosain Rumjahn (eds.), *Religion in Multi-cultural Education*, (USA: IAP), 2006, p. 49.

[9]   Abū ʿĪsā Muḥammad ibn ʿĪsā at-Tirmidhī, *Sunan at-Tirmidhī, Kitāb al-Muqaddimah*, 184, (Beirut: Dar al-Kutub al-Ilmiyyah), 1996. This is a *gharib ḥadīth* according to at-Tirmidhī. Also see: Seyyed Hossein Nasr, *Knowledge and the Sacred*, (New York: State University of New York Press), 1989, p. 93 and Muḥammad ibn ʿAbdullāh Khatib at-Tabrīzī, Abdul Hameed Siddiqui (tr.), *Mishkāt al-Maṣābīḥ, Kitāb al-ʿIlm*, Vol. 1, No. 216, (Lahore: Islamic Publication), 1979, p. 136.

Brief Biography of Scholars

‘Umar Khayyām, (1050-1123): A Persian polymath: philosopher, mathematician, astronomer and poet, who also wrote treatises on mechanics, geography, mineralogy, music, climatology and theology. He is most famous in English speaking countries for his *Rubay‘āt* Quatrains.

Abū al-Aswad ad-Du’alī (d. 688): Traditionally seen as the pioneer who established the first grammatical rules for the Arabic language and who invented the scriptural vocalisation for the Qur’anic text.

Abū al-Layth as-Samarqandī (d. between 983-993): A Ḥanafī theologian and jurist.

Abū ‘Ubaydah Ma‘mar ibn al-Muthannā (728-824/5): A pioneering Arabic philologist from Basra.

Aḥmad Sirhindi (1563-1624): A Sufi theologian from India, well known for the letters about the renewal of Islam that he sent to the Ottoman rulers of his time.

Al-Baghdādī, Abū Manṣūr ‘Abd al-Qāhir ibn Ṭāhir (d. ca. 1037): A scholar of theology and arithmetic.

Aṭ-Ṭūsī, Nāṣir ad-Dīn (1201-1274): Shiite scholar of astronomy.

Az-Zuhrī, Muḥammad ibn Muslim ibn Shihāb (670-ca. 737): Biographer of the Prophet ﷺ, teacher of Ibn Isḥāq and one of the earliest *ḥadīth* scholars.

Al-A'mash, Abū Muḥammad Sulaymān ibn Mihrān (680/1-765): An early *ḥadīth* scholar and a Qur'an 'reader' of Persian origin. He learnt *ḥadīth* from scholars such as az-Zuhrī and Qur'an reading from scholars such as Mujāhid.

Al-Aṣma'ī, Abū Sa'īd 'Abd al-Malik ibn Qurayb (d. 828): A pioneering Arabic philologist, and an associate of Abū 'Ubaydah who lived in Baghdad.

Al-Bīrūnī, Abū Rayḥān Muḥammad ibn Aḥmad (973-1048): Born in the city of Kheva near "Ural". Associated with the court of Sultan Maḥmūd Ghaznawī, al-Bīrūnī was a physician, mathematician, geographer and historian. He learnt Sanskrit, Hindu philosophy, mathematics, geography and studied the Hindu religion in India.

Al-Bukhārī (810-870): A scholar of *ḥadīth*, he compiled one of the six well known sound collections of *ḥadīth*.

Al-Fārābī Abū Naṣr Muḥammad ibn al-Farākh (b. 870): In Latin he was known as Alpharabius. Born near Fārāb in Turkistan. He was a philosopher, scientist and linguist.

Al-Ghazālī, Abū Ḥamīd ibn Muḥammad ibn Muḥammad aṭ-Ṭūsī ash-Shāfi'ī (1058-1128): Born in Iran. Known as one of the greatest scholars of Islam, Ghazālī's major contribution lies in religion, philosophy and Sufism.

Al-Ḥallāj Abū al-Mughīth al-Ḥusayn ibn Manṣūr ibn Mahamma al-Bayḍawī (858-922): A theologian and Sufi who was executed for alleged heresy. A student of the great Sufi scholar Abū al-Qāsim al-Junayd.

Al-Ḥarrānī, Thābit ibn Qurrah ibn Marwān aṣ-Ṣābi'ī (836-901): Born in Ḥarrān (in present-day Turkey). Thābit contributed to several branches of science, notably mathematics, astronomy and mechanics.

Al-Ḥasan al-Baṣrī (642-728): Born in Basra, early scholar of religion and Sufism.

Al-Ḥasanī, Abū 'Abdullāh Muḥammad ibn Muḥammad ibn 'Abdullāh ibn Idrīs al-Qurṭubī (1099-1166/80): Born in Spain, Cordoba. His major contribution lies in the science of medicinal plants as presented in his several books.

Al-Junayd, Abū al-Qāsim ibn Muḥammad (d. 910): Acknowledged as a respected scholar and Sufi. He is known to have associated with one of the earliest Sufi scholars, al-Muḥāsibī.

Al-Khalīl ibn Aḥmad al-Farāhīdī (d. 791): Born in Oman. An early Arab philologist, author of the first Arabic dictionary *Kitāb al-'Ayn.*

Al-Kindī, Ya'qūb ibn Isḥāq (800-873): In Latin he was known as Alkindus. A philosopher, mathematician, astronomer, physician, geographer and even an expert on music. He was known as the philosopher of the Arabs.

al- Khwārizmī Abū 'Abdullāh Muḥammad ibn Mūsā (d. 840): Born at Khwārizm (Kheva), south of the Aral Sea, he was a mathematician, astronomer and geographer; he is known to be the founder of several branches of mathematics such as Algebra, and transmitted basic concepts of mathematics such as the Arabic numerals and the zero to Europe. His name is the origin of the term 'Algorithm'.

Al-Mubarrad, Abū al-'Abbās (826-900): Born in Basra. A scholar of literature and a celebrated philologist.

Al-Muḥāsibī, Abū 'Abdullāh al-Ḥārith ibn Asad al-'Anazī (781-857): Born in Basra, he lived mostly in Baghdad. A theologian, jurist and one of the earliest scholars of Sufism.

Al-Muqaddasī, Muḥammad ibn Aḥmad Shams ad-Dīn (d. 1000): Traveller and geographer.

Ar-Rāzī, Abū Bakr Muḥammad ibn Zakariyā (864-930): Born at Ray, Iran. He was a physician, philosopher, mathematician and astronomer.

Aṭ-Ṭabarī, Abū Jafar Muḥammad ibn Jarīr (839-923): One of the greatest scholars of history and Qur'anic exegesis.

Aṭ-Ṭabarī, 'Alī Rabban (838-870): Physician, psychologist, philosopher, climatologist and zoologist.

Az-Zahrāwī, Abū al-Qāsim Khalaf ibn al-'Abbās (936–1013): Famed Andalusian physician and surgeon.

Az-Zarnūjī, Burhān ad-Dīn (thirteenth century): Arab educationalist.

Fakhr ad-Dīn 'Ajamī (d. 1460): Known in Turkish as Molla Fahrettin Acemi. He was the third Shaykh al-Islam of the Ottoman Caliphate. He was first assigned the office of Mufti by Sultan Murād II in 1422 CE and appointed Shaykh al-Islam in 1436 CE.

Ḥunayn ibn Isḥāq al-'Ibādī (808-873): Christian scholar of science who translated an immense number of Greek works into Arabic. He was also a physician with a special interest in ophthalmology.

Ibn Abī Uṣaybi'ah (1203-1270): An Arabic physician and historian well known for his biographical history of physicians, *'Uyūn ul-Anbā' fī Ṭabaqāt al-Aṭibbā'.*

Ibn al-Haytham, Abū Alī al-Ḥasan ibn al-Ḥasan (d. 1039): A scientist who made significant contributions to the principles of optics, as well as to physics, astronomy, mathematics, ophthalmology, philosophy, visual perception and to the scientific method.

Ibn an-Nadīm (ca. 936-995): He lived in Baghdad. A Shiite scholar who is famous for his index of all books written in Arabic.

Ibn al-Muqaffa', 'Abdullāh (720-756): Born in Persia, he was a scholar of literature and a pioneer in Arabic literary prose.

Ibn 'Arabī (1165-1240): Born in Spain, he was a celebrated Sufi, both attacked for heresy and defended by well known scholars.

Ibn Butlan (d. 1066): Born in Baghdad, a Christian theologian and physician.

Ibn Ḥayyān, Abū Mūsā Jābir (d. 803): In Latin he was known as the alchemist Geber. He is known as the father of chemistry. He practised medicine and alchemy in Kufa around 776 CE.

Ibn Jurayd (837-933): Arab philologist and lexicographer.

Ibn Kathir, 'Imād ad-Dīn (ca. 1200-1373): A historian and scholar of *ḥadīth* and *tafsīr* who lived in Syria.

Ibn Khaldūn, 'Abd ar-Raḥmān ibn Muḥammad (1332-1406): Born in Tunisia. Ibn Khaldūn's chief contribution lies in the philosophy of history and sociology.

Ibn Khallikān (1211-1282): Born in Iraq, author of a famous biographical dictionary.

Ibn Kamāl (1468-1534): A polymath scholar who influenced Ottoman thought by his writings on history, theology and jurisprudence.

Ibn Māsawayh, Yūḥannā (d. 857): Christian physician and translator of Greek works.

Ibn Maymūn, Mūsā (Maimonides) (1135-1204): Medieval Jewish philosopher and one of the greatest Torah scholars and physicians of the Middle Ages. He was born in Córdoba, Spain.

Ibn Qutaybah (828-889): A theologian, philologist and scholar of literature.

Ibn Rushd, Abū al-Walīd Muḥammad (1126-1198): Known as Averroes in Latin, Ibn Rushd was born in Cordoba and is recognised as a philosopher who had a strong impact on European philosophy; it is less well known that he was also a *qāḍī* and a jurist of Islamic law.

Ibn Sīnā, Abū 'Alī al-Ḥusayn ibn 'Abdullāh (980-1037): Known as Avicenna in Latin, Ibn Sīnā was born near Bukhara. A polymath, he was the most famous physician, philosopher, encyclopaedist, mathematician and astronomer of his time.

Ibn Sīrīn (654-728): One of the early *ḥadīth* scholars and scholars of *fiqh* who is also famous for a book on the interpretation of dreams.

Ibn Taymiyyah (1263-1328): One of the leading Ḥanbalī theologians and jurists of his period.

Ibn an-Nafīs (d. 1288): A distinguished physician and author of books on medicine.

Imam Abū Ḥanīfah, Nu'mān ibn Thābit (689-759): Born in the city of Kufa, he is reputed to have lived there at the same time as Companions of the Prophet ﷺ such as Anas ibn Mālik, 'Abdullāh ibn Abī Awfā and Sahl ibn Sa'd ؓ and to have seen them, although people differ as to whether he learnt from them. Abū Ḥanīfah is known as the founder of the Ḥanafī *madhhab*, one of the four surviving Sunni guilds of law.

Imam Ibn Ḥanbal, Aḥmad ibn Muḥammad (780-855): Known as Imam Ibn Ḥanbal, he was born in the city of Baghdad. One of his teachers in Islamic law was Imam ash-Shāfi'ī. Imam Ibn Ḥanbal is known as the founder of the Ḥanbalī *madhhab*, one of the four surviving Sunni guilds of law.

Imam Mālik, Abū 'Abdullāh, Mālik ibn Anas (715-795): Born in Madīnah, Imam Mālik studied *ḥadīth* and *fiqh* and is known as the founder of the Mālikī *madhhab,* one of the four surviving Sunni guilds of law.

Imam ash-Shāfi'ī, Abū 'Abdullāh Muḥammad ibn Idrīs (767-820): Known as Imam ash-Shāfi'ī, he was born in Gaza. He studied Islamic law under Imam Mālik and others. Imam ash-Shāfi'ī is known as the founder of the Shāfi'ī *madhhab*, one of the four surviving Sunni guilds of law.

Kuscu, 'Alī (d. 1474): Mathematician and astronomer during the period of Sultan Mehmed al-Fātiḥ. A teacher at the *Samâniye medrese* and seen as the main influence on Mehmed al-Fātiḥ's interest in rational sciences.

Molla Ebu's-Su'ud (Abū as-Su'ūd) Effendi (1490-1574): The Shaykh al-Islam (1545-1574) during the Caliph Sulaymān I Kanuni's period.

Molla Husrev (d. 1480): The fourth Shaykh al-Islam of the Ottoman Caliphate, he was appointed by Sultan Mehmet II and was followed by Molla Gürani in 1480 CE. Molla Husrev was known as a brilliant Ottoman jurist; his works on jurisprudence were used as standard textbooks in Ottoman *medrese*. He was the second Mufti of Istanbul following Khiḍr Beg (d. 1459) in that post. Mehmet II is known to have stated that, "Molla Husrev is the Abū Ḥanīfah of our times."

Molla Luṭfī (d. 1494): A scholar of mathematics and scholastic theology in the Ottoman Empire.

Molla Shemseddin (Shams ad-Dīn) Mehmed Fenari (1350-1431): The first Shaykh al-Islam (1424-1431) of the Ottoman Caliphate, he was appointed by Sultan Murād II in 1424 CE.

Mirim Celebi (d. 1525): A scholar of mathematics and scholastic theology in the Ottoman Empire.

Muḥammad ibn Isḥāq (704-767): First to write a biographical work with regard to the Prophet ﷺ entitled, 'Life of the Messenger of Allah ﷺ'.

Rābi'ah al-'Adawiyyah (714-801): Possibly the earliest and most famous woman Sufi, renowned for her doing without the world and devotion to Allah.

Tashkopruluzade Aḥmad (1495-1561): An encyclopaedic Turkish scholar and *medrese* lecturer of the Ottoman Caliphate.

Bibliography

Adamson, John, A *Short History of Education,* Cambridge: University Of Cambridge Press, 1991.

Aksan, Virginia H. and Goffman, Daniel (Eds.), *The Early Modern Ottomans: Remapping the Empire,* Cambridge: University of Cambridge Press, 2007.

ʻAlī, Y., *The Holy Qur'an: English translation of the Meaning and Commentary,* Madinah: King Fahad Holy Printing Complex, 1995.

Al-Bukhārī Muḥammad ibn Ismāʻīl ibn al-Mughīrah, Muhammad Muhsin Khan (tr.), *Ṣaḥīḥ al-Bukhārī - The translation of the meaning of Ṣaḥīḥ al-Bukhārī,* New Delhi: Kitab Bhavan, 1984.

Aldafairi, Fahad, *Evaluating the Islamic Education Curriculum in Elementary Schools in the State of Kuwait,* PhD: Oxford University, 1997.

Al-Fahad, ʻAbdullāh, *Classical Educational Thought, Curriculum and Methods of Teaching in Islam,* PhD: Cardiff, 1998.

At-Tabrīzī, Muḥammad ibn ʻAbdullāh Khaṭīb, Abdul Hameed Siddiqui (tr.), *Mishkāt al-Maṣābīḥ,* Lahore: Islamic Publication, 1979.

At-Tirmidhī, Abū ʻĪsā Muḥammad ibn ʻĪsā, *Sunan at-Tirmidhī,* Beirut: Dar al-Kutub al-Ilmiyyah, 1996.

Al-Qāsim, ʻAbd ar-Raḥmān (comp. and ed.), *Ibn Taymiyyah Fatāwā,* Vol. 18, Beirut: Dar al-Kutub al-Ilmiyyah, 1398 AH.

Az-Zarkāshī, Muḥammad *Ibn Taymiyyah Fatāwā*, Beirut: Dar al-Kutub al-Ilmiyyah, 1406 AH.

Anderson, Olive, 'Great Britain and the Beginning of the Ottoman Public Debt: 1854-1855', *The Historical Journal*, Vol. 7, No. 1, 1964, pp. 47-63.

An-Nawawī, Imam Abū Zakariyyā Yaḥyā ibn Sharaf, S. M. Madni Abbasi (tr.), *Riyāḍ aṣ-Ṣāliḥīn*, New Delhi: Kitab Bhavan, 1986.

Armstrong, Karen, *Muḥammad; A Western Attempt to Understand Islam*, London: Victor Gollancz, 1991.

Attas, Syed M. Naquib, *The Concept of Education in Islam: A Framework for an Islamic Philosophy of Education*, Jeddah: Hodder and Stoughton, 1979.

Avrin, Leila, *Scribes, Script and Books*, (Chigago: ALA Editions), 2010.

Azra, Azyumardi, *Islam in the Indonesian world: An Account of Institutional Formation*, Indonesia: Mizan, 2006.

Babinger, Franz, *Mehmed the Conqueror and His Time*, Princeton: Princeton University Press, 1959.

Baldick, Julian, *Mystical Islam*, London: I. B. Tauris, 1992.

Bammate, Haider, *Muslim Contributions to Civilization*, Takoma Park: Crescent Publication, 1962.

Bashier, Zakaria, *Sunshine at Madīnah*, Leicester: The Islamic Foundation, 1990.

Baynes, N. H. and Moss, L. B., *Byzantium: An Introduction to East Roman Civilization*, Oxford: Clarendon Press, 1949.

Baysan, Ibrahim Vehbi, *State Education Policy in the Ottoman Empire during the Tanzimat Period*, PhD: University of Manchester, 2004.

Berkey Jonathan P., *The Transmission of Knowledge in Medieval Cairo*, New Jersey: Princeton University Press, 1992.

———, *Popular Preaching and Religious Authority in the Medieval Islamic Near East*, USA: University of Washington Press, 2001.

———, *The Formation of Islam: Religion and Society in the Near East 600-1800,* Cambridge: Cambridge University Press, 2003.

Berkey, Jonathan, 'The Transmission of Knowledge in Medieval Cairo: A Social History of Islamic Education', *Journal of Semitic Studies,* Princeton: Princeton University Press, Vol. 39, No. 2, 1994, pp. 361-364.

Bilge, M., *Ilk Osmanli Medreseleri,* (Istanbul: Istanbul Universitesi Edebiyat Fakultesi),1984.

Bloom J. and Blair, S., *Islam: A Thousand Years of Faith and Power,* London: Yale University Press, 2002.

Bosworth, C. E., Bearman, P. J., Bianquis, Th., Van Donzel, E., and Heinrichs, W. P., (eds.),,*Encyclopaedia of Islam,* 12 Vols., (Leiden: E. J. Brill), 1997.

Bowersock, Brown and Grabar (eds.), *Late Antiquity: A Guide to the Post-Classical World,* Cambridge: The Belknap Press, 1999.

Boyd, Williams, *The History of Western Education,* Edmund J. King (ed.), Edinburgh: Black, 1966.

Brockelman, Carl, *History of the Islamic Peoples,* London: Routledge and Kegan Paul, 1949.

Burke, Peter, *History and Social Theory*, Oxford: Polity Press, 1992.

Buttler, Alfred J., *The Arab Conquest of Egypt,* P. M. Fraser (ed.), Oxford: Clarendon Press, 1978.

Charette, Francois, *Mathematical Instrumentation in Fourteenth-Century Egypt and Syria: The Illustrated Treatise of Najm Al-Din Al-Misri,* Leiden: Koninklijke, 2003.

Corsi, Pietro and Weindling, Paul, *Information Sources in the History of Science and Medicine,* London: Butterworth Scientific, 1983.

Carlebach, Julius, *Karl Marx and the Radical Critique of Judaism,* London: Routledge and Kegan Paul, 1978.

Dawud, Abu, Ahmad Hasan (tr.), *Sunan Abu Dawud,* New Delhi: Al-Madīnah Publications, 1985.

Denfer, Ahmad Von, *Research in Islam,* Leicester: The Islamic Foundation, 1985.

Deringil, Selim, *The Well Protected Domain: Power in the Ottoman Empire 1876-1909,* London: I.B. Tauris, 1998.

Dodge, Bayard, *Muslim Education in Medieval Times,* Washington: The Middle East Institute, 1962.

Doi, Abdur Rahman I., *Shari'ah: The Islamic Law,* London: Ta-Ha Publishers, 1997.

Dols, Michael W., *The Black Death in the Middle East,* Princeton: Princeton University Press, 1977.

Dunn, Ross E., *Adventures of Ibn Battuta: A Muslim Traveler of the 14th Century,* Los Angeles: University of California Press, 1986.

Ebrey, P.B., Walthall, A. and Palais, J. P., *East Asia: A Cultural, Social, and Political History,* USA: Houghton Mifflin Company, 2008.

Eickelman Dale F. and Piscatori James (eds.), *Muslim Travelers,* Los Angeles: University of California Press, 1990.

Esposito, John L., *The Oxford Encyclopedia of the Modern Islamic World,* Oxford: Oxford University Press, 1995.

Ezel and Shaw, *History of the Ottoman Empire and Modern Turkey,* Cambridge: University Press, 1977.

Farah, Caesar E. (ed.), *Decision Making and Change in the Ottoman Empire,* Missouri: The Thomas Jefferson University Press, 1993.

Faroqhi, Suraiya, McGowan, Bruce, Quataert, Donald and Pamuk, Sevket, *An Economic and Social History of the Ottoman Empire 1600-1914: Volume 2*, Cambridge: Cambridge University Press, 1997.

Faruqi, Ismail R. and Lois Lamya, *The Cultural Atlas of Islam*, New York: Macmillan Publishing Company, 1986.

Faruqi, Ismail R. and Nassef, 'Abdullah Omar (eds.), *Social and Natural Sciences: The Islamic Perspective,* Jeddah: Hodder and Stoughton, 1981.

Faruqi, Z. H., 'Madrasah Nizamiya of Baghdad', *Studies in Islam,* Vol. 17, 1980, pp. 1-7.

Fernandes, Leonor, *The Evolution of a Sufi Institution in Mamluk Egypt: The Khanqah,* Berlin: Klaus Shwarz Verlag, 1988.

Frye, Richard N., *The Golden Age of Persia,* London: Phoenix Press, 2000.

Ghaffar, Abdul, *The Rise of Muslim Schools in London*, PhD: Lampeter University, 1997.

al-Ghazāli, H. M. Fazlul Karim (tr.), *Ihya Ulum ad-Din Vol.1,* New Delhi, Kitab Bhavan, 1982.

Gibb and Kramers, *Shorter Encyclopaedia of Islam,* Leiden: E. J. Brill, 1974.

Goddard, Hugh, *A History of Christian-Muslim Relations,* Edinburgh: Edinburgh University Press, 2000.

Gutas, Dimitri, *Greek Thought, Arabic Culture,* London: Routledge, 1998.

Hameed, Fahmeeda, *A Critical Study and Analysis of Scholarly Achievements of 'A'ishah,* PhD: Lampeter, 2000.

Hamidullah, Muhammad, *Khutabat-e-Bahaawalpoor (Essays of Bahaawalpoor),* Islamabad: Idarah Tahqiqat Islami, 1997.

————, 'Signs of Punctuation in the Copies of the Holy Qur'an: A Suggestion', *Al-'Ilm Journal of the Center for Research in Islamic Studies*, South Africa: University of Durban-Westville, January 1994, Vol. 4, pp. 1- 4.

Harery, Ghulam Aḥmad, *Islami Dastor-i-Hajaat (Islamic way of Life)*, Lahore: Takhliq Markaz, 1991.

Hasan, Ahmad, *Principles of Islamic Jurisprudence,* Islamabad: International Islamic University, 1993.

Hasan, Mas'ud ul, *History of Islam Vol. 1,* Lahore: Islamic Publications, 1998.

Hefner, R. 'Introduction: the Culture, Politics and Future of Muslim Education', in *Schooling Islam: The Culture and Politics of Modern Islam*, Hefner and M. Q. Zaman (eds.), Princeton: Princeton University Press, 2007.

Hill, Donald Routledge, *The Book of Ingenious Devices by the Banu Musa ibn Shakir,* Dordrecht: D. Reidel Publishing, 1979.

Hitti, Philip K., *History of the Arabs,* London: Macmillan and Co., 1968.

Hodgson, Marshall G. S., *The Venture of Islam,* Chicago: The University Of Chicago Press, 1974.

Hojjati, Abbolmajd, *Zoroastrianism and Ancient Persian Education,* PhD: University of Saint Louis, 1965.

Holt, P.M., 'Some Observations on the "Abbasid Caliphate of Cairo', *Bulletin of the School of Oriental and African Studies,* University of London, Vol. 47, No. 3, 1984, pp. 501-507.

Hourani, Albert, *A History of the Arab People,* London: Faber and Faber, 1991.

Husaini, S. W. A. S., *Qur'an for Astronomy and Earth Exploration from Space,* India: Lazwal, 1996.

Ibn Batuta, *Ibn Batuta, Travels in Asia and Africa,* London: Routledge and Kegan Paul, 1984.

Ibn Ishaq, A. Guillaume (tr.), *The Life of Muhammad,* Karachi: Oxford University Press, 1970.

Ibn Khaldun, Franz Rosenthal (tr.), *The Muqaddimah,* London: Routledge and Kegan Paul, 1967.

Ibn Majah, Abu 'Abdullāh Muhammad ibn Yazid, *Sunan Ibn Majah*, Beirut: Dar al-Maarifah, 1996.

Ihsanoglu, Ekmeleddin and Gunergun, Feza (eds.), *Science in Islamic Civilisation,* Turkey: IRCICA, 2000.

Imamuddin, S. M., *Arabic Writing and Arab Libraries,* London: Ta-Ha Publishers, 1983.

Inalcik, Halil and Quataert, Donald (eds.), *An Economic and Social History of the Ottoman Empire,* Cambridge: Cambridge University Press, 1994.

Inalcik, Halil, *The Ottoman Empire: The Classical Age 1300-1600,* London: Weidenfeld and Nicholson, 1973.

Imber, Colin, *The Ottoman Empire 1300-1650,* London: Palgrave Macmillan, 2002.

Islam, A. U., 'The Educational Philosophy of Muḥammad Iqbal', *Muslim Education Quarterly,* Cambridge: The Islamic Academy, Vol. 18, No. 2, 2001, pp. 4-17.

Jawad, H. A., 'Muḥammad, the Educator: An Authentic Approach', *The Islamic Quarterly,* London: The Islamic Cultural Centre, 1990, Vol. xxxiv, No. 2, pp. 115-120.

Karpat, Kemal H., *Ottoman Past and Today's Turkey,* Brill: Leiden, 2000.

Keddie, Nikki R. (ed.), *Scholars, Saints and Sufis: Muslim Religious Institutions in the Middle East since 1500,* Berkley: University of California Press, 1972.

Khan, Hamiuddin, *History of Muslim Education Vol. I (712-1750),* Karachi: Academy of Educational Research, 1967.

Khan, M. M., *The Translation of the Meanings of Sahih al-Bukhari Vol. 1,* New Delhi: Kitab Bhavan, 1984.

Kraemer, Joel L., *Humanism in the Renaissance of Islam,* New York: E. J. Brill, 1992.

Kuper, Adam and Jessica, *The Social Science Encyclopedia,* 2nd edition, London and New York: Routledge, 1996.

Labarta, Emilio Calvo (ed.), *A Shared Legacy: Islamic Science East and West: Homage to Professor J. M. Milas Vallicrosa,* Barcelona: University of Barcelona, 2008.

Lane, E. W. (ed.), *Arabic-English Lexicon vol. II,* London: Islamic Texts Society, 1984.

Lapidus, Ira M., *A History of Islamic Societies,* Cambridge: Cambridge University Press, 2002.

Leiser, Gary, 'Medical Education in Islamic Lands from the Seventh to the Fourteenth Century', *Journal of the History of Medicine and Allied Science,* Ankara, Vol. 38, 1983, pp. 48-75.

Lewis, Bernard (ed.), *The World of Islam,* London: Thames and Hudson, 1980.

———, *Istanbul and the Civilization of the Ottoman Empire,* Norman: University of Oklahoma Press, 1963.

Lindner, Rudi Paul, *Nomads and Ottomans in Medieval Anatolia,* Bloomington: Indiana University, 1983.

Lings, Martin, *Muḥammad,* Hemel Hempstead: George Allen and Unwin, 1983.

Makdisi, George, 'Muslim Institutions of Learning in the 11th Century', *Bulletin of the SOAS Studies,* Vol. 24, 1961, pp. 1-56.

———, *The Rise of Colleges,* Edinburgh: Edinburgh University Press, 1981.

———, *The Rise of Humanism in Classical Islam and the Christian West*, Edinburgh: Edinburgh University Press, 1990.

Mango, Cyril, *Byzantium, the Empire of New Rome,* London: Weidenfeld and Nicholson, 1950.

Mardin, Şerif, *Religion, Society, and Modernity in Turkey,* Syracuse, NY: Syracuse University Press, 2006.

Maududi, Sayyid Abu 'Ala, *Ta'limiat (Edification),* Lahore: Islamic Publishers, 1981.

Merry, Michael S., 'Islamic Philosophy of Education and Western Islamic Schools: Points of Tension' in Salili, Farideh and Hoosain Rumjahn (eds.), *Religion in Multicultural Education,* USA: IAP, 2006.

Meyerhof, M., *Studies in Medieval Arabic Medicine,* London: Variorum Reprints, 1984.

Morsi, Mohammed Monir, *The Islamic Education: Its Foundation and Development in the Arab World,* Cairo: Alam al-Kutub, 1974.

Muhammad, Abdul Aziz, *Zakat and Rural Development in Malaysia*, Malaysia: Berita Publishing, 1993.

Muir, William, *Life of Mahomet*, Osnabruck: Biblio Verlag, 1988.

Mulhern, James, *A History of Education,* 2nd edition, New York: Sheed and Ward, 1956.

Munir-ud-Din, Ahmad, *Muslim Education and the Scholar's Social Status up to the 5th Century Muslim Era,* Zurich: Verlag Der Islam, 1968.

Muslim, Abul Husayn Muslim ibn al-Hajjaj Qushayri al-Nishapuri, Abdul Hamid Siddiqi (tr.), *Sahih Muslim,* New Delhi: Kitab Bhavan, 1984.

Nahlawi, Abdul Rahman, *Usul al-tarbiyah al-Islamiyah wa-asalibuha fi al-bayt wa-al-*madrasah *wa-al-mujtama* (*The Foundations and Styles of Islamic Education in the Home, the School and Society*), Damascus: Dar al-Fikr, 1983.

Nakosteen, Mehdi, *History of Islamic Origins of Western Education,* Colorado: University of Colorado Press, 1964.

Naqeeb, Abdul Rahman, *Educational and Psychological Thought in Islamic and Arab Culture,* Egypt: Dar al-Fikr, 1979.

Nasr, Seyyed Hossein (ed.), *Islamic Spirituality*, London: SCM Press, 1985.

———, *Islamic Science,* England: World of Islam Festival Publishing, 1976.

———, *Knowledge and the Sacred,* New York: State University of New York, 1989.

———, *Traditional Islam in the Modern World,* London: KPI, 1987.

Ngah, Zaid bin, *The Practice of the Prophet Muḥammad in Tarbiyyah: Its Significance for the Formation of the First Muslim Community*, MPhil: University of Birmingham, 1996.

Oadah, Khalid F., *The* Madrasah *System in Mediaeval Time*, PhD: Cardiff University, 1998.

Otaibi, Moneer M. and Rashid, Hakim M., 'The Role of Schools in Islamic society', *The American Journal of Islamic Sciences: Education,* Washington and Kuala Lumpur: The International Institute of Islamic Thought, Vol. 14, Winter 1997, pp. 1-19.

Outhwaite, W. and Bottomore, T., *The Blackwell Dictionary of Twentieth Century Social Thought,* USA: Blackwell, 1933.

Palmer, Michael F., *Jung and Freud on Religion,* London: Routledge, 1996.

Parry, V. J., *A History of the Ottoman Empire to 1730,* Cambridge: Cambridge University Press, 1976.

Pedersen, Johannes, *The Arabic Book,* Geoffrey French (tr.), New Jersey: Princeton University Press, 1984.

Petry C. F. (ed.), *The Cambridge History of Egypt Vol. I,* Cambridge: Cambridge University Press, 1998.

Philip, Thomas and Haarmann, Ulrich, *The Mamluks in Egyptian Politics and Society,* Cambridge: Cambridge University Press, 1998.

Philips, Abu Ameenah Bilal, *The Evolution of Fiqh,* Riyadh: International Islamic Publishing House, 1988.

Qadhi Abu Amina Yasir, *An Introduction to the Sciences of the Qur'an*, Birmingham: Al-Hidayah, 1999.

Rahman, Afzalur, *Muḥammad The Educator Of Humankind,* London: The Muslim Schools Trust, 1980.

Raymond, Andre, *Cairo - City of History*, Egypt: American University in Cairo Press, 2000.

Riche, Pierre, *Education and Culture in the Barbarian West: From the Sixth through the Eight Century,* Colombia: University of South Carolina Press, 1978.

Robinson, Francis, 'Ottoman-Safavids-Mughals', *Journal of Islamic Studies*, Vol. 8, No. 1, January 1997, pp. 151-184.

Robinson, N., *A Concise Introduction to Islam*, Surrey: Curzon Press, 1999.

Sa'adah, Ibrahim, *Islam wa Tarbyat-ul-Insan (Islam and the Education of Humankind),* Jordan: Maktab al-Munar, 1985.

Sabra, Adam, *Poverty and Charity in Medieval Islam: Mamluk Egypt, 1250-1517,* Cambridge: Cambridge University Press, 2000.

Saggs, H. W. F., *Civilization before Greece and Rome,* London: B.T. Batsford, 1989.

Saygii, Arikan Tarik, 'Impacts of Wrong Financial Decisions on the Collapse of an Empire: The Ottoman Case', *African Journal of Business Management,* Vol. 3, April 2009, pp. 151-159.

Saunders, J. J., *A History of Medieval Islam,* London: Routledge and Kegan Paul, 1965.

Seemaan, Khalil I. (ed.), *Islam and the Medieval West,* Albany: State University of New York Press, 1980.

Seeman, K., 'Education in Islam, From the Jahiliyyah to Ibn Khaldun', *Muslim World,* Binghamton: State University of New York, Vol. 56, 1966, pp. 188-198.

Shaban, M. A., *Islamic History: A New Interpretation,* Cambridge: Cambridge University Press, 1971.

Shalaby, Ahmad, *The History of Muslim Education,* Karachi: Indus Publication, 1979.

Shaw, S. J. and Shaw, E. K., *History of the Ottoman Empire and Modern Turkey,* Cambridge: Cambridge University Press, 1995.

Shoshan, Boaz, *Popular Culture in Medieval Cairo,* Cambridge: Cambridge University Press, 1993.

Siddiqi, Muhammad Zubayr, *Ḥadīth Literature,* Cambridge: The Islamic Texts Society, 1993.

Silverstein, Adam J., *Islamic History: A Very Short Introduction,* Oxford: Oxford Press, 2010.

Skerrit, O. Z., *Quality in Post-Graduate Education,* London: Kegan Paul, 1994.

Smart, Ninian, *Atlas of the World's Religions,* Oxford: Oxford University Press, 1999.

Somel, Selçuk Akşin, *The Modernization of Public Education in the Ottoman Empire 1839-1908*, Brill: Leiden, 2001.

Sonn, Tamara, *Islam, A Brief History,* 2nd edition, Oxford: Wiley-Blackwell, 2010.

Stanton, Charles Michael, *Higher Learning in Islam,* Maryland: Rowman and Littlefield, 1990.

at-Tabari, Ismail K. Poonawala (tr.), *The History of at-Tabari,* Los Angles: State University of New Press, 1990.

Ṭaḥāwī, Aḥmad ibn Muḥammad, Yusuf, Hamza (tr.), *The Creed of Imam al-Tahawi,* USA: Zaytuna Institute, 2007.

Tibawi, A. L., *Islamic Education*, London: Luzac and Company, 1972.

Turner, Howard R., *Science in Medieval Islam,* Austin: University of Texas Press, 1997.

Ullman, Manfred, *Islamic Medicine,* Edinburgh: Edinburgh University Press, 1978.

Waddy, Charis, *The Muslim Mind,* London: Grosvenor, 1990.

Waghid, Yosuf, 'Islamic Educational Institutions: Can the Heritage be Sustained?', *The American Journal of Islamic sciences: Education,* Washington and Kuala Lumpur: The International Institute of Islamic Thought, Vol. 14, Winter 1997, pp. 35-51.

Waldman, Marilyn Robinson and McNeil, William H., *The Islamic World*, New York: Oxford University Press, 1973.

Watt, W. M., *Muḥammad at Mecca,* Karachi: Oxford University Press, 1953.

————, *Muslim Intellectual: A Study of al-Ghazali,* Edinburgh: Edinburgh University Press, 1963.

Winter, T. J. (ed.), *The Cambridge Companion to Classical Islamic Theology,* Cambridge: Cambridge Press, 2008,

Young, M. J. C. and Serjeant, R. B. (eds.), *Religion, Learning and Science in the 'Abbasid Period,* Cambridge: Cambridge University Press, 1990.

Zarnuji, Burhan Al-Din, *Instruction of the Student: The Method of Learning,* Chicago: The Star Latch Press, 2001.

Internet References

FSTC Limited, *The An-Nūrī Hospital,* 20 December 2002, http://www.muslim heritage.com/topics/default.cfm?ArticleID=325, (accessed 10/07/2010)

FSTC Limited, *Knowledge, Learning Institutions and Libraries in Islam: Book Publishing and Paper Making,* 11 January 2007, http://www.muslimheritage.com/topics/default.cfm?articleID=642, (accessed 12/07/10)

Ihsanoglu, Ekmeleddin, *The Medreses of the Ottoman,* http://www.muslim heritage.com/uploads/madrasahs.pdf, (accessed 18/03/11)

Ihsanoglu, Ekmeleddin, *Ottoman Educational Institutions during the Reform Period,* (FSTC), 2004, http://www.muslimheritage.com/uploads/reformottomans.pdf, (accessed: 18/03/11)

Overbye, Dennis, 'How Islam Won, and Lost, the Lead in Science', *New York Times,* October 30, 2001, http://www.jonathantan.org/handouts/Islam/Islam-H111af-sciences.pdf, (accessed 20/07/2010)

Savage-Smith, Emilie, 'Attitudes toward Dissection in Medieval Islam', *Journal of the History of Medicine and Allied Sciences* Vol. 50, No. 1, pp. 67-110, 1995, http://jhmas.oxfordjournals.org/cgi/reprint/50/1/67, (accessed 09/07/2010)

Savage-Smith, Emilie, *Islamic Culture and the Medical arts*, Maryland: National Library of Medicine, 1994, http://www.nlm.nih.gov/exhibition/islamic_medical/islamic_00.html#toc (accessed: 11/08/2011)

Sayili, Aydin, *Central Asian Contributions to the Earlier Phases of Hospital Building - Activity in Islam*, FSTC Limited, 2005, pp. 9-10, http://www.muslimheritage.com/uploads/Central%20Asian%20Hospital%20Building.pdf, (accessed: 22/07/10)

Sayili, Aydin, *Certain Aspects of Medical Instruction in Medieval Islam and its Influences on Europe,* FSTC Limited, 2005, http://www.muslimheritage.com/topics/default.cfm?TaxonomyTypeID=11andTaxonomySubTypeID=57andTaxonomyThirdLevelID=-1andArticleID=1005#ftn6 (accessed: 27/07/10)

Ocak, Ahmet Yasar, *The Ottoman Empire and Islam: Framework For a New Interpretation*, (Hacettepe University, Ankara), http://humanities.uchicago.edu/orgs/institute/sawyer/archive/islam/ocak.html, (accessed: 07/01/12)

Index

B